WILD LA

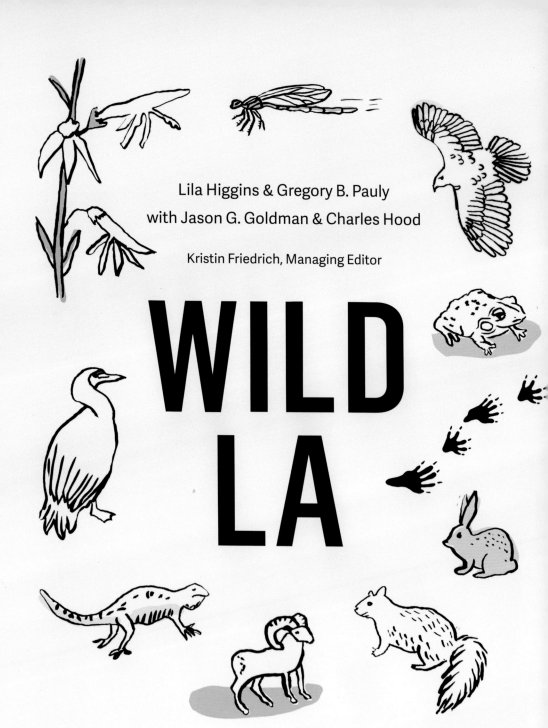

Lila Higgins & Gregory B. Pauly
with Jason G. Goldman & Charles Hood

Kristin Friedrich, Managing Editor

WILD LA

TIMBER PRESS • PORTLAND, OR

FINISH UP
THE LOOP

EXPLORE THE
AMAZING NATURE
IN AND AROUND
LOS ANGELES

GOOD
VIEWS

NATURAL
HISTORY
MUSEUM
LOS ANGELES COUNTY

Dedicated to all people curious about nature, whether they find it in a national forest or their own neighborhood. And especially to those whose passion has inspired them to become community scientists, helping study urban nature in ways unimaginable just a few years ago.

Frontispiece artwork by Martha Rich.
Copyright © 2019 by the Natural History
    Museums of Los Angeles County.
    All rights reserved.
    nhm.org/wildla
Photo and illustration credits appear
    on page 329.

Published in 2019 by Timber Press, Inc.
The Haseltine Building
133 S.W. Second Avenue, Suite 450
Portland, Oregon 97204-3527
timberpress.com

Printed in China
Text design by Anna Eshelman
Cover design by Adrianna Sutton and Martha Rich

ISBN 978-1-60469-710-0
Catalog records for this book are available from the
Library of Congress and the British Library.

CONTENTS

FOREWORD

Nature in Los Angeles is diverse and fascinating, and the Natural History Museums of Los Angeles County want to share its stories.

For over one hundred years, the Natural History Museum in Exposition Park has been devoted to the history of the planet—fossils, gems and minerals, the evolution of plants and animals, and the transformation of Los Angeles from tiny pueblo to metropolis. In 2013, we increased our focus on living nature when we turned asphalt parking lots into our outdoor Nature Gardens, and delved into Los Angeles's wildlife in our interactive Nature Lab. Our work offsite is just as important to us: we bring scientists, educators, and people of all ages together to explore local green space and collect data through our many community science projects.

Today, most people on this planet live in cities. The plants and animals that share city space are understudied by scientists and, sometimes, undervalued by human city dwellers. When we think of nature, we often think of sparsely populated, faraway places little disturbed by urbanization. Many people don't realize Los Angeles is teeming with incredible nature, or that Ice Age Los Angeles is revealed at the La Brea Tar Pits.

We want to shift that thinking, not only because we are passionate about Los Angeles but because we believe—and research is beginning to show—that urban nature exploration is linked to conservation. When we understand what's out there, we better appreciate it. When we appreciate it, we protect it.

These stories of local nature will draw you in. They are marked by native and non-native species making a go of it in our mild Mediterranean climate, some challenged by urbanization and habitat change and others benefitting from it. The stories unfold in parks and hiking trails throughout the city, and in your backyards, courtyards, and schoolyards. Through these stories, we want people to see the nature close to them, not a distant, exotic phenomenon only available to experts and naturalists. It's here for everyone—it's right outside, right now.

....

Dr. Lori Bettison-Varga, President and Director,
Natural History Museums of Los Angeles County,
Natural History Museum, La Brea Tar Pits, and Hart Museum

INTRODUCTION

This is a book that celebrates the nature all around us each and every hour of every day. Despite jokes that Los Angeles is a concrete wasteland, the truth is that it's actually an area of astounding biological diversity, with many powerful and interesting stories about how the "wild" and the "urban" are more interconnected than most people guess.

What do we mean by "LA nature"? When we refer to "Los Angeles" or "our area," we mean much more than city or county limits—our focus is on the Los Angeles River and San Gabriel River watersheds (plus some of the smaller coastal watersheds draining the Santa Monica Mountains). A watershed is an area whose streams, gullies, creeklets, and canyons all drain into the same place. If rain falls on the ground and eventually flows to the Pacific Ocean via the San Gabriel River, then this ground is within the San Gabriel watershed. "Our area" includes most of LA County, some of Orange County, and slivers of Riverside County and Ventura County. Our focus is on most of the Santa Monica and San Gabriel Mountains, the San Fernando Valley, the San Gabriel Valley, and all of the main Los Angeles Basin from Malibu to northern Orange County. This is not a beach and tide pool book (though we do explain how to see wild sea turtles in Long Beach). Instead, we're interested in nature on land—in our creeks, rivers, ponds, and air—all the plants and bugs and other animals you can discover from high in the mountains all the way down to the sand.

Biologists and naturalists have strong opinions, but the four writers of this book had to agree on some ground rules. We wanted it to be different from the usual natural history guide—easier to read, easier to understand. Our mission was to create a book that could live on your shelf, but also fit in your backpack when you're out exploring.

The book has three main parts. The first section reviews the ecology and natural history of the LA area in ten easy-to-read chapters organized by topic. There are chapters on the roles of fire and water, for example, and an exploration of wildlife after dark.

The middle section is the field guide. We selected over one hundred species not because they are beautiful, native to California, or endangered—although many of them are—but because they're important to the LA nature story and they're the plants and animals you're most likely to notice on your nature adventures. Some species you may not have seen yet, but some you surely have—we hope this book will help you identify and understand why their presence in the city is so fascinating.

The final section is field trips. We chose our twenty-five trips because they're accessible for a broad range of nature lovers. Most parts of Los Angeles are covered; any LA reader should live fairly close to at least one site—hopefully less than half an hour away.

A note on the common species names. Scientists capitalize animal names in different ways. Scientists who specialize in birds, lizards, snakes, and amphibians use capitals (Acorn Woodpecker), but scientists who specialize in mammals, insects, fungi, and plants don't (striped skunk). To be conversational and make the book consistent, we lowercase everything except for place names and proper names. All scientific names follow the usual rules: written in italics, with the genus name uppercase and specific name lowercase. So, the acorn woodpecker is *Melanerpes formicivorus*, which means "black creeping ant eater."

We hope this book inspires you to take a closer look at the wildness around you. We highlight plenty of Los Angeles's wilder spots, like Griffith Park and the San Gabriel Mountains, but our main message is that nature is everywhere. It's in your backyard, it's beside your porch light, it's on the sides of the freeway, and it's atop the highest downtown skyscrapers. Scientists have only recently begun to fully appreciate the abundance and diversity of wildlife in urban areas. How lucky is it that we have a front row seat to nature's newest discoveries?

WILD
LOS ANGELES

Los Angeles is Full of Nature

When Miguel Ordeñana was little, he loved going to the University of Southern California football games with his mom Adilia. He'd cheer for the Trojans and dream about becoming a football star. That dream changed eventually into becoming a wildlife biologist—but he still likes watching games. In the 2015 season opener, he sat with his mom and two little brothers, the whole family rooting for the Trojans to beat the Arkansas State Red Wolves.

During the game, Miguel's thirteen-year-old brother Aaron spotted a creature flitting above their heads in the night sky.

"Miguel, bat!" he yelled.

Shifting his attention from the field to the sky, Miguel looked up and spotted the bat. Then another and another. They were swooping and arcing in front of the stadium's massive lights—hunting. Bats love to eat moths, and because these tasty bugs are attracted to light, all a hungry bat needs to do is hang out near a bright spotlight and wait for dinner.

Miguel was prepared for moments like this. He pulled a bat detector from his pocket, plugged it into his iPhone, and waited to see if it could pick up bat sounds over the screaming fans.

Because bats are active at night, they need more than just their eyes to find dinner. Bats also "see" food with their ears, using a trick called echolocation. They send out ultrasonic squeaks, which bounce off trees, buildings, and bugs. The echo lets them distinguish things that are good to eat from things that aren't food at all.

Miguel's bat detector contains a miniature microphone tuned to the frequencies bats use to echolocate. Because each type of bat makes different calls, scientists can use recordings of the calls to figure out which species made them. Back in his office at the Natural History Museum, Miguel used special software to analyze the 105 bat sounds he recorded during the game. Half came from just one species: the Mexican free-tailed bat.

▲ The Mexican free-tailed bat can eat hundreds of mosquitos per hour.

Los Angeles County is home to at least twenty different bat species. Most prefer more undisturbed areas, like Griffith Park or the Santa Monica Mountains, but the Mexican free-tailed bat is really good at adapting to the big city. It can make a home for itself by roosting inside man-made structures instead of caves. Before 2013, nobody realized that free-tailed bats spent time near Exposition Park, but thanks to Miguel and his brother, we now have a better understanding of how these animals interact with our city.

Put Your Nature Eyes On

The bats at the football game are a good reminder that wildlife can be found anywhere. There's no line where nature stops and city begins. Nature can be found under your sofa, where an alligator lizard has snuck in and cornered a cricket; in the potted plant on your balcony, where

The Mexican free-tailed bat is the most common bat in urban Los Angeles. It's also the jet of the bat world, capable of flying faster than any other bat (60 mph), higher than any other bat (over 10,000 feet), and migrating over 1,000 miles.

13

ladybug larva chow down on aphids; or in the park down the street, where a Cooper's hawk turns a pigeon into breakfast.

Gaze down on the landscape from above and you'll notice Los Angeles is more than just paved roads and manicured lawns. It's a patchwork of tame and wild spaces. Rugged mountains give way to carefully groomed beaches, and surging rivers are enclosed by tons of concrete. Oak trees, hundreds of years old, rest beside newly laid soccer fields. As you'll see, it's not just bats who find a way to thrive in this patchwork landscape:

Coyotes cruise the tree-lined streets of Los Feliz and Silver Lake.

Mule deer ramble about NASA's Jet Propulsion Lab campus in La Cañada-Flintridge, just steps away from where the Mars Curiosity Rover was built.

Red-tailed hawks perch on light poles along the 101 Freeway.

Red-crowned parrots, descendants of escaped pets, feast on fruit trees in Pasadena, hundreds of miles from their native northeastern Mexico, where they're considered endangered.

Geckos from Europe hide near porch lights in El Segundo, Chatsworth, and Pomona, and frogs from the Caribbean hop among potted plants in a Torrance greenhouse.

Nineteen species of snakes, eighteen lizards, nine frogs, six salamanders, and three resident freshwater turtles (plus at least six more introduced turtle species) call the LA area home.

Endangered fish like the unarmored threespine stickleback and steelhead trout swim alongside one another in our streams and creeks.

▲ The view from Echo Park's Vista Hermosa Park reminds us that in cities, trees and skyscrapers can dot the horizon, and urban wildlife is all around us.

▶ Introduced to our area in the 1930s, black bears can now be found in our mountains and foothills.

Thousands of species of insects live in Los Angeles—estimates vary from approximately four thousand to more than twenty thousand—with many still awaiting discovery and description.

Eastern fox squirrels travel all over the city thanks to an aerial highway system made of telephone and electrical wires that transports them safely above speeding cars and barking dogs.

And then there's the most famous furry Angeleno, the mountain lion dubbed P-22, who somehow crossed two of the nation's busiest free-ways and survived to settle in Griffith Park.

Many of the animals listed above are relatively easy to see if you put your nature eyes on. Get to Griffith Park around sunset and watch the space where picnic grounds meet the hillsides—coyotes come down on evening adventures to scavenge food left behind from the day's picnics and bar-becues. Spend enough time outside and you could run into sphinx moths, horned lizards, parakeets, and even bears or bobcats.

Why Is There So Much Nature in Los Angeles?

The incredible diversity of species in our area results from a combination of factors. First, Los Angeles has always been biologically diverse. Not that long ago, it was home to three species of bears, three species of ground sloths, five species of big cats (of which the mountain lion was the smallest), two kinds of elephant relatives (the mastodon and mammoth), plus most of the animals still in the area today.

Add to this all the species we humans introduced, both on purpose and by accident. Our streets, hillsides, and parks are home to non-native trees, grasses, and birds. Our streams are home to non-native fish, turtles, and

crayfish. A few hundred years ago, many of these species would not have found Los Angeles to their liking—the long, dry summers would be deadly for most. But now in many parts of Los Angeles, it "rains" twice a week or more when the sprinklers turn on. We import so much water that even some tropical rainforest species are comfortable here. In these urban oases, living can be easy and the number of native and non-native species high.

A bird's-eye view from Elysian Park highlights the diversity of LA habitats.

Green sea turtles swim in the lower San Gabriel River near Long Beach.

Animals like Los Angeles for the same reasons humans do: our comfortable Mediterranean climate. Deadly winter freezes and long, triple-digit summer scorchers aren't a concern here. Then there's the dizzying array of LA habitats, from mountains and streams to forests and grasslands, deserts and tide pools, beaches and backyards. A few claims to fame:

Los Angeles is the only city in the United States with a major mountain range running through it. Thank you, Santa Monica Mountains!

LA County has the greatest difference between its lowest and highest points of any county in the United States, ranging from sea level to 10,064 feet at the top of Mount Baldy.

Los Angeles is the birdiest county in the country, with over five hundred recorded species. How did we get so many birds? We have huge numbers of native species, lots of non-native species that thrive thanks to our climate, plus lots of visitors passing through as they migrate along the Pacific Coast.

Californians brag that they can ski and surf in the same day. LA naturalists can brag too—here, you can see wild bighorn sheep and sea turtles in the same day! Within these diverse habitats, there's a perfect place for just about anyone.

◀ Bighorn sheep can see downtown Los Angeles from some of their clifftop hangouts in the San Gabriel Mountains.

LOS ANGELES IS IN A BIODIVERSITY HOTSPOT

Many people don't know that Los Angeles is part of a biodiversity hotspot called the California Floristic Province, which stretches from southern Oregon to Baja California and includes most of California except the deserts. It's one of thirty-six biodiversity hotspots in the world. The list includes places we think of as the wildest on Earth—the Tropical Andes, New Zealand, the islands of Indonesia, and Madagascar.

To qualify as a biodiversity hotspot, a region needs two things. First, it must have at least 1,500 endemic plant species. *Endemic* means a species is found in one place and nowhere else on the planet. Plants don't move around, so they're easier to count than animals. Plus, lots of endemic plants in an area usually means lots of endemic mammals, fish, birds, fungi, insects, and other groups.

The second biodiversity hotspot qualification is that at least 70 percent of the area's original habitat must have been lost—this is the hotspot part of the definition. Much of Los Angeles was trampled by cows in the early 1800s, then plowed under for the agricultural booms of the late 1800s and early 1900s, then hidden under pavement, houses, and skyscrapers throughout the 1900s. The area's unique biodiversity—whether plants, animals, or fungi—is at risk of disappearing forever.

The trouble is that half the humans within the California Floristic Province live in the Greater LA area. And the very things that made Los Angeles's human population growth possible also made things hard for the wild plants

Bio means *life*, so biodiversity is literally *the diversity of life*. This diversity can occur at all levels of biology—genes in a population, individuals in a species, species in an ecological community, and communities across a landscape.

and animals that lived here first. Some, like the Mexican free-tailed bat, adapted to life among humans. Some have been less lucky: one hundred years ago, fifty types of butterflies fluttered about the peaks and valleys of Griffith Park—today ten of them have disappeared, victims of urban development and the changing frequency and intensity of fires.

Los Angeles Loves Change

Consider this: the city's official tree, the coastal coral tree, and its official flower, the bird of paradise, both hail from South Africa.

Or this: though a grizzly bear adorns our state flag, the species was hunted out of the Santa Monica Mountains sometime in the late 1800s and was gone from the state entirely by the early 1920s.

Or this: the world's northernmost resident population of green sea turtles, typically thought of as tropical critters, splashes around in the brackish water where the San Gabriel River empties into the Pacific Ocean near Long Beach. A power plant on the river sucks in cold seawater to keep equipment cool; the warmed water then gets flushed into the river—at perfect sea turtle temperature.

As we put greater and greater pressure on our environment, nature finds ways to surprise us, by adapting, transforming, and compromising. Humans haven't driven nature out of cities. Instead, nature has adapted to survive alongside us.

Bats changed their habits by learning to hunt insects attracted to bright stadium lights. Frogs from halfway around the world hop around in our sprinkler-moistened gardens. Snakes soak up the heat from our sunbaked asphalt roads. The more we change the landscape, the more nature in the landscape adapts.

La Brea Tar Pits Tell the LA Story

What is the single coolest thing about Los Angeles?

Hint: It's not our sports teams or our beaches, Griffith Observatory or the Hollywood sign. It's not any movie star or the fact that Los Angeles invented the hot rod, the lowrider, the French dip sandwich, and the Korean fusion pork belly taco.

▶ Beneath Wilshire Boulevard and Hancock Park lie vast fossil beds, where the remains of hundreds of species are jumbled together. The deposit pictured here was discovered during construction of a parking lot at the Los Angeles County Museum of Art.

No, what Los Angeles has that other cities don't is a time machine. It's accurate and reliable, and it lets us travel back in time to understand what the area was like during the Earth's most recent glacial period—a time when temperatures were cooler and much of the planet was covered in ice. The La Brea Tar Pits have preserved millions of fossils in near perfect condition—so many and in such detail, we can identify species of plants, for instance, based on their preserved leaves, thorns, and seeds. From mammoths and saber-toothed cats all the way to tiny beetles and grass seeds, the La Brea Tar Pits have created an encyclopedia of past life. No city in the world matches Los Angeles for quality and quantity of fossils. The La Brea Tar Pits make up the single best Ice Age fossil site in the world, and it just happens to sit along Wilshire Boulevard.

A clarification: some people think dinosaurs are preserved at La Brea—the time scale isn't right for this. Dinosaurs (not including birds, who descended from dinosaurs) lived 66 to about 231 million years ago. Most La Brea fossils are only 10,000 to 50,000 years old, from the very end of a time known as the Pleistocene (ply-stuh-seen) epoch, which lasted from 11,700

19

This is a copy, called a *cast,* of a baby American mastodon skull that was excavated in 1914. American mastodons are rarely found in the tar pits; Columbian mammoths are more common. Mastodons are distant relatives to modern elephants, but mammoths are much closer on the family tree. In fact, today's Asian elephants are more closely related to the extinct mammoths than they are to African elephants.

to about 2.6 million years ago. This wasn't one stable, uniform phase—it was comprised of a series of glacial-interglacial cycles. The Pleistocene and our current epoch, called the Holocene, together form the current ice age (for you trivia buffs, named the Quaternary Glaciation). Because ice sheets and glaciers exist today, we're technically living in an ice age, it just happens to be a warmer, interglacial period.

Just like today, the end of the Pleistocene was marked by dramatic climate change—the Earth was leaving a colder glacial period and entering a warmer interglacial period. By studying the fossil record, we gain insight into how the environment in Los Angeles reacted to ancient climate changes, and how it might react in the future.

On the Channel Islands, just off the coast of Southern California, fossilized human and mammoth remains date to around 13,500 years ago, about the same time as La Brea fossils. Did humans hunt mammoths in Southern California? There is no direct evidence of this yet, but archaeologists are working hard to understand how and when people first arrived to the Americas and what impacts their arrival had on the species already here.

Welcome to the Ice Age

Imagine that you have just stepped out of a time machine into Pleistocene Los Angeles. Rub your eyes, stretch your legs, and get ready for an adventure.

The first thing you notice is the air. How cool it feels on your face, and how much it smells like a pine forest. Things feel wetter, a bit more "mountainy" than present-day Los Angeles. It feels similar to today's coastal Northern California around Monterey or Santa Cruz.

That Northern California feeling is due in large part to the trees: lots of iconic Monterey cypress, plus familiar Southern California oaks, juniper, and gray pine. In the distance, you notice dense trees lining the canyons of the Santa Monica Mountains. Their height gives them away: these are coastal redwoods, then and now the tallest trees in the world.

Between you and the trees sprout large clumps of green grass standing three to four feet tall. Nothing about today's Southern California landscape prepared you for this: a bunchgrass prairie stretching across the lowland plain for miles in every direction, lush like Africa's Serengeti in the rainy season.

This grassy plain is dotted with brown blobs, ambling on all fours and occasionally standing up to browse the tops of trees. Are they some kind of slow, tired bison? No. You recognize one as a lumbering ground sloth, ten feet long and weighing over a ton, bigger than any bear alive today. And look, over there! A Columbian mammoth, a relative of modern elephants, using its trunk to pull up bunchgrass one clump at a time. To your right is a herd of hundreds of bison. The adults are enormous—larger than modern bison—standing six to seven feet tall and weighing over 2,500 pounds. They're bigger than the largest rodeo bull you've ever seen, bigger even than the cape buffalo of Africa.

The sun blinks out, and for a split second you think a plane has flown overhead. But here in the Pleistocene, it's actually a massive condor-like bird, *Teratornis*, soaring above you with wings that stretch twelve feet wide. When it lands in a nearby oak, it stands nearly three feet tall—taller than a Great Dane.

Something is moving a short distance in front of you—a large animal crouched down, prowling through the bunchgrass. Then there's another, and a third, and a fourth. It's a pride of saber-toothed cats, known also as *Smilodon*. Each is roughly the size of an African lion, with two elongated dagger-like teeth that give the animal its common name. You're no longer the top predator—in Pleistocene-era Los Angeles, you're prey.

▼ A western horse is scavenged by saber-toothed cats, while dire wolves and a coyote impatiently wait their turn. This image is from a larger mural by Mark Hallett on display at the La Brea Tar Pits.

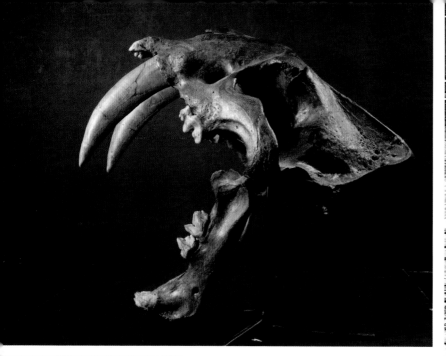

What's in a Name?

The name *La Brea* comes from an 1828 Mexican land grant. The 4,500-acre expanse was called Rancho La Brea (the tar ranch). The black substance oozing out of the ground here technically isn't tar—which is a human-made material—it's asphalt, a heavy crude oil that comes from petroleum. Asphalt can be gooey and almost liquid when warm, but when it cools, it hardens like a rock.

Deep underground, below the surface streams and pools, sits the Salt Lake Oil Field. The petroleum in this hidden oil field comes from tiny algae, called diatoms, that lived millions of years ago when the LA Basin was beneath the sea. Over time, sediments piled on top of the dead diatoms, causing intense pressure and heat, which converted their organic matter into crude oil. When crude oil bubbles up through cracks in the Earth's surface—which happens a lot in this part of earthquake-prone Los Angeles—some of the thinner part evaporates. What's left behind is sticky black asphalt.

The Gabrieleño/Tongva community and their neighbors to the north and west, the Chumash, knew about this tar and found it useful. They used it to attach arrowheads to shafts and hooks to fishing line. Filling black walnut shells with the tar created a kind of dice for games. They also applied it as waterproofing on all kinds of objects, including their sea-going canoes. European settlers followed their example and used it to waterproof roofs. In the 1860s and 1870s, Angelenos mined it for building roads. The big Lake Pit that faces Wilshire

▲ Long-trapped gasses still bubble to the asphalt surface at the tar pits.

▼ A *Smilodon* skull fossil, stained dark by the asphalt of the La Brea Tar Pits.

◀ Workers excavate fossils from the tar pits during one of the first major excavations (1913–1915). In the background are oil derricks pulling up black gold from the Salt Lake Oil Field. The city has changed dramatically, but the tar pits remain.

Boulevard in front of the La Brea Tar Pits is the remains of an early mine.

It wasn't until 1875 that a scientist realized the bones in the tar weren't all from modern sheep and cattle, but from ancient creatures trapped long ago. Still, the value of the deposits remained largely unknown until 1901, when petroleum geologist William W. Orcutt started excavating the pits and quickly amassed a collection of Ice Age animal bones. The secret was out, and scientific excavations have gone on there ever since.

In Spanish, *la brea* means *the tar*. When people say *the La Brea Tar Pits*, they're really saying *the the tar tar pits*. It's a linguistic nightmare, but the name (forgive the pun) sticks around.

Fossil Treasure

Scientists have recovered millions of fossil specimens from the tar pits, making it the richest Ice Age fossil site in the world. In all, they've recorded evidence of over six hundred plant and animal species. Besides the

❓ Entrapment: How the Tar Pits Kill

A visit to the La Brea Tar Pits might make you think that animals became stuck in deep pools of asphalt. The pits you see today, however, are the result of more than one hundred years of scientific and commercial excavations. Thousands of years ago, the sticky asphalt trap was likely a small seep, not much more than a shallow puddle of ooze.

In winter, the asphalt was cold and hard. Even the heaviest animals could walk across safely most of the time. But in the warmth of summer, the asphalt warmed and softened. The path an animal walked without a problem a few weeks earlier—or maybe even earlier that morning—became a death trap. The asphalt was probably camouflaged beneath wind-blown dust and drying leaves; passing wildlife wouldn't recognize anything unusual until their feet sank into unstable ground. Just a few inches could be enough to trap a big mammal long enough for it to die of dehydration or exhaustion, or be killed by a passing predator. Sometimes, that predator would get caught too—causing an entrapment pileup.

This story is told in the fossils found today. The most common large animal species found in the tar pits are predators and scavengers. A trapped bison or mammoth could attract dire wolves, saber-toothed cats, coyotes, eagles, and vultures. If some of these latecomers also got trapped, there'd be a weeks-long buffet of carrion (dead animal meat) in various stages of decomposition. The pileup would likely continue until the bones sank deeper into the pit or the weather cooled and the asphalt hardened again. A prolonged entrapment event like this only had to happen about once a decade to yield the number of large animal fossils found today.

well-known mammoths, dire wolves, and ground sloths, they've found horses and bison, tapirs and peccaries, and camels and llamas—animals whose relatives can be found elsewhere in the world but are long gone from Los Angeles. Not everything here is extinct though—from coyotes to lizards to oak trees, most species found in the tar pits still live here today.

La Brea fossils are special because the tar provides a "glue" that captures an organism's finer details. Fossils are usually made when plants or animals die and sink into silt or mud that eventually turns to stone, preserving only the bones. And many fossil beds elsewhere in the world contain only large creatures, because heavy animals or rough conditions destroyed smaller, more delicate ones. But because the La Brea Tar Pits capture organisms of all sizes and preserve a variety of materials (bone, cellulose, chitin), we get a much richer mix of fossils than usual. In fact, the pits can preserve just about everything—researchers can even study pollen and insects, specimens known as microfossils. It's usually not great to be a hoarder, but when it comes to studying fossils, all scientists agree: the more we have, the better!

► These fossil bones were excavated from the tar pits between 1913 and 1915. They were stored in the basement of the Natural History Museum before they were moved to their new home at the La Brea Tar Pit Museum.

LITTLE GUYS TELL THE BIGGEST STORIES

The fossils excavated from the La Brea Tar Pits can tell us a lot about entire ecosystems—something that most fossil beds can't do. There's just one problem. All the critters that got trapped inside the tar ended up floating around like ingredients in a big bowl of soup. There's no rhyme or reason to the placement of the animals within the deposits, so a paleontologist digging up fossils today might find a 35,000-year-old mastodon tusk alongside a 10,000-year-old coyote skull. To figure out which plants and animals lived together at the same time, scientists use a procedure called carbon-14 dating.

Carbon-14 is a type of chemical found in all living plants and animals. When an organism dies, carbon-14 decays at a very predictable rate. By measuring how much carbon-14 is left inside a fossil, paleontologists can estimate how long ago it died. This trick allows researchers to make educated guesses about the communities of animals that lived and died together. And by using it on the tiniest fossils, they can learn what the climate was like thousands of years ago.

While fossils from big animals might be awe inspiring, those animals tend to need a lot of space, so their remains don't usually give us much detail about the environment in smaller geographic areas. Insects, rodents, plants, small birds, and reptiles usually stick to a small territory, so they can tell us a lot more about local environmental conditions. As a result, beetles can reveal more about ancient climate patterns than, say, mammoths can.

The Decline of the Big Mammals

Starting around 50 million years ago—long before the asphalt seeps at La Brea began trapping animals—most of the world's wildlife communities, including the ecosystem right here in Los Angeles, began looking something

◄◄ Microfossils from the La Brea Tar Pits include seeds, insects, bark, and bones of small animals.

◄ This beautifully preserved shrew jaw, roughly half the size of a penny, is an example of a microfossil that helps scientists understand changes in climate and biodiversity through time.

like modern African ones. There were a few tiny mammals and a few giants, but most were small or medium-sized. That arrangement lasted for millions of years, right up until around 50,000 years ago when the planet began to lose its big mammals. The exact timing of these megafaunal extinctions varies around the globe, but in North and South America they occurred between approximately 15,000 and 11,000 years ago. In a relatively short period of time, dire wolves, short-faced bears, four species of big cats including *Smilodon* and the American lion, mammoths, sloths, camels, horses, bison, the teratorn, several species of eagles, and other big species all went extinct. The fauna of Los Angeles started changing—and it happened fast.

The jury is still out on what caused this rapid extinction, but an increasing number of scientists think it was a one-two punch of changing climate and the arrival of humans. The world was going through a period of severe climate change at that time, not unlike the one we're experiencing today. The planet was coming out of a glacial period. The atmosphere was warming, and melting ice made the world's oceans rise. Plus, humans had crossed into the Americas from eastern Asia and were spreading out, occupying new territories and increasing their populations.

TROUBLE IN THE FOREST

Before the continent's megafauna began to die off, the world was colder and drier than it is now. Ice sheets covered huge parts of North America, and much of the rest, including Southern California, was covered with savannahs (wide-open grasslands dotted with trees) rather than with forests.

The ice receded as the planet warmed, and the once-endless savannahs were carved up by expanding forests. Many of the region's big mammals needed the wide-open spaces to survive—closely clustered trees are not optimal if you're a camel.

The Pleistocene era was defined by constant shifts between warm and cold, wet and dry. The landscape bounced back and forth while forests

► A short-faced bear statue in Hancock Park reminds us of the megafauna who lived here before us.

shrunk back then spread out over and over again. As forests grew thicker, groups of savannah animals became isolated as their habitats shrank and became disconnected. These are the same problems plaguing wildlife today: habitat loss and reduced habitat connectivity.

HUMANS COME INTO THE PICTURE

The planet teetered back and forth between these two extremes like a see-saw many times during the Pleistocene, but it was only toward the end that big animals became unable to survive the isolation created by encroaching forests. Why was the most recent transition from glacial to interglacial and savannah to forest so different than the previous transitions? Scientists believe human activity exerted pressure on wildlife populations already impacted and stressed by climate change.

It's tempting to imagine small bands of hunters with bows and arrows slaughtering hordes of wild animals into extinction, but that's not what's necessary to lose a group of animals. People, other predators, diseases, and accidents just have to cause more deaths each year than there are births. Given enough time, the population will eventually vanish.

By the time our species began interacting with the megafauna of ancient Los Angeles, the animals were already suffering from the effects of fragmented, smaller populations. The massive beasts of the time were at a tipping point and an efficient new predator coming onto the landscape—that's us—may simply have been the straw that broke the ancient camel's back.

Using the Past to Figure Out the Future

The Rancho La Brea story is one of change. Because the asphalt seeps were actively trapping animals before and during the megafaunal extinction, they offer a unique glimpse at how ancient life was affected by changing climate and the arrival of humans. The tar pit fossils teach us that the dramatic changes faced by wildlife in Los Angeles during these last few hundred years of rapid urbanization are part of sweeping environmental changes that began long ago.

Comparing animals that did or didn't survive the Pleistocene-era extinction helps us understand what makes a species better at surviving changes to the environment. The fossils at La Brea allow us to peer far into our future, showing us what Los Angeles could look like in one hundred, one thousand, or even ten thousand years. And if we're fast enough, and clever enough, we just might be able to use the lessons of the past to create a better, more sustainable, more comfortable future. Not just for us, but for all the plants and animals with whom we share this planet.

◀ Inside the La Brea Tar Pits Museum, visitors can watch scientists and volunteers in the Fossil Lab sort and identify fossils every day.

▶ A photo of the LA River taken sometime between 1890 and 1900.

▶▶ Museum scientist Miguel Ordeñana (pictured in the Glendale Narrows near Sunnynook Park) studies LA River wildlife.

Water Writes the History of Los Angeles

Those who don't really know the LA River may be inclined to think of this urban waterway as a concrete-lined, trash-filled storm drain. It wasn't always so. Los Angeles only exists as a metropolis today because of the river, which played a big role in shaping its evolution. Today the river is an unlikely gem in the city—still a place for wildlife to survive and for humans to thrive.

What was the LA River like over two hundred years ago? Father Juan Crespí, a Franciscan missionary in Gaspar Portolà's Alta California expedition, kept a diary as his team searched for good places to build what would become California's network of colonial missions. On Wednesday, August 2, 1769, the

expedition headed west from the San Gabriel Valley and approached the river near modern-day Lincoln Heights; Crespí wrote, "After traveling about a league and a half through a pass between low hills, we entered a very spacious valley, well grown with cottonwoods and alders, among which ran a beautiful river from the north-northwest."

The next afternoon, Crespí and his companions traveled sixteen or so miles and reached modern-day Ballona Creek. Friday they camped near Santa Monica Beach, then turned north to navigate Sepulveda Pass into the San Fernando Valley. At the northeast end of the valley, Crespí's fellow Franciscan friars would eventually build Mission San Fernando at a spot near a Native American settlement, where Crespí described the water as "sufficient for the animals though not over abundant."

◄ Great blue herons, with a wingspan that can reach over six feet, are common LA waterbirds.

The Early Days of LA Water

The Los Angeles Crespí experienced was much wetter than the city we know today. Streams running down the mountains in V-shaped canyons carried water, sand, silt, gravel, and boulders from higher elevations into broad, lowland plains.

The river-fed valleys were full of rich soil, perfect for the agriculture that would come to dominate the LA area through the early twentieth century. But the loose, orchard-ready earth was no match for raging floods, which regularly sent surges of muddy water across the landscape, carving new channels as it raced towards the Pacific. Mounds of sediment or uprooted trees would choke off one channel and a new one would form, carrying water and sediment in a different direction. As these lowland rivers routinely altered their course, they re-engineered the landscape over and over again.

Deep within the jumbled rocks and boulders under Los Angeles are natural reservoirs called aquifers. It is believed that the aquifer beneath the San Fernando Valley can hold a whopping one trillion gallons of water, almost more than all one thousand of California's man-made reservoirs! That may seem like a lot, but it's not an endless amount; years of pumping to supply farmland and people has greatly depleted this aquifer.

As still happens today, the LA area suffered massive storms once every ten years or so. The major rivers overflowed and spread out to form broad floodplains, sometimes nearly twenty miles wide. After the waters receded, the river re-emerged with a new path.

Sometimes the LA River drained into Santa Monica Bay via Ballona Creek. Other times, it flowed south, as it does today, emptying into San Pedro Bay at Long Beach. The San Gabriel River moved around too, draining into San Pedro Bay some years and into Los Alamitos Bay in others. The rivers wandered, and everything that lived around them adapted—until European settlers arrived.

THE RIVER STRIKES

The Great Flood of 1862 was the largest in California's recorded history. In Los Angeles, rain fell for a mind-boggling twenty-eight days straight, from December 1861 into January 1862. Floodwaters washed away entire towns. The area's three rivers (including the Santa Ana River) merged to form an eighteen-mile-wide flood flowing from Signal Hill to Huntington Beach. Most of the San Fernando Valley was covered with a shallow lake.

▼ This is the first aerial image of Los Angeles, taken at 9,000 feet by Edwin Husher in 1887 from a hot air balloon. Note the sandy wash of the LA River before it was channelized.

But it wasn't until 1938 that everything changed. A storm began late on February 27, 1938, a Sunday night. Monday forecasts warned Angelenos the weather would be "unsettled with rain" through Tuesday. It was a terrible understatement. Seven days after the storm started, a *Los Angeles Times* reporter described the scene: "Disaster, gutted farmlands, ruined roads, wrecked railroad lines . . . a kaleidoscope of human misery."

Thousands of properties were lost and more than 140 people died. In Long Beach, a wooden pedestrian bridge over the LA River collapsed, and witnesses saw ten people drowned. Farther upriver, a section of the Lankershim Boulevard Bridge also collapsed, killing five. A massive landslide washing through Beverly Glen took out a house containing a mother and her toddler. The father was in a different room taking a bath. The bathtub broke from its footing and floated, with the man inside, several hundred yards down the canyon. He broke both his elbows but survived.

▲ Railroad tracks and bridges caught in a 1914 LA River flood.

▼ Early Angelenos ignored the region's flood history and built close to the river, sometimes with costly consquences.

THE CONCRETE SOLUTION

These horrific scenes led Los Angeles to resolve it would never again suffer the whims of Mother Nature. The Army Corps of Engineers showed up, armed with the concrete that continues to confine the rivers today. It took three million barrels of concrete, poured by some 10,000 workers, to pave the LA River (the San Gabriel River faced a similar fate). The goal was to move water off the landscape and into the ocean as quickly as possible so heavy rains wouldn't cause destructive floods.

Until the rivers were encased in concrete, rainwater made it all the way to the ocean only in flood season. Usually, snowmelt would flow to valleys and basins then soak into the ground, filling the aquifers. The older, river-dominated LA Basin (and nearby valleys) contained many types of wetlands: tidal flats and marshes, wet meadows, freshwater marshes, vernal pools, willow thickets, floodplain forests, and more. By surrounding the river in concrete, engineers ensured the Los Angeles inhabited by Native Americans and later encountered by Crespí and Portolà ceased to exist. What remains today can be considered an engineering success, but that success came at the expense of the watershed's natural plant and animal life.

> It took about twenty years to channelize the LA River; over 800,000 dump truck loads of soil were moved!

THE BEEF ON EARLY LA RANCHES

▲ Seven species of native fish once inhabited the LA River, including steelhead trout—like this impressive twenty-five-inch specimen caught in 1940.

◀ Where it all begins: the LA River's headwaters are upstream of the concrete, in tree-lined Calabasas Creek.

With the Gold Rush in 1849, California's human population quickly grew and so did the demand for beef. Landowners in Southern California were growing into wealthy cattle barons, and cattle needed space to graze and water to drink. A system of man-made wells drained the massive underground aquifers beneath Los Angeles to nourish the herds. The wetlands that once absorbed large storms and replenished the aquifers were trampled under cattle hooves.

These changes contributed to flooding—soil pressed flat by herds (not to mention that covered by roads and sidewalks) can't soak up as much rainwater as loose, natural soil. Grass played a part too. Before the cows came, the landscape was dominated by native bunchgrasses. These perennial plants lived as long as two hundred years, surviving the dry summer thanks to deep roots that extend fifteen feet or more into the soil, and grew in spaced out clumps separated by patches of bare dirt (hence the name bunchgrass). But

It's tough to picture a version of Los Angeles in which the main challenge to getting around was wetlands and muddy paths, not bumper-to-bumper traffic. Still, evidence of this earlier, soggier time still exists. Consider La Cienega Boulevard, which runs from the Santa Monica Mountains to the LA International Airport. *Ciénega* is Spanish for swamp. The area north of the Baldwin Hills where the street runs today was once a massive ten-mile-long boggy wetland.

▲ People still fish in the LA River, mostly for non-native carp.

cows are some of nature's best lawnmowers, gobbling up all the grass in sight. When native bunchgrasses were unable to survive season to season because of overgrazing, exotic annual grasses took over. These grasses live a single season and die after reseeding, so they survived grazing much better than native grasses.

Los Angeles's cattle boom eventually went bust, thanks to the area's other recurring water issue—long-lasting droughts. One particularly severe drought lasted three years, from 1862 to 1864. Wild animals were finding food and water in short supply already, thanks to cattle overgrazing, but the drought made water even scarcer. Swarms of the ominously named devastating grasshopper chewed up what remaining vegetation they could find. Cattle barons, faced with dying herds, were forced to sell their properties, making the land available for purchase and development. It was during this short fifteen-year period, from the Gold Rush through the drought, that the LA area witnessed one of its most dramatic transformations. If not for the combination of drought and grasshoppers, Los Angeles would be a very different place today.

People Versus Nature

Los Angeles's water story includes intense flooding and severe drought, extreme overabundance and agonizing, life-threatening shortage. Perhaps no other place embodies this paradox better than Beverly Hills. Once upon a time, the streams that flowed through Coldwater, Franklin, and Benedict canyons joined near modern-day Beverly Hills to form a wetland called *Rodeo de Las Aguas* (Gathering of the Waters). Today Rodeo Drive is famous for celebrities and high-end boutiques like Gucci and Prada. But the street's name reminds us that, in this town, the most important gatherings always have been, and always will be, about water.

Permanent surface water is historically unusual for coastal California. Early Los Angeles, with its natural rivers, may have been a wetter place overall, but Southern California still grew hot in summer. Despite the variety of wetlands covering the southland, most aquatic habitats dried up each year—by August, surface water was rare and freshwater ponds remained only in the largest wetlands.

As the human population's demand for year-round water grew and underground aquifers were drained, surface reservoirs and man-made ponds began to dot the landscape, and aqueducts were built to import water from far away—all to ensure a steady supply of water throughout the long, hot summer. But when we created this permanent surface water, we also provided a habitat for invasive critters that would otherwise be unable to survive a dry Southern California summer—including bullfrogs, African clawed frogs,

► These pipes were installed in 1912 to bring water from the Owens Valley to the growing city. This 419-mile pipeline, termed the LA Aqueduct, remains a major source of water for the LA area.

◄ African clawed frogs are able to thrive in our human-made aquatic habitats.

red-eared slider turtles, bass, and crayfish. Thanks to these newcomers, four of our seven native fishes have disappeared entirely from the southland, while the remaining three are protected with special conservation status.

Take a moment to reflect on this. To combat destructive storms and floods, we seized control of the rivers by brute force, encasing them in corsets of concrete. Because we forced storm water directly into the sea, it couldn't replenish our aquifers. To quench the thirst of cows, citrus trees, and people after we exhausted the aquifers, we created an elaborate system of surface ponds, reservoirs, and aqueducts that brings fresh water from hundreds of miles away. Some say the next world war will be fought over water. The history of Los Angeles is a lesson in just how far people will go to control it.

Fire, Past and Future

Southern California, with its hot, dry weather, has always been fire prone. Summer fires, which burn from June through September, are calmer and generally not propelled by wind. But in autumn, the Santa Ana winds really pick up, blowing hotter, drier air from the desert down the coastal slopes of our local mountains. They can occur throughout the year but are worst October through April and can generate devastating wind-driven fires. Though the two types of fires have very different temperaments, this means fire season in Southern California lasts from June through April. Be thankful for May.

The Deadliest Fire in LA History

In 1933, Los Angeles was, like the rest of the country, in the depths of the Great Depression. A government program loaned LA County money to pay unemployed workers forty cents an hour to clean up horse trails in Griffith Park, carve out new roads, and remove weeds. That fall Los Angeles was walloped by hot, dry, west-blowing winds from the deserts in the east: the infamous Santa Anas. Months without rain turned the grassy slopes of the park dry. It seemed they could ignite if you just looked at them wrong.

Nearly four thousand workers were in the park on October 3. By mid-day, temperatures in downtown Los Angeles hit 100 degrees. Workers on their lunch break listened to the radio as the New York Giants defeated the Washington Senators in the first game of the World Series. Two hours later, they noticed smoke rising from the north side of the park.

It seemed there was enough manpower to fight the fire, but the workers—who were either forced or asked to help, depending on who you ask and what you read—were armed only with shovels and weren't trained firefighters. The Santa Ana winds whipped the fire up further, and flames multiplied faster than workers could beat them down. Trained firefighters eventually showed up, and the fire was controlled later that evening.

By the time it was put out, the fire had claimed the lives of at least twenty-nine workers—because recordkeeping was poor, it's difficult to

▲ After a fire, plants like this scrub oak will re-sprout from their still-living roots.

◀ Griffith Park and the historic Griffith Observatory have faced the threat of fire multiple times throughout their history.

establish how many people were working in the park that day, and how many survived—some estimates suggest the death toll was closer to fifty-eight. It remains the deadliest fire in LA history, and to this day, nobody knows how it started.

In 2007, the skies above the Observatory were dark orange the night that Griffith Park burned again. This time, the brushfire scorched more than 800 acres, about a fifth of the park. But by the time five hundred firefighters contained it after two brutally hot days, not a single person was seriously injured and the observatory, zoo, and merry-go-round escaped unharmed. At the time this book was published, the 2018 Medocino Complex Fire to the north of Los Angeles had become the largest in California history. We may be getting better at saving lives and structures, but we'll always have fire.

Not all Fire Is Bad

In the immediate aftermath of wildland fires, the landscape appears charred, still, and lifeless. Fallen ash gives the soil a gray tint. Any trees still standing are often blackened beyond recognition.

◄ Poodle-dog bush is a fire follower—it only grows the first few years after a fire. Despite its cute name and purple flowers, keep back. Touching any part can give you a serious rash.

But fire has a way of making the landscape stronger, and without it, many animals and plants wouldn't survive at all. The endless loop of burning and recovery is called the fire cycle, and plants have come to depend on its predictability.

Plants that need exposure to smoke or fire to trigger the release or sprouting of seeds are called *pyriscent*. For example, lodgepole pines, which grow at high elevation in our local mountains, have cones that open in response to fire, releasing their well-protected seeds. Most Southern California fires occur in summer and fall, before winter rains. Once the rains arrive, the seeds of pyriscent plants kick into action. Many manzanita species need a fire to tell them to sprout and grow fast while there is little competition for space. Their seeds are hiding just below the surface, and they'll only start to grow if the ground above them burns. Some seeds can last a hundred years or more, patiently waiting for fire.

Similarly, most chaparral shrubs have a structure at the base, just above the root system, called a burl. The burl stores water and energy. Once it detects that a fire has burned the above-ground portion of the shrub, the burl gets to work, sending new growth up through ashy soil. It only takes two months for new green shoots to push through the charred soil after a fire. These shoots give way to flowers, followed by new trees and shrubs. Eventually, these plants will burn again, and the cycle will continue.

One of the most mysterious fire-dependent animals is the fire beetle. They can detect fires from up to twenty miles away using their very own infrared detectors. Because fire beetles only lay eggs on freshly-singed branches, they must gather in groups by the fire to mate. Very little is known about where the beetles live when there aren't any fires.

FRIENDS OF FIRE

▲ Plants like fire poppies thrive after wildfires.

◀ This western fence lizard explores its home after a fire.

Animals have evolved to take advantage of the fire cycle too. After a fire, small rodents take advantage of the open ground to forage for seeds hiding in the soil. Rabbits munch on green shoots pushing through the soil. Birds of prey hunt across the now open ground for the lizards, snakes, and rodents that survived but are now conspicuous as they search for their own food. Deer can often be found at the edges of burned land, using surviving chaparral for cover from predators, while also eating the fresh new vegetation. If burned and unburned areas are found close together, deer reproduction and survival is especially high.

The decade following a fire is a period of change, with different kinds of plants dominating at different times. Changing plants offer changing leaves, seeds, flowers, and fruits, which all attract different sorts of insects, birds, reptiles, and mammals. Some of these plants and animals can't survive in fully recovered chaparral. These critters depend on routine fires for their very existence.

Geological evidence shows that Southern California chaparral was burning up to twenty million years ago. But archaeological evidence indicates that fires began to change eleven thousand years ago, when people showed up. As humans got better at setting and putting fires out, Southern California and its wildlife communities changed forever.

SMALL FIRES GOOD, BIG FIRES BAD?

In an effort to save our homes and businesses, we try to extinguish wildfires as soon as they begin—a practice called fire suppression. The problem is, when we put out fire this efficiently, large areas don't burn for a long time. Instead, they accumulate fuel. When they finally do light up, the resulting fire is much more intense, aggressive, and hotter than it would normally be.

Fire suppression might actually make things worse, because infrequent, large fires are more dangerous than frequent, smaller fires. Fire-prone chaparral and active fire suppression can be a dangerous mix.

On the other hand, a group of scientists recently pored through nearly one hundred years of California fire records and found that large, hard-to-control wildfires have always been a feature of the Southern California landscape, and that fire suppression activities have little impact on them. The increase in wildfires, they say, instead reflects an increase in the number of smaller man-made blazes. Ending fire suppression protocols would not necessarily mean that wildfires would suddenly become more manageable.

▲ A helicopter draws water from the LA Aqueduct to battle the 2009 Station Fire in the San Gabriel Mountains.

When it comes to fire in Southern California, two facts remain:

1. Where there is chaparral, there will be fire. It's both inevitable and necessary.

2. The number of human-caused fires is increasing, and they aren't so easy to put out.

People Make Fires

The natural cause of fire is lightning. Because lightning strikes are more common on California's interior mountains and at elevations above five thousand feet, most lightning-ignited wildfires begin inland and may be swept toward the coast by wind. These natural fires tend to burn for only a short time before they're naturally extinguished.

These days, lightning is the least likely firestarter—behind arson, careless cigarettes and campfires, car fires, and other human activities. While natural fires mostly happen in the mountains, human-caused fires occur at lower elevations, near cities, and along freeways. And while natural fires are seasonal, people can spark fires all year long. We have changed both where and when fires happen.

It's not just people today. In the past, Native Americans were frequent fire starters too. They burned brush to drive wildlife into open fields where they could hunt easily. They used it to burn off some plants in order to strengthen others useful for food, tools, and medicine. They also knew freshly burned areas supported different plants and animals than older, unburned areas. A combination of burned and unburned habitats ensured diverse resources. Part of today's Southern California nature was a product of Native American landscape management through fire.

BURNING GRASSES

Even natural fires burn differently nowadays. The plants we've introduced often provide better wildfire fuel. The grasses of Southern California used to grow in bunches, with plenty of open dirt between them. But a look at our hillsides in July or August today shows a continuous blanket of dry, brown grass. These are mostly non-native species, introduced to Los Angeles from around the Mediterranean and Middle East.

Unlike bunchgrasses, which can survive season to season, non-native grasses sprout after winter rains, release their seeds in summer, then die with the hope that those seeds will begin the cycle again after next year's rains. Most of these grasses were introduced by Europeans exploring California—probably accidentally as supplies and people (with their mud-encrusted boots) came on and off ships along the coast. Unfortunately, the carpet of dead, brown, exotic grasses provides more fuel and allows fire to spread much better than land sprinkled with living, green, native bunchgrasses.

Though it can seem scary, destructive, and even cruel, fire is an essential element of life for most plants and animals in Southern California, including humans. As with most natural elements of Los Angeles, people have changed the way wildfire works, but we'll never eliminate it entirely.

Native Species

"Bears are made of the same dust as we," wrote the naturalist John Muir, "and breathe the same winds and drink of the same waters." If Muir had lived in Los Angeles in 2012, he might have also written that bears eat of the same meatballs.

In spring and summer that year, a California black bear turned up at least three times in a Glendale neighborhood at the base of the San Gabriel Mountains. His first appearance was at 3 a.m. in a home garage. The home-owner heard noises and opened the door, only to come face to snout with a four hundred-pound bear raiding his fridge, snacking on cans of tuna and Costco-brand meatballs.

Black bears aren't technically native to the San Gabriel Mountains—they're native to California but were introduced to this area by humans after grizzly bears were hunted out in the early 1900s. But this bear's story is illustrative of the challenges facing wildlife in urban and urban-adjacent environments.

The bear came to be known as Meatball (some called him Glen Bearian). Officials from the California Department of Fish and Wildlife tranquilized him, gave him an ear-tag so he would be recognizable to other wildlife offi-cials, then relocated him deep within the Angeles National Forest.

When he woke up, Meatball walked back into town, and the whole story repeated. Wildlife officials realized Meatball had become too clever for his own good.

Bears usually do a good job keeping to themselves, but in 2009, the Station Fire burned through quite a bit of quality bear habitat in the San Gabriel Mountains. Rather than explore new parts of the forest, bears like Meatball explored neighborhoods in Glendale and La Crescenta.

When bears (and other large carnivores) become too comfortable around humans, it's usually a death sentence. There's the danger of getting hit by a car, and the reality of getting caught by wildlife officials. Even when we try to relocate animals like Meatball to more remote areas, it's nearly impossible

► Black bears are omnivores and have a broad diet. In urban areas, they may raid trashcans and dumpsters in search of easy food.

to keep them from the irresistible scent of easy-to-find human food. Unless there's a wildlife sanctuary with the resources to take them in, these animals are usually euthanized.

Meatball's story ends on a happier note. On his third jaunt through Glendale, he was caught (officials baited the trap with French fries, a cheeseburger, and bacon) and sent to a wildlife sanctuary near San Diego. Meatball is thriving in his new home and eating much healthier these days—his favorite foods are avocados, grapes, and raw nuts.

How Charismatic Megafauna Survive in Los Angeles

In heavily urbanized places like Southern California, animals have to compete with humans for food and space. It may seem like Los Angeles has a lot of green space, but these patches of more natural habitat are isolated, scattered across the landscape in small- and medium-sized pieces. Scientists refer to it as a connectivity problem—if these habitat patches aren't linked somehow, animals have a hard time traveling safely between them and are more likely to wander across roads and highways, or venture into our neighborhoods.

Eating trash and raiding garage refrigerators aren't the only ways animals try to survive in the big city. The best animal survivors in urban and suburban areas usually rely on one of two strategies: adapt or exploit.

URBAN ADAPTERS

Coyotes are shy about cities but clever about taking advantage of them. They have modified their schedules, coming out at night and rarely spending more than a few hours at a time in our neighborhoods. While we sleep, they

roam the streets, gobbling up fallen fruit in our yards or rummaging through our garbage cans.

Cooper's hawks, on the other hand, have truly embraced city living. They actively take up residence in Los Angeles, because it's chock full of their favorite foods—tasty doves, sparrows, finches, pigeons, and other birds that backyard birdwatchers invite into gardens. It's as if we're setting the table and ringing the dinner bell.

Southern California poultry farmers, who mistakenly believed their chickens were threatened, used to shoot Cooper's hawks. Eventually, the hawks stopped hanging out around humans—or were killed before they could raise chicks. But in the last few decades, after shooting them became illegal, Cooper's hawks have realized humans aren't a threat anymore. Today, they're one of the most common birds of prey in Los Angeles, often seen perched in backyard trees scanning the urban forest for prey.

Peregrine falcons have also adapted to city life. In their more natural habitats, they nest on ledges along sheer cliffs. But cities offer a lot of substitute nesting sites—bridges and tall buildings with narrow window ledges. They like to eat the same prey as Cooper's hawks, so the city has become prime habitat for them.

Then there are Vaux's swifts (rhymes with *foxes*). Each spring and fall, thousands of these four-inch-long birds, each weighing less than a slice of bread, cruise through Los Angeles as they migrate between breeding grounds in the Pacific Northwest and wintering grounds in Mexico and Central America.

Cooper's hawk
oys its mourning
ve meal.

Once endangered,
egrine falcons
n be spotted
lowntown Los
geles.

Before Los Angeles was built up, these cigar-shaped birds would have rested in hollowed-out trees. When buildings replaced trees, the swifts didn't seem to mind. Bricks provide enough texture for them to cling to, so now they catch their much-needed shut-eye in brick-lined chimneys. Walk through downtown Los Angeles between April and May while the birds are flying north, or between September and October when they're flying south, and you may see one of the city's greatest wildlife spectacles: thousands of swifts settling into a chimney or elevator shaft for the night.

After spending the day snatching up insects while flying, they arrive at their roosting site and spend a few minutes circling. Eventually, one bird decides to take the plunge and the rest follow. To the observer, it looks like hundreds of birds swirling into a funnel or being flushed down a drain. In just a few minutes, the show is over, and the birds are resting inside the chimney.

For many years, their preferred roost was at the downtown Chester Williams Building near the intersection of Fifth Street and Broadway. A few years ago, developers renovating the building capped the chimney, and the birds had to move their rest stop to the Spring Arts Tower at Fifth and Spring streets. As time goes on, the swifts will likely have to move again.

URBAN EXPLOITERS

Think of urban exploiters as super-adapters. They haven't just discovered a way to survive among humans; they truly thrive alongside us. The best examples? Probably the cockroach or the brown rat, but let's go with someone local and a bit more showy. Meet the Allen's hummingbird.

There are two types of this fast-flapping species: migratory and sedentary. The first kind migrates each year along the California coast, breeding from the Oregon border to Santa Barbara, and wintering on the Pacific coast of Mexico. But the sedentary type is the city exploiter—content to stay home all year long, they're the fastest-moving couch potatoes you've ever seen.

These green, red, and bronze-winged homebodies used to be found only on the Channel Islands off the coast. But sometime in the 1960s or 1970s, they turned up on the Palos Verdes Peninsula. Most ornithologists (bird scientists) agree they probably got from the islands to the mainland without any help from us. Once they got comfortable in Palos Verdes, they began to expand. Today, they live between Santa Barbara and San Diego and as far east as Riverside, and their range continues to expand.

Hummingbirds eat up to eight or nine times their body weight every day, and they're happy to find lots of food in the city. When you combine hummingbird feeders in backyards with all the exotic, decorative flowering plants Angelenos like—Cape honeysuckle, eucalyptus, and the bottlebrush shrub, for example—Allen's hummingbirds have the unending buffet their incredibly fast metabolisms demand.

▼ Allen's hummingbirds, once rare, are now common garden birds in Los Angeles. They take advantage of ornamental plants.

▲ Rattlesnakes like warm roads on cool evenings, which makes them vulnerable to getting run over.

The Lucky and the Unlucky

Los Angeles was once home to Pacific tree frogs, California newts, Western toads, and California red-legged frogs. All these native amphibians declined rapidly as the area was urbanized, but none more dramatically than red-legged frogs. As recently as one hundred years ago, red-legged frogs, which are the biggest of all California's native amphibians, were found hopping around creeks in Beverly Hills. But the last ones were spotted in the Santa Monica Mountains in the mid-1960s and the San Gabriel Mountains in the mid-1970s. Nobody knows exactly why they disappeared, but there are several likely causes.

Human-built reservoirs and urban ponds are one. These open, permanent water sites allowed the introduction of non-native fish and crayfish, which quickly learned to gobble up native frogs' eggs, tadpoles, and even the adults—non-native bass and bullfrogs both love to eat red-legged frogs.

A frog-killing fungus called chytrid also contributed to the red-legged frog's decline. The fungus doesn't kill bullfrogs or Pacific treefrogs, but they can still carry chytrid around with them, spreading it to species vulnerable

to the infection. Even red-legged frog populations that managed to hang on in mountain canyons while the valleys below urbanized couldn't make it through the fungus epidemic.

There's a glimmer of hope, though. While red-legged frogs disappeared from the Santa Monica Mountains, a few populations persisted in the Simi Hills. Biologists from the National Park Service have successfully relocated eggs from the Simi Hills to the Santa Monica Mountains, where they hatched tadpoles that grew into full-size frogs. As long as the small creeks where they were reintroduced remain protected (and free of non-native fish), the frogs seem able to take care of themselves.

Southern Pacific rattlesnakes tell a similar story. Once you leave the LA Basin and venture into the mountains, rattlesnakes are plentiful. Where there is chaparral, there are rattlesnakes—with one exception: the Baldwin Hills, near Culver City. There hasn't been a single rattlesnake here for at least half a century. As one of the most persecuted animals in Southern California, they were probably killed off. Even as other snakes—like gophersnakes and California kingsnakes—found ways to survive, the Southern Pacific rattlesnake disappeared.

Most snakes are hammered by urban development, especially by trying to cross roads and becoming roadkill. But rattlesnakes have an added disadvantage: all too often, a hiker or homeowner comes across a rattlesnake and, rather than leaving it alone, he or she grabs a stick or a shovel and kills it. Most animals that disappear from the urban jungle suffer from indirect effects of human behavior, like habitat loss or pollution. The Southern Pacific rattlesnake is somewhat unique—a target of intentional human aggression.

Wildlife Communities

All species are part of a bigger community. It sounds a little sentimental, but the truth is, in a healthy ecosystem, each species plays a role. In LA chaparral, mountain lions are the top, or apex, predators. They feast on deer, but also raccoons, coyotes, rats, mice, and probably the odd squirrel or two. Coyotes and foxes are called *mesopredators*, which means they're medium sized, not at the top of the food chain, but still able to make a meal of rodents and rabbits.

Imagine what might happen if the mountain lions disappeared. Without any large predators, the mesopredator populations would go through the roof. Small herbivore populations (rabbits and rodents) would shrink, while large herbivore populations like deer would expand. The whole system would go a little nutty.

In some ways, urban wildlife communities are mixed up. Some plants and animals have been driven out of town, while others have discovered incredibly clever strategies for adapting. But rather than think of these animal communities as incomplete, it makes sense to think of them as new ecosystems entirely, with relationships that have never existed before (and often have not been well studied). The ecological frontier isn't in a remote rainforest or deep ocean. It's right here, at home.

Exotic Species

The subject line of the email was simply, "Bird?"

It's not unusual for researchers at the Natural History Museum to receive requests like this. Local residents aren't shy about asking for help identifying critters they encounter on hikes, in a local park, or in their backyards. What was unusual about this email, sent in August of 2012, was its timestamp: 1:48 a.m.

Megan was losing sleep. A very loud, very nocturnal animal had taken up residence in her backyard. For several weeks, starting after sunset and continuing throughout the night, the critter would shriek every thirty minutes or so. In her frustration, Megan fired off an email to Kimball Garrett, the Museum's longtime bird collections manager, asking for help identifying the culprit. The noise had become such a nuisance her husband and son had taken to sleeping in the living room, the farthest they could physically get from their backyard.

Megan used her smartphone to record the sound and attached it to the email. After hearing the squawk, Kimball was positive it wasn't a bird. He thought it might be a frog, and he wrote to colleague Greg Pauly, the Museum's curator of herpetology (reptiles and amphibians), who quickly recognized the call as that of the tokay gecko.

There are hundreds of kinds of geckos all around the world, but their name—the word *gecko* itself—is derived from the call of a single, very loud, Southeast Asian species, the tokay gecko. Both *tokay* and *gecko* are onomatopoeias, words that sound like the noise they describe. The sound is the animal's calling card. *To-kay!* Or *ge-ko!* To others of its kind, it might mean something like, "keep away, this is *my* tree," but to us they may as well be shouting, "Hey! Over here! I'm a gecko!"

How did a Southeast Asian gecko wind up in Megan's backyard? It was probably an escaped pet. Pet stores buy and sell hundreds of them. When they get loose, all they really need to survive is enough bugs to eat and water to drink. With our backyard sprinkler systems, we've created habitats similar enough to their native rainforest to make them quite comfortable.

By the time Greg solved the puzzle, Megan's gecko had gone quiet. Perhaps it had moved on to a new neighborhood, or maybe it had been caught by an unfamiliar predator: a pet cat.

Frog Invaders

Non-native animals like the tokay gecko are introduced to habitats all the time, all over the world. But for a species to successfully colonize its new habitat, it must survive long enough to reproduce and for its offspring to reproduce as well. It needs to thrive, not just scrape by. Once individuals are successfully reproducing, biologists would call it an established population.

An established non-native species may not always be labeled invasive—this classification is reserved for species posing some harm to the environment, or to our economy. While the tokay gecko is certainly non-native, exotic, and introduced, it probably isn't invasive in Los Angeles—at least not yet. Let's hope it doesn't follow the footsteps of the tiny and very loud coquí frog.

Two years after Megan sent her late-night note, bird expert Kimball received another memorable email. This one was sent by a skilled birder unable to identify a call she kept hearing outside her home. Kimball confirmed it wasn't a bird, then passed it on to Greg, who identified it as a coquí frog, native to Puerto Rico.

▶ The coquí is a small frog with a big voice—some say too big.

Coquí frogs move around the world in shipments of potted plants for nurseries. They invaded Hawaii's big island sometime in the late 1980s. Then they spread to Oahu, Kauai, Maui and now, it seems, California.

Unlike many frogs, coquís don't have a tadpole stage; they emerge from their eggs as tiny froglets, making them excellent invaders. All it takes is for a gravid female (*gravid* means full of fertilized eggs) to stow away in one potted plant and—boom! Dozens of baby frogs are ready to spread out in a new territory. No streams or ponds necessary.

Adult coquí frogs are usually about 1 to 1.5 inches long—about the size of a silver dollar—but when the froglets hatch, they're small enough that several could sit on a pinky fingernail. They can stow away easily, but they don't stay hidden for long. When the males decide it's time to find a friendly female and make froggy babies, they aren't shy about advertising themselves.

Coquí is another onomatopoeia referring to the animal's call, *ko-KEE*. At home, Puerto Ricans cherish the sound as part of their natural heritage. In fact, Puerto Ricans living far from home miss the sound so much there's a market for coquí frog calls—everything from ringtones to sleep aids. But in Hawaii the hoppers are considered a nuisance. Why is a symbol of pride in Puerto Rico a problem in Hawaii? The frogs don't have any natural predators in Hawaii (or in California), and they breed with abandon. In some places in Hawaii, their density has been estimated as high as ten thousand per acre or up to fifty times more dense than in Puerto Rico. That many frogs can gobble up some fifty thousand insects each night—bad news for the bugs, and bad news for other species that rely on those bugs.

The nocturnal chorus also causes people to lose sleep. Some compare the frog chirps to the sound of a jet engine, and it's not an entirely ridiculous comparison. Despite their tiny size, coquí frogs can produce sounds around ninety decibels. That's roughly how noisy a motorcycle is from twenty-five feet away.

It's impacting the economy. The noise is so bad that people have started moving away from the frogs. A new Hawaiian law requires sellers to tell prospective home buyers if coquí frogs live on the property, and they've driven down property values on the Big Island to the tune of 0.16 percent. It might not sound like much, but if the frogs eventually infest all residential neighborhoods on the island, that's a combined loss of some $7.6 million in real estate value.

Knowing the impact of coquí frogs in Hawaii, Greg took care to document the possible invasion in Southern California. He eventually traced the frogs to a Torrance nursery that regularly receives shipments of tropical plants from Hawaii. Then he rounded up a dozen community scientist volunteers to go on a frog hunting expedition. In just two hours, the group collected more than one hundred chirpers from the nursery's greenhouse—and a quick listen made it clear there were many more still hopping about. A few months later the story repeated. This time, Greg had to inform a Beverly Hills resident—another frustrated emailer losing shuteye—that the mystery car alarm keeping him up at night was actually a coquí frog.

California already has two well-established populations of coquí frogs. Both populations are at nurseries, and no populations have been found outside of the greenhouse environments, although the occasional calling male does show up following landscaping projects, wrecking the sleep of the unsuspecting homeowner. It's unclear if coquís will become a problem in California and equally unclear whether anything could be done about it. In Hawaii, several islands continue control efforts, but, despite millions of dollars spent tackling the problem, the Big Island has given up.

Pet Invaders

Coquí frogs have introduced themselves to our area through a mix of accident and adaptability. However, many non-native species are introduced on purpose. Plants and animals kept in gardens or as pets often escape or are "set free" by owners, only to wreak havoc in the local ecosystem. There are countless examples in Los Angeles.

▲ Red-crowned parrots were generally brought here as pets. Escaped birds have led to an established breeding population in Los Angeles.

The tall, spiky organ pipe-like cacti you see on Griffith Park hillsides? Non-native. Maybe some escaped from the folk-gardens in Griffith Park, or perhaps fifty years ago somebody had a potted cactus that got too big for their apartment, so they replanted it in the wild. It's the same with the dozens of different parrot species that squawk across Los Angeles. They're all descendants of escaped or abandoned pets.

FROM CUTE TO COLOSSAL

The classic example of an invasive pet is the red-eared slider. Sliders start out life as adorable inch-long turtles. They've been the standard pet store turtle for decades. In the 1950s, they were *the* dime store turtle, often sold in a small aquarium with a little plastic palm tree island.

Though many red-eared sliders die in captivity due to unsuitable living conditions, those that survive quickly grow—big. When pet owners realize they're unprepared to care for these foot-long giants for the next couple decades, they often release them into a local pond or waterway.

Be a responsible community member. Never release pets into the wild or plant non-native species where they could escape and spread. You never know what effect they might have.

This scenario has played out in cities around the world. Red-eared sliders are native to the central United States, but they are now the most widespread freshwater turtle species on the planet. They can be found in almost every state (including Hawaii and also in Guam and Puerto Rico), in Mexico,

Canada, South Africa, Australia, and multiple countries in Europe, Asia, and South America.

Once abandoned, red-eared sliders can introduce diseases to native turtle populations. They also might compete with native turtles for food and basking sites. The International Union for Conservation of Nature lists the red-eared slider as one of the world's worst invasive species.

Leafy Invaders

Some invaders wind up playing less destructive roles—even resulting in positive outcomes. One of the most complicated interlopers in California is the ubiquitous eucalyptus tree.

Originally from Australia, the blue gum eucalyptus took root in California in the mid-1850s, as farmers planted them along fields and orchards to act as windbreaks. After the "eucalyptus craze" of the nineteenth and early twentieth centuries, California fell out of love with the trees, but by then, it was too late—there are hundreds of thousands of acres growing across the state.

In sunny California, the blue gum didn't have to contend with any of the diseases, insects, birds, or leaf-munching koalas it evolved with across the Pacific. A perfect storm for biological invasion. But whether or not the blue gum is invasive depends on who you ask—and where.

Critics point to how dangerous the tree is, dropping loads of flammable bark and leaves on the ground throughout the year. But removing them could do more harm than good. Blue gums are hard to kill—they regrow easily from a chopped stump. Chemical herbicides are the only real option for eradication, and many folks find chemical control problematic. Others argue that any plants that might replace blue gums could be just as flammable, or worse.

The tree's impact on native wildlife doesn't help clarify things. Some native birds, including herons, egrets, red-shouldered hawks, and red-tailed hawks, seem content to nest or take shelter in eucalyptus groves, but cavity nesters like woodpeckers are kept out because the trees are so resistant to rot that they rarely have suitable cavities. Birds that forage for insects in the canopy are also out of luck—most native insects just don't find the leaves all that tasty. Several studies have found that fewer birds use eucalyptus groves than they do native tree stands. However, blue gums have become important roosting sites for imperiled monarch butterflies as they overwinter in Southern and Central California. Blue gums also become infested with tiny insects called lerp psyllids, an important food source for overwintering warblers. When it comes to blue gums in California, like some relationships, it's complicated.

An Ongoing Invasion

Large-scale movement of wild animals and plants around the world is the new normal. Checkpoints in airports and on interstate highways are an essential way to prevent unwanted plants and animals from getting into California. However, the tiniest stowaways will always evade the eyes of inspectors.

► Plant quarantine inspectors at Glendale Airport in 1937 check for hitchhiking insects on a flight from Mexico.

► The vedalia ladybug still helps us out with biological control of cottony cushion scale today.

►► An adult female of cottony cushion scale. The white structure is her egg case containing 600–800 eggs!

Some newcomers are deemed dangerous enough to warrant quarantines, pesticides, or biological control. In 1869 a citrus pest, the cottony cushion scale, found its way to California. Entomologists (insect scientists) found a beetle from its homeland of Australia, the vedalia ladybug, and introduced it in 1888, saving California's citrus industry. Many consider this the beginning of modern biological control, the practice of finding a natural enemy of a pest in its homeland, then importing and releasing it to kill the pest. Biological control can cut down on pesticide use, but it takes a lot of time and good science to get right.

Invasive species scientists study these newcomers (once we know they're here—many go unnoticed until their populations get large enough), looking at the impacts the new plant or animal will have on our environment and economy. This information can then be used to assess whether control efforts are needed. The vast majority of species don't have major impacts. They simply become one more local species with a story to tell.

Migration

Birdwatchers can look a bit odd, with their floppy hats and dangling binoculars, but on certain nights in spring and fall, Los Angeles's birding tribe looks stranger than usual. Donning dark glasses and aiming their telescopes at the full moon, they watch a migration in progress.

Migrating birds like thrushes, warblers, and sandpipers fly all night, landing to feed and rest once the sun rises. By watching carefully, you can see them pass overhead, backlit by the moon. On a clear night, when the moon is *too* bright, sunglasses cut down the glare.

Sometimes you can tell which species is passing overhead by their call; other times, by shape and flight style. Moon-watching may seem odd, but according to bird expert Kimball Garrett, it's a great chance to compare the

▼ Double-crested cormorants fly over downtown in V formation. Like bicycle racers, each one drafts off the one before.

► A humpback whale shows its flukes as it starts a deep dive.

patterns of nocturnal migration across the city. Do more migrant birds pass along the foothills than over the flat LA Basin? Are many birds moving right along the coast? Scattering observers over the region allows us to answer these questions.

Migration Mysteries

All animals travel during their lifetimes, but some animals take truly magnificent journeys of dozens, hundreds, or even thousands of miles. Southern California in general—and the Greater LA area in particular—holds vital resources for these long-distance migrants, who take advantage of our cities and suburbs to rest and refuel before continuing their long treks or flights.

Each year, in every habitat and ecosystem across the globe, some tiny voice inside various animals big and small compels them to leave everything behind and walk, fly, or swim to a distant land. Migrating animals have long puzzled humans. Before we had technology to track them, they seemed to appear without warning and disappear just as fast. Nobody knew where they came from or where they were going.

Many migrants aren't consciously aware of the cues telling them it's time to move. Even the simplest of creatures with barely a brain to speak of—like microscopic plankton in the ocean—use environmental triggers to precisely time their travel. Those triggers might include temperature, day length, the availability of food, the drive to mate, or dozens of other cues. To be considered a true migration, an animal's movements should be part of an annual or seasonal cycle: birds in the Northern Hemisphere that migrate south for winter and north for summer, for example.

Some of the world's most impressive migrators are the great whales—like the gray whale, the humpback, and the fin whale—some of which travel from the warm tropics to the icy poles and all of which can be seen off our coast (see Trip 25). The most massive of these ocean giants is the hundred-foot blue whale, as long as a jumbo jet, with a heart the size of your car. The California population of this mega marine mammal spends its winters breeding near Costa Rica and its summers gorging on food off the California coast.

DRAGONFLIES ON THE MOVE

One of the largest dragonflies in the LA area is the common green darner. It's also one of the best-known migrating dragonflies, but the migration itself is shrouded in scientific mystery—no one knows exactly where they come from, or where they're going.

We do know they appear in early spring before other, non-migrating dragonflies begin to take flight. Some green darners stop here in Los Angeles for a quick break on their journey north, others stay and set up shop.

Because their young develop in wetlands, they find a nice spot to hang out near water then set about finding a mate and laying eggs in streams and ponds. By the end of the summer, their nymphs have morphed into adults who begin their own migration south. Some scientists think they spend their winters in Mexico or the Caribbean. Though nobody knows their destination for sure, many entomologists think they aim for areas their parents came from.

Only 16 of the 326 species of dragonfly that call North America home routinely migrate.

Green darners aren't the only dragonflies that migrate through Los Angeles. Others making epic flights include black saddlebags, wandering gliders, and variegated meadowhawks. In late summer you can sometimes see

◄ Millions of green darner dragonflies migrate north in the spring and south in the fall. They can fly up to thirty miles per hour!

large groups of dragonflies congregating on hilltops as they journey south. In some cases, hundreds of thousands of dragonflies have been seen flying, as if carried by a river of air, along our coasts, mountain ridges, and waterways.

MIGRATING MONARCHS

Though they weigh only as much as six sheets of printer paper, monarch butterflies make a mighty migration. Populations in the eastern United States famously fly an epic two thousand-plus miles from summer feeding grounds in Canada to overwintering spots in Mexico.

Monarchs in California are a separate population from those east of the Rockies and migrate along a different path. Like their eastern cousins, they may fly as far north as Canada in summer, but during winter they settle along California's coastline. The Golden State's wintering population, seen from Ensenada, Mexico, all the way to Sonoma County, numbers in the hundreds of thousands.

On cool days, wintering monarchs stick to their roosting trees, sitting motionless, with their wings closed as if pretending to be leaves. But on sunnier days, you can see them flying about until late afternoon, when they return to their roosts for the night.

Many monarch roosts in Los Angeles are located on private property and can be tough to see, but some are publicly accessible. In October and November, visit Leo Carrillo State Beach for a look at these gold and black stunners (watch the eucalyptus trees along the creek, near the campground), or head even further north to the Monarch Butterfly Grove in Pismo Beach. An hour beyond Pismo Beach, you can see more amazing migrators: northern elephant seals at the Piedras Blancas rookery. They migrate as much as 13,000 miles in a year.

▼ Monarchs returning to their roosting tree.

LADYBUGS LOST AT SEA

Some impressive migrations span thousands of miles, but other, smaller migrations occur entirely within Los Angeles. Meet the convergent ladybug and its altitudinal migration. This species of everybody's favorite beetle looks familiar—its *elytra* (the hard front wings that protect their more delicate flying wings underneath) are the classic reddish orange with black spots—and you can find them in just about any garden or backyard from late spring through early fall. But once the weather starts to cool, these ladybugs head for the hills—literally.

Groups of several hundreds or thousands congregate in mountain canyons, where they bulk up by eating pollens and nectar, just like bears preparing to hibernate. The fat they pack on helps them survive winter. They'll spend up to nine months hibernating, often buried beneath the snow where the earth keeps them just warm enough. Once the snow melts, the ladybugs emerge and fly back to lowland valleys and coastal areas to begin feasting on aphids again.

Some ladybugs have been seen migrating too far, though. The Santa Ana winds, which tend to blow through early spring when ladybugs are emerging from hibernation, can blow them well past the coast and out to sea—a hazard of their migration style.

▲ Ladybugs gathering for winter in our local mountains.

Ladybug migration isn't sophisticated. It's governed by fairly simple—and rigid—rules. Once they've eaten up all the aphids, exhausting their food supply, the ladybugs pack up and fly toward the mountains. If lots of aphids are around, the ladybugs have no reason to go anywhere.

Convergent ladybug migration is also directed by the amount of daylight. When days become shorter at the end of the summer, it's time to begin the winter migration towards the highlands. When days become longer in the spring, it's time to begin the spring migration towards the lowlands.

If the Santa Anas threaten to push the ladybugs out to sea, they can't wait it out or alter course and head back toward the mountains. The rules that dictate their migration are too inflexible. The lost ladybugs might find a piece of driftwood or boat to cling to, but it's usually too late. Before long, they'll either starve or drown.

The dead and dying ladybugs often get washed up on the beach. Life is tough for a wayward beetle.

Freeways in the Sky

▲ In winter, mountain birds like this chickadee come down from higher elevations to investigate foothill yards and parks. This is called altitudinal migration.

◄ A greater yellowlegs begins its spring journey north after refueling in LA wetlands.

Los Angeles sits right in the middle of a four thousand-mile bird highway, a sort of endless conveyor belt of feathered critters coming and going throughout the year. Every year, at least a billion birds use this migration highway. Some travel the whole length, others just dip in and out along small sections.

There are four bird highways crossing North America from south to north: the Atlantic Flyway, which connects the Caribbean with Greenland; the Mississippi Flyway, which connects the Gulf Coast with Central Canada along the river for which it's named; the Central Flyway, which connects South and Central America with central Canada through the Great Plains; and our very own Pacific Flyway, which connects Patagonia with Alaska along the Pacific coastline.

In some places, the Pacific Flyway is one thousand miles wide. The animals that use it need quality habitat to rest in along their journey. If too much of that habitat gets paved over, converted into farmland, or degraded, the long-term survival for these species starts to look bleak. Some more adaptable birds, like the Vaux's Swift, might be able to substitute an urban chimney for a hollowed-out tree trunk, in which to roost, but others are more picky, or less lucky.

This is why many biologists have started to think about conservation not just in terms of preserving quality habitat, but in terms of preserving the links—or connections—between those habitats.

It's useful to think of nature in a place like Los Angeles as an ever-changing mosaic rather than a simple collection of native and introduced species. Even though some animals only visit a few days or weeks, the habitat they find in Los Angeles is just as critical for their survival as the habitats at either end of their migration.

We're lucky to have the opportunity to coexist with these visitors. They remind us that the environment is always changing, animals are resourceful, and nature can be found everywhere. Even within a Northridge backyard garden, or a chimneystack downtown.

After Dark

It's a sunny afternoon. Camille Boag and her dog Rue begin their regular walk around Echo Park Lake. They've only just started when Camille stops to take a closer look under the bushes.

She grabs a stick and pokes at a mystery item, but it's not what she's looking for. "Domestic dog," she says to herself, and continues along the path. As a volunteer for a community science project, Camille has agreed to come here each month to document coyote scat (the scientific term for poop). Coyotes pass through the park unseen at night, but they leave behind scat to mark their territories.

With practice, she's become something of an expert at telling the difference between dog and coyote droppings. Coyote scat has a lot more hair and fur in it, is much more likely to contain bones and seeds, and is usually twisted and tapered at one end. Dog poop, on the other hand, contains mostly mushy pet food and is shaped like blunt logs.

It might seem strange, but this is one of the best ways for researchers to learn about the lives of nighttime animals. You can tell a lot about an animal from its poop.

A Day in the Life of a Night Animal

Coyotes were once called the ghosts of the plains, because they were heard more than they were seen. This is still true. Their calls, familiar to anybody who lives near our hills and mountains, help coyotes keep in touch with their pack-mates, even when they can't see each other. Perhaps they're wishing each other a good morning or warning their comrades to be careful.

Most coyotes follow a daily routine: patrolling their territory while looking for food. Imagine a coyote as it reaches a familiar rock near the edge of its home range. Like a domestic dog on a fire hydrant, it uses urine to mark its turf. Think of it as a note written with pee, sending a message to unfamiliar coyotes who might be nearby. "Stay away," the coyote declares as it sprays the rock. "This seat is taken."

Los Angeles isn't the only city with urban coyotes. Biologist Stan Gehrt researches the city-dwelling coyotes of Chicago. One coyote he studied was not only successfully navigating Chicago's streets but also waiting for traffic lights to change before trying to cross!

▲ A coyote out in the early morning.

▲ A coyote's-eye-view of Los Angeles from the Hollywood Hills.

Let's imagine a coyote wandering through a golf course. Food is abundant in the hills and yards of Los Angeles. While coyotes will eat a huge variety of plants and animals, living or dead, one of their favorite meals in urban areas is the cottontail rabbit. Rabbits have fewer places to hide on the golf course than in the brush-covered hillsides—the coyote spots breakfast hopping along near the ninth hole. But the coyote just isn't fast enough, and the rabbit escapes.

In the early a.m. hours, the coyote emerges from the hills to saunter down Sunset Boulevard. This is risky business—like every other animal that calls Los Angeles home, coyotes often become roadkill. But it is more likely to survive a crossing in the middle of the night than during the day.

Because it's a quiet night, our coyote crosses easily. Safely back on the sidewalk, it turns its head to the left and sees driveway after driveway. Having missed breakfast, the coyote is hungry. And it knows that where there are driveways, there are backyards. The coyote listens but hears nothing.

61

The coast is clear. As it jogs down one driveway, it notices the porchlights, attended by light-seeking insects. Small non-native lizards are enjoying a feast thanks to those lights. While a lizard might make a good appetizer for a hungry coyote, ours knows it can find food more easily in the backyard.

As homeowners and families sleep soundly inside, the coyote quietly moves from yard to yard. Fruit trees have dropped oranges and grapefruits, and one yard has a garden with ripe strawberries. It's not rabbit, but fruits and berries make a fine feast, and, unlike lizards and rabbits, they don't run away.

One hour and a dozen backyards later, the coyote gets lucky. A dog owner has left out a big dish of water. Raccoons were at the dish first, but when they sniffed the coyote's scent, they were off in a flash of black and gray fur. The coyote drinks in total privacy.

At dawn the sky turns pink and road traffic starts to pick up. As the city's nocturnal critters settle into sleep, people are waking up to their alarms and getting ready for work and school. Having survived the big city another night, the coyote makes its way home to the protection offered by dense chaparral. (But not before leaving a smelly gift behind for some community scientist like Camille to find!) The coyote hears its siblings and parents yipping and yahooing. It returns their calls with one of its own. "I found some tasty food," it might say. "But now I'm heading home. See you soon!"

▲ Fan palms silhouetted against the setting sun mean that the night shift is about to come on duty.

Internal Clocks

As long as there have been critters on this planet, there have been those that sleep through the heat of the day and emerge to go about their lives at night.

The Earth's daily rhythms have continued more or less unchanged for billions of years. Night is darker and cooler; day is brighter and warmer. Animals—including humans—have evolved to expect these predictable cycles. Plants, fungi, and bacteria also have these internal clocks, known as circadian rhythms.

At night, our artificial lights make parts of the city bright as daylight, altering the night sky with what's known as light pollution. Changing the basics of night and day can alter the circadian rhythms of animals, insects, and other organisms, even people.

Most birds sleep at night, and hunt and sing during the daytime. In the wild, male robins start singing just before dawn. But in cities like Los Angeles, streetlights can mess with their timing, causing them to start a few hours too early. And male northern mockingbirds usually only sing to find a mate during the day, but those in lighted areas continue to warble at night. Researchers suspect artificial lights trick the mockingbirds into believing it's still daytime.

A little extra singing might not seem like a big deal, but it is. The birds could be wasting energy singing before their potential mates are ready to listen. Every calorie they burn by singing must later be replenished by eating.

Other changes happen when we have too much light. One study found that female frogs, which normally breed at night, were less choosy about their potential mates in brighter areas. The hypothesis is that they would rather mate quickly and then hide, because bright lights increased the risk that they would become somebody else's dinner. Another researcher noticed that frogs near a football stadium stopped mating on game nights. If the frog pond was covered, blocking the glow from the bright lights, the frogs were happy to mate.

Some moths can use the light of the moon to navigate. When they mistake artificial lights for the moon they can circle endlessly. Of course, this is great for bats—a cloud of moths hovering around a light is

Bird legs have special tendons that lock into place while they perch so they don't fall off their branch while sleeping.

▶ The Yuma myotis bat prefers ponds and streams. Thanks to the lake at the La Brea Tar Pits, you can sometimes spot them along Wilshire Boulevard.

a heavenly feast for them. However, if our communities were to switch to more efficient, darkness-protecting light sources, the bats would go back to finding moths the old-fashioned way. They find the lights useful, but not essential—a handy life-hack for surviving in the city. Without the lights, the bats would still be out there, using their sonar to chow down.

The good news is that there are some kinds of lights that cause a lot less light pollution than other kinds; if your city or neighborhood is talking about making the switch to these more efficient types, it's worth supporting. Darker skies are good for humans and animals, and they help us see the stars more clearly, too.

▲ A white-lined sphinx moth feeds at night.

Do Plants Have Bedtimes?

Plants are different at night than they are during the day. They may look the same from the outside, but their internal power systems run differently. In daytime they soak up sunshine for photosynthesis, the chemical process that creates energy for them and oxygen for us.

At night, plants can't photosynthesize because moonlight is too weak (imagine trying to read a book by candlelight—if the candle was a block away). But plants aren't just chilling out at night, getting bored. Many need nocturnal insects to visit their flowers and pollinate them. They may not be running their energy systems, but they're still open for business and hoping for customers.

► Datura blossoms are open at night and early morning, often closing up during midday heat.

You can find one such plant, the sacred datura, in Los Angeles's foothills and weedy lots. Nicknamed moon flower or, less charitably, jimsonweed or stinkweed, it's an attractive plant that resembles a pumpkin vine growing low to the ground. Its dark, gray-green leaves, about the size of a child's hand, have large, white blossoms, often displaying a purple inner core. These blossoms are pollinated by sphinx moths—insects about the size of a hummingbird, which are active mostly at night.

A Good Reason to Get up Early (Once in a While)

Want to see a sphinx moth, coyote, bat, or maybe even a bobcat? Many nocturnal animals go to bed before the sun is fully up, but if you're out early enough, you may see the night shift before they clock out. Before most of the city is awake, you'll have the roads and hiking trails to yourself and could be the first to find animal tracks or scat (the end of the night shift is also the start of the day shift, so you'll see twice as much nature as usual). Though they can be harder to spot, the animals and insects that take to the night are important members of our wildlife communities. Without them, Los Angeles would be a very different place, even during the day.

▼▲ Common night shift members include skunks and opossums.

Backyards

Michael Gronwold lives in a downtown LA apartment. He doesn't have much room, but that didn't stop him from creating a wildlife habitat. He set up two wooden window boxes four floors up from the busy street, hoping his little garden would attract the bees, butterflies, and other pollinators he'd seen flying around downtown. They showed up right away. So did a hummingbird. Inspired, Michael installed a hummingbird feeder.

As more hummingbirds found his garden, he increased his feeders to four. Two species routinely show up: Anna's hummingbird and Allen's hummingbird. On one particularly cloudy day, he counted thirty-six hummingbirds feeding or perched outside his window. Michael describes his experience as being "visited all day long by the beautiful flying residents of downtown Los Angeles."

Backyards Are Critical Habitat

Individuals have the power to make Los Angeles work better for wildlife. Urban and suburban green space can be divided into two categories: parks and other protected spaces, and privately-owned yards and lawns. We can show city officials how altering the ways parks and preserves are managed will benefit humans and wildlife, but in urban settings, more than a third of green space is backyards and private property. Studies have shown that when yards become more wildlife friendly, even habitats as small as Michael's, the payoffs can be huge.

According to a study conducted on backyards in Illinois, one backyard can provide a small benefit to wildlife, but when multiple neighboring houses—within 150 feet of each other—use wildlife-friendly landscaping strategies the combined benefits are tremendous. One example: neighborhoods like these attracted more birds than those where homeowners didn't create critter-friendly habitats. And streets with multiple bird-friendly yards had almost twice as many bird species as those without.

Green Space Is Good for Us Too

▲ Acorn woodpeckers specialize in acorns, but they won't say no to a well-placed bird feeder.

◄ Cabbage white butterflies are among the most commonly spotted in Los Angeles. They have been recorded flying every month of the year.

In the early 1980s, the Japanese Ministry of Agriculture, Forestry, and Fisheries began to promote a practice they termed *shinrin-yoku*. Loosely translated as forest bathing, it involves taking in the atmosphere of the forest: essentially, a nature walk. Research shows that this improves mental and physical well-being and promotes relaxation.

The Japanese aren't the only ones making this sort of argument. American biologist E. O. Wilson argued that humans have a strong "urge to affiliate with other forms of life," something he termed *biophilia*. And the idea that spending time in nature can be good for the soul is wrapped up in the establishment of the nation's National Park system, often described as America's best idea. Newton B. Drury, director of the National Park Service between 1940 and 1951, once said that by exposing Americans to the natural world, the parks offer "an opportunity to grow mentally and spiritually, as well as physically."

It would be nice if we could all take time every week to hike in mountains, or even stroll through a city park, but sometimes work, school, and family obligations get in the way. Soccer practice, conference calls, trips to the dentist—given the pace of life in the City of Angels, staring out the window at songbirds and hummingbirds for a few minutes or noticing the nature on your way to the grocery store can do a world of good.

Of course, there's also the ecological benefit of biodiversity. Without a wide variety of species, the things we need to survive—oxygen, clean water, food—could be in short supply. Since it seems we don't plan to stop cities from growing, allowing biodiversity some space in our yards seems like a reasonable compromise.

67

The Backyard Crew

A wild predator shifts silently in and out of lush, green shadows. Its sole purpose, at this moment, is to eat. Finding a target, she closes the distance quickly, snatching her prey between ferocious mouthparts.

This scene could describe lions on the prowl in Africa, but it also unfolds every day in LA backyards, courtyards, and parks. The humble ladybug is the lioness of your backyard garden, stalking aphids as voraciously as lions do antelope. Los Angeles's raccoons, foxes, hummingbirds, lizards—and, yes, even the insects—live in a world just as inspiring and brutal as the dramatic Serengeti. Great horned owls crush cottontail rabbits in their talons, applying some three hundred pounds per square inch of pressure to drain the life from their furry prey. Parasitic wasps lay their eggs in caterpillars so their young larvae can have fresh meat when they hatch. And beetle grubs make juicy snacks for Southern alligator lizards, which are themselves hunted by California scrub-jays.

Spend enough time in your backyard or apartment complex courtyard and you'll see more than just the drama of predator versus prey, you may be lucky enough to see what stays hidden from most people. Animals use your yard to court, have sex, lay eggs, and give birth—maybe just a few feet from your own bedroom. They defend their territories, raise their young, grow old, and eventually die. Animals go about their lives unknown to us, unless we look closely.

▲ Seven-spotted ladybugs feast on aphids.

BACKYARD WILDLIFE SANCTUARY

▲ This California towhee bathes to stay parasite free. After splashing around, it will sit in the sun to dry out and preen its feathers, adding a protective oil coating to each one.

◄ Black-bellied slender salamanders will eat small insects and worms in your garden.

There's so much we can do to make our homes, schools, parks, and neighborhoods critter-friendly, whether we've got a small apartment with a window box, or a house with a few acres of yard. A few changes to your backyard or garden can make it more wildlife friendly. Start by providing basic needs—food, water, shelter, and space. Here are some good ideas:

The National Wildlife Federation runs the Certified Wildlife Habitat® program to help homeowners make their backyards wildlife friendly (check **nwf.org** for details).

- Plant native species—they use less water, are adapted to our climate, and their leaves, seeds, and flowers provide the best food and shelter for local wildlife.

- If you have space for trees, plant a mix of evergreens, like pines, and deciduous trees, like oaks. Trees don't just add habitat, they add complexity—a variety of habitats stacked vertically one on top of the other.

- Put in a small water feature like a simple bird bath—birds like to bathe in it, and insects and other animals will drink from it in the heat of summer.

- If you have a swimming pool, consider installing a "frog log." It's a little escape ramp that allows small animals, including frogs, squirrels, lizards, baby birds, and others, to avoid drowning if they fall in.

- Create shelters—a brush or rock pile is a great place for lizards and other small critters to hide. If you put logs out, you can also look for mushrooms and slime molds growing on them after it rains.

- Don't clean up too much! Let plants go to seed—birds rely on them for food. Allow leaves to accumulate; it helps build soil and provides cover for soil-dwelling creatures.

You can take your wildlife-friendly yard to the next level by installing an owl box, a bee hotel, or a bird feeder. Rather than simply making it possible for animals to use your yard, these devices can actually attract them. Owl boxes and bee hotels also provide space for babies. Imagine having an owl nursery in your backyard!

INDOOR CATS MAKE GOOD NEIGHBORS

It's worth mentioning that your good work creating a wildlife-friendly backyard can be undermined by certain actions. For example: letting your cat outside. Specifics vary from study to study, but biologists agree that outdoor cats kill a staggering number of birds, reptiles, and mammals each year. Keeping your tiny leopard inside could have a big impact on your neighborhood's biodiversity.

If you do have an outdoor pet, and you keep a food dispenser outside, make sure it is critter proof. Same goes for your trashcans. Raccoons can develop gout if they eat too much pet food, and easy trash pickings can attract coyotes to your yard. Coyotes may also choose to make your pet into dinner (another reason to keep Whiskers inside), so work to make your yard as coyote unfriendly as possible.

Though squirrels and other rodents can be a nuisance, don't use rodenticides or rat poisons. While these poisons do kill their intended targets, they also work their way up the food chain. Predators like bobcats, mountain lions, hawks and owls, and pets like cats and dogs can all get secondary poisoning—it accumulates in their systems after they eat animals that ate the poison or if they scavenge a poisoned animal's carcass.

In studies conducted by local National Park Service biologists, over 80 percent of coyotes and over 90 percent of bobcats and mountain lions had been exposed to rodenticide poisons. Even if the poison doesn't kill these predators directly, it can still impair immune function—increasing the risk of catching mange and other diseases.

▲ Green fruit beetle swarms are often found on ripe fruit. They are most active in summer.

▼ Raccoons won't hesitate to eat any pet food left out—but it's not good for them.

Try natural options for pest control. Many of our non-human neighbors have survived the relentless march of urbanization for generations. But that doesn't mean we can't give them some neighborly help. Plus, the local predator population will return the favor—less poison means more hawks, owls, and others taking care of your rodent problems.

We're All in It Together

Leo Politi Elementary School sits just two miles from downtown Los Angeles, in one of the densest parts of the city. This means there's not that much room for nature to grow or kids to play. A few years ago, then-principal Brad Rumble decided to take an empty part of campus and grow a garden.

▲ One off-beat suggestion is to sprinkle coyote urine here and there around your yard—you might just convince the squirrels to leave your herb garden alone.

With the help of students from a nearby high school, they planted sages, oaks, monkey-flowers, and other native species. They dug a vernal pool. Then they waited for the birds and insects to show up. Teachers began using the space for lessons, and Brad took students there to talk things through when they were troubled.

Not long after the garden grew in, wildlife turned up—the students counted dozens of species of birds in the garden, and hundreds of insects—but that was expected. The surprise was that student disciplinary issues dropped to almost zero and science test scores skyrocketed. Brad said they went "from the basement to the penthouse in science." Before the garden, 9 percent of Leo Politi students tested proficient in science. After the garden was planted, 54 percent did. Gardens don't just benefit wildlife. They also benefit us.

What would our city look, sound, and smell like if every school and property owner provided a bit of quality wildlife habitat? If enough people landscape their yards with wildlife in mind, those gardens could become corridors for traveling between larger green spaces, allowing animals to hop-scotch safely across the city from backyard to backyard. Los Angeles has a good amount of undeveloped green space, but, acre for acre, the nature of Los Angeles is the nature of the backyard.

► Students from Leo Politi Elementary survey their schoolyard garden for birds. The data they collect are uploaded to eBird, so scientists and others can answer questions about birds in Los Angeles.

Science by the People

At just twelve years old, Reese Bernstein became a published scientist. All because of his observation skills and a tiny gecko.

Reese always loved lizards. He'd search for them in his backyard, at school, and on every family hike. His parents encouraged his obsession, and his dad, Will, gave him a field guide to the reptiles and amphibians of the LA area. They would pore over the book together, studying the pictures and noting the different lizards they found on their adventures.

One night at a family barbecue in Chatsworth, Reese found a lizard he'd never seen before. Its feet made him think it was a gecko.

When they got home that night Reese pulled out his field guide to figure out what type of lizard it was. The western banded gecko was the closest match.

Reese and his dad sent a photo of the gecko to the Natural History Museum's community science project Reptiles and Amphibians of Southern California, or RASCals. Museum scientists confirmed that the lizard was in fact a gecko, but not a native western banded gecko. Instead, the gecko was from the Mediterranean. Reese and his dad went back to Chatsworth and found more of the geckos. This was an important scientific discovery—the first time anyone had found an established population of this species in LA County.

When professional scientists make discoveries like this, they share the news with other researchers by writing up their findings and publishing them in scientific journals. Greg Pauly worked with Reese and his dad to do just that. Reese and Will co-authored the research paper that described the discovery of these Mediterranean house geckos, in Los Angeles. How many twelve-year-olds have done that? Thanks to the rise of community science, people like Reese can help professional scientists like never before.

What Is Community Science?

Community science, also known as citizen science, is the name for the collaboration between professional scientists and the general public as they work together to answer questions about our world. Whatever you call it, it's

▲ The Mediterranean house gecko is one of several non-native geckos you can find in urban Los Angeles.

as diverse as the people participating in it. In the United States, people have been monitoring stream quality and counting birds for decades. Today, some projects in Africa have people use smartphones to document wildlife in and around their lands.

Community science often has a big outreach and education goal, but it's also a research method. Projects should provide results that are published in the scientific literature or that impact conservation or management. In the best studies, the research questions cannot be answered with any approach other than community science. Consider Reese's gecko. No biologist was ever going to find it hidden away on private property, but Reese was able to find it because he had access to the location and he had his nature eyes on.

In some community science projects, the scientists ask the question; other times, it comes from the community. The RASCals project began because Greg wanted to know what reptiles and amphibians live in Los Angeles today, and where they are found. By comparing Museum records to modern-day surveys, he can start to understand how species have shifted their ranges in response to urbanization. Reese participated in the project

Seven species of non-native geckos and three species of native geckos live in Southern California. Of the native species, only the western banded gecko is found in LA County.

The Natural History Museum has multiple community science projects. You can find information on all of them and learn how to help at **nhm.org**.

1. **RASCals** (Reptiles and Amphibians of Southern California) is designed to improve our knowledge of native and non-native reptiles and amphibians in Southern California.

2. **BioSCAN** (Biodiversity Science: City and Nature) works with families and landowners to set up insect traps across Los Angeles, to help us understand which species live here.

3. **SLIME** (Snails and slugs Living in Metropolitan Environments) seeks to better understand the distribution of Southern California's snail and slug populations.

4. **Southern California Squirrel Survey** aims to learn more about the distribution and behavior of local squirrel species, especially the expanding, non-native eastern fox squirrel and the declining native western gray squirrel.

5. **LA Spider Survey** participants have sent in almost 6,000 spiders from all over the county so scientists can understand which species live where.

▲ Why did the tarantula cross the road? Most likely to find a mate. This male tarantula got his iNaturalist.org portrait taken while patrolling for receptive females.

▼ When taking photos of plants, animals, or fungi for scientific identification, some angles are better than others. Mushroom gills are an important characteristic for identification of fungi.

You can get started sharing photos of any plant, animal, fungus, or other evidence of life (scat, tracks, bones) with the Museum by using **#NatureinLA** on social media, emailing photos to **nature@nhm.org**, or by downloading the free iNaturalist app.

because he had a question about the lizard he found. While Reese's question was answered during the process, Greg's question needs a lot more data—non-native species are showing up all the time, and the best way to find them and track their movements is through community science.

You can help Greg and scientists like him find answers by sending pictures to RASCals, SLIME, and many other community science projects. Even if you're not sure what kind of critter you've seen, share it anyway, and somebody will help you identify it. Every bit of data helps.

BIG QUESTIONS NEED BIG DATA

Imagine you're a professional scientist with the question: What nature lives here? In a wilderness area, you'd simply survey the plants and animals around you. But how do you do that in a city where most of the land is privately owned? Getting permission to go into everyone's backyard would be very time consuming, if not impossible. Even with permission, imagine how many scientists you'd need to survey the entire LA area!

Getting homeowners involved allows scientists to build large datasets (big collections of information). When thousands of Angelenos send in pictures of creatures from their backyards, scientists begin to see trends, like which lizards only live close to natural areas, or which snails are only active during certain times of year. Scientists get data and community scientists gain something too. Reese learned more about his favorite subject—lizards. Other people learn new skills, meet friends who are also interested in plants and animals, or get a hands-on experience with real science.

COMMUNITY SCIENCE STORIES:
THE INDO-PACIFIC GECKO

In the summer of 2013, Glen Yoshida snapped a photo of a lizard hanging out on the wall above his front door in Torrance. He uploaded the photo to the iNaturalist app on his phone. Because smartphones have clocks and GPS chips, it automatically included the photo's time and location. Those essential pieces of information are critical when researchers turn to community science to help answer questions.

Glen knew his lizard wasn't from Southern California, but like Reese he wasn't sure exactly what it was. At the Museum, Greg identified it as the Indo-Pacific gecko—a native to Southern and Southeast Asia. Knowing it was a species new to California, Greg wanted more information. He asked Glen to keep photographing the geckos and to record the temperature at his home each day he saw them.

All Indo-Pacific geckos are female. They reproduce using parthenogenesis, a reproductive strategy in which females produce clones of themselves without having to mate with a male.

Together, Greg and Glen made several astonishing discoveries: the geckos were active year round as long as the day was warm, and the geckos' eggs could incubate and hatch even in Los Angeles's colder winter months. That's surprising for a species from the tropics.

◄ Community scientist Xan Sonn observed these alligator lizards in a Pasadena apartment courtyard and contributed his photo to RASCals.

As with Reese's discovery, Greg worked with Glen to publish the finding, and Glen co-authored a scientific paper. Not only did they discover another non-native species in Los Angeles they also worked together to understand how the tropical gecko is surviving in Los Angeles.

COMMUNITY SCIENCE STORIES: LIZARD LOVE BITES

Mating behavior is a fundamental component of how animals survive in their environments. But for some species, it's difficult to study in the wild. Through community science, researchers benefit from the power of the crowd.

Take alligator lizards. Courting alligator lizards are an odd sight. The male lizard bites the female behind her head, sometimes holding her in this position for more than a day. While in this lizard love bite, the pair seems less aware of their surroundings and can end up in the open. When people stumble upon this scene, they are usually curious and sometimes take pictures.

When the Museum first asked Angelenos to send in their lizard love pictures (on Valentine's Day in 2016), the response was huge. Greg collected over one hundred images of mating alligator lizards. At the time, only one research paper mentioned the behavior at all, so very little was known about it. Greg had a lot of questions: What season does the mating ritual happen in? Does the fact that urban areas are warmer than rural ones cause urban lizards to mate earlier? How does the timing of mating vary across elevation, latitude, or years? Though he's still never seen mating alligator lizards with his own eyes, with his new crowdsourced data, Greg can begin asking and answering these questions and more.

COMMUNITY SCIENCE STORIES:
THE DINNER-PARTY BET

In 2007, Brian Brown, the Museum's curator of entomology, was chatting with a donor at a dinner party. Brian boasted that he could find a new species of fly in Los Angeles, one entirely unknown to science, just as easily as he could

▲ Brian Brown sets up a Malaise trap.

in the tropics where he does a lot of his field work. The donor challenged him to discover a new species in her backyard.

A few weeks later, he found himself in her Brentwood backyard setting up an insect Malaise trap. Bugs fly into what looks like a tent and get funneled towards an opening at the top, where they fall into a jar filled with alcohol. Brian calls it the jar of death—not a warm, fuzzy name, but an essential tool for preserving insects for scientific study.

When Brian retrieved the bug-filled container and took it back to his lab at the Museum, the very first critter he examined with his microscope was a tiny yellowish fly—about the size of a pinhead. He compared it to known species of phorids, the tiny humpbacked flies he specializes in, but couldn't find a match. It was a new species, unknown to the world until that moment.

Just one insect into his experiment and he'd already won the bet! After sorting through the other phorids in the jar, he ended up with this new species, a European species never recorded in North America, and an African species also unrecorded on this continent. The truth is, Brian had known he'd win the bet. Very few people study these flies around the world, and no one had ever looked in Los Angeles before.

Brian's discoveries inspired BioSCAN (Biodiversity Science: City and Nature), a project in which people across Los Angeles allow the Museum to set up Malaise traps in their backyards. After just three months of sorting through thousands of tiny flies, Brian and his team discovered thirty new species. Twenty-seven were found in backyards, one in the Museum's own Nature Gardens, one in a community garden, and one at an elementary school. Then they found twelve more. Then another one. A whopping 43 of 110 phorid flies in the LA area were new to science. The more they look, the more they find. LA backyards are teeming with undiscovered life.

How to Help

Participating in a community science project is a simple way to help scientists learn more about our neighborhoods. Your smartphone photos of squirrels, snails, slugs, reptiles and amphibians are invaluable to scientists all over Southern California. If you have a backyard or other property, letting researchers use it as a field site is another great way to help—they might install a wildlife camera or an insect trap in your yard.

But even if you don't have a yard or you missed the perfect shot of that lizard under your car, there are plenty of ways to pitch in. There are thousands of volunteer opportunities in Los Angeles. At public gardens like those at the Natural History Museum, the Huntington Library, or Descanso Gardens, volunteers help care for the resident plants and animals. In wilder places, many local Parks and Recreation departments, the US Forest Service, the National Park Service, and organizations like Tree People or Friends of Ballona Creek will train volunteers to remove invasive species and assist with habitat restoration. Local non-profits like Friends of the LA River and Heal the Bay host regular river and beach clean-ups, and LA Waterkeeper needs volunteers to help monitor ecological health and water quality along the LA River.

▲ Community scientists capture data about LA nature.

BUILDING BRIDGES

Creating backyard habitat and redesigning city parks to support native species has a measurably positive impact on wildlife. But not every animal is able to take advantage. Take the mountain lions living in the Santa Monica Mountains. The area around Liberty Canyon boasts great lion habitat on both sides of the 101 Freeway, but the dangerous crossing keeps the populations mostly separate. Some particularly courageous cats have risked life and limb to reach new territory, but they're often hit by cars. In the fifteen years researchers have studied them, only four lions are known to have survived the crossing.

Young lions need to be able to move north in search of new opportunities, and older lions need to be able to move south, bringing new genes. Starved of new genetic material, this tiny mountain lion community could disappear in a matter of decades as inbreeding takes its toll. If we want our mountain lions to have a future, they must be able to safely traverse Southern California.

Community members and conservation groups have partnered to create the #SaveLACougars campaign. Their goal is to build a wildlife crossing across the 101 Freeway in Liberty Canyon. Once completed, it's likely to be the largest urban wildlife crossing anywhere in the world and something of an experiment. Just about everything from butterflies to lizards to bobcats would benefit, not just mountain lions. Wildlife crossings have been built elsewhere with great success, but not in one of the world's biggest cities on top of one of its busiest highways. This bridge will be a model for human-wildlife coexistence in heavily urbanized areas.

BECOME AN ADVOCATE

Getting involved in advocacy is another way to be a champion for wildlife. You can start by getting informed, signing up for local wildlife nonprofits' newsletters, or following their social media accounts. Once you know about the issues, share them with your friends and family, attend local city council meetings, and vote in local elections. Show your support for local wildlife-friendly efforts like building new parks or redesigning old ones, or switching to less light-polluting street lights. It all helps to make our cities work better for wildlife.

Even in today's connected world, full of billions of people and thousands of scientists, new discoveries are being made. Questions about nature still need answers, and we can work together to find them. How can a future Los Angeles work better for humans and wildlife? How can backyard habitats help our city? How will our volunteer hours affect wildlife? Answering the questions about how our city works in concert with nature is essential for the future of Los Angeles, and for cities around the world. We're all part of a grand, global ecological experiment in urbanized living. The best part is, we can all help guarantee the experiment ends with success.

Birds
82

**Insects and
Spiders**
106

Mammals
130

**Reptiles and
Amphibians**
148

101 LA SPECIES TO KNOW

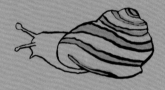

Snails and Slugs
162

Mushrooms, Slime Mold, and Lichen
166

Plants
172

Acorn Woodpecker

Melanerpes formicivorus

▲ An acorn woodpecker inspects the acorns in its granary.

Red cap and clown expression

White patches in middle of otherwise dark wings as it flies

Usually in groups on trees (not often on ground)

The loud calls and antics of acorn woodpeckers inspired animator Walter Lantz to create Woody Woodpecker.

Unlike most other woodpeckers, an acorn woodpecker is rarely seen on its own. You may hear one before you spot it: Acorn woodpeckers are often encountered in raucous groups, everybody calling *YAK-ah, YAK-ah,* back and forth.

Dressed boldly in black and white, with large white patches on the rump and each wing, and wearing a red crown, acorn woodpeckers have an outfit few animals can match. Single birds often display to each other by spreading their wings to expose those white patches.

Through binoculars, their pale eyes look like sewn-on buttons, giving them a pop-eyed look, like a birthday clown who's had too much espresso.

Woodpecker Community

These oak specialists focus on acorns, which are gathered and stored by small groups working together. They also breed communally: up to three females may lay eggs within a single nest. After the eggs hatch, other birds act as

> Like other woodpeckers, acorn woodpeckers fly with a burst of wingbeats and short glides, rising up and dropping down in a flight pattern that resembles a roller coaster.

helpers to care for the young. The helpers are often closely related to the breeding birds they assist—think siblings, aunts, and uncles.

They store their acorns in granaries—hundreds (even thousands) of small holes drilled into trees, phone poles, fences, and buildings. The birds jam acorns into the holes, to be retrieved later. As the acorns dry and shrink, the woodpeckers move them to smaller holes to make it harder for other critters to steal them. When other foods are in short supply, woodpeckers use their stash to remain well fed.

Although acorns form a large part of their diet, they eat other food too. The scientific name *formicivorus* means ant-eating, and this is indeed one of several woodpecker species that eats ants. They also sally, or charge suddenly, into the air to catch flying insects. Sometimes, they visit seed feeders and even hummingbird feeders.

Where to See Them
Acorns grow on oaks—find the trees and you'll probably find the birds. **Trips 1**, **2**, **8**, **14**, and **16** are reliable places to start.

Black Phoebe
Sayornis nigricans

Phoebe numbers are undoubtedly greater now in the LA Basin than they were prior to urbanization. They need mud for nest building, and thanks to how lushly we water urban landscapes, they've gotten comfortable in our residential areas and parks.

However, you won't ever see a flock of black phoebes crowding around. They're territorial birds that don't put up with rivals, so you'll usually see single birds or pairs. Late in the nesting season (May to August), you'll sometimes also see juveniles accompanying adults as they learn to fly. By fall, though, they'll have moved on, looking for their own slice of home turf. You can recognize juveniles by the cinnamon-colored bars on each wing.

Black Tie Optional
They're called phoebes because of their call, which sounds like *fee-BEE*? Although, if you're thirsty, you may hear it more like *fee-BEER*!

Black above, white below ("tuxedo")

Upright posture on fence posts and branches

Hunts by chasing flying insects then returning to perch

Actually, the song tends to alternate both phrases—*fee-bee?, fee-beer!, fee-bee?, fee-beer!*, and so on.

No matter the song, an adult black phoebe's dress code never varies: black head, back, wings, and tail, and a white belly that reaches up to a point in the center of the breast—like a tiny, fancy tuxedo.

Bugs and Mud

Black phoebes are one of four hundred kinds of flycatchers. These birds hunt by sallying—perching on branches or fence posts, waiting, waiting—then ZIP!—darting off to catch a passing bug and landing nearby to whack the prey into submission and gobble it down. They catch moths, bees, dragonflies, and grasshoppers and will also nab crawling insects or minnows near the surface of a pond. Whiskers around their bills help them sense and catch flying insects.

Phoebe nesting requirements include mud for building and an overhang for shelter. Urban areas, with their constant irrigation and variety of manmade structures, provide an abundance of both. Phoebes embody the phrase, "If you build it, they will come."

Where to See Them

Throughout the LA Basin and up to about 4,000 feet elevation in the foothills, especially in residential areas, well-watered parks and gardens, and near any streams or canyons with standing water. This is not a hard bird to find, and is quite likely at **Trips 1**, **3**, **7**, **8**, **10**, **14**, **18**, **19**, **21**, and **24**, among others.

Black-necked Stilt

Himantopus mexicanus

Black and white head and body, year-round

Long, pink legs

Black-necked stilts look like baby flamingos dressed up like penguins. To feed, they stalk through shallow water on long, pink legs, ready to jab down with a beak to catch insect larva, tadpoles, or water beetles.

They build their nests just above the water, often on small islands or matted clumps of vegetation at the water's edge. Typical of ground-nesting shorebirds, this stilt's sandy-colored, black-speckled eggs (usually a set of four) are remarkably well-camouflaged, but if a would-be predator gets too close to a stilt nest, the adult bird puts on a distraction display. It flies a short distance away and pretends to be injured—diverting attention away from the vulnerable nest. They nest in late spring and summer—runoff from rare summer storms can also be a danger to the eggs.

Where to See Them

The best places to find black-necked stilts are usually around other shorebird species—find one, you'll find others. They turn up in shallow ponds and river margins anywhere in the lowlands but are seen in greatest numbers along the lower LA River. The flow of shallow water through the wide concrete channel creates an ideal platform of sediment and algae, which in turn is home to flies, beetles, and other insects that are tasty treats to hungry, wading shorebirds. They can be seen on **Trips 10**, **19**, **22**, and **23**, with 23 being a world-class urban birding adventure from June to October.

Bushtit

Psaltriparus minimus

Hiking along the LA River or in our local parks, you might have noticed the bushtit's distinctive nest—a woven pouch hanging in a large shrub or tree. About ten inches long, it looks like somebody tried to make a bag out of twigs, lichen, and dryer lint. Despite its dirty-sock nest, this dainty bird is one of North America's busiest songbirds.

Bushtits float through bushes in chittering flocks, inspecting twigs and undersides of leaves for tasty insects. Plain gray, with a tiny ink-dab of a bill, they are casual acrobats, hanging upside-down while hunting. Other songbirds will often join a bushtit flock, adding to the twitters and chirps.

A Good Friend to Have

Because many insect-eaters leave our area in summer to breed, only the bushtit is on bug duty year-round. It consumes large numbers of aphids, scale insects, and other garden pests, making it an important friend to gardeners.

Bushtits are also great at spotting hawks and will trill a warning call that scatters the flock. Other birds join them in diving for cover inside shrubs or the leafiest parts of trees. This behavior is often a bird-watcher's first clue that a hawk is nearby.

Where to See Them

A common resident of the LA area, bushtits live here year-round from sea level to the lower mountains, including in parks, gardens, and chaparral. Expected at many sites in the LA Basin, including **Trips 1**, **3**, **6**, **7**, **8**, **11**, **14**, **15**, **19**, and **21**.

The word *tit* came from the Vikings and means pin in Old Norse—it describes any small songbird.

Dinky bill

Females have yellow eyes

Small and gray

Head lacks a crest

Gray saddle across top of blue back

Often in noisy, inquisitive flocks

Large, gray-bellied, blue-colored jay

California Scrub-Jay

Aphelocoma californica

You may hear this bird before seeing it—its screechy, scolding call carries a long way, even in dense brush. The scrub-jay is jaunty and bold. Though it's a jay and also blue, don't call it a blue jay—the true blue jay (*Cyanocitta cristata*) is an Easterner not normally found in California.

Scrub-jays are omnivores and eat a wide range of food—fruit, insects, worms, seeds, and perhaps an unattended piece of your lunch. They're also predators of small lizards, snakes, and birds, and they will raid nests, steal eggs, and even eat nestlings.

You'll often find jays around oak trees, gathering and storing acorns, which makes them major competitors with acorn woodpeckers. Woodpeckers have to keep a close watch on their granaries to make sure jays don't steal an easy meal. And jays have to be doubly cautious when they're storing acorns—other jays sometimes watch and steal the acorn after its owner flies off.

Where to See Them

Anywhere there are oaks, from scrub-oak chaparral through live oak woodlands and valley oak savannahs. They also turn up in residential neighborhoods and urban parks. **Trips 1**, **2**, **4**, **8**, **9**, **14**, and **20** will usually have this species, among many other sites.

In birds, red and yellow feathers get their color from pigments, called carotenoids, that are absorbed from the bird's food. However, blue colors come, not from pigments, but from the way the feathers are structured. Blue feathers have tiny air pockets inside the cells that scatter light in such a way that we perceive the color blue.

California Towhee

Melozone crissalis

While we think of large birds such as eagles and hawks as being fierce, many smaller birds are just as spirited. As California towhee females build nests, the males stand guard, prepared to drive off rivals. They will even attack their own reflections in windows, hubcaps, or car side mirrors. Their warning call is a sharp, metallic *chink*!—if you hear it, scan the tops of nearby bushes or fence posts to find a towhee standing watch.

At first glance, this is yet another brown bird—birders call them little brown jobs or LBJs. Often the California towhee is one of the first LBJs a novice bird-watcher learns. They're common in many large parks, chaparral slopes, oak woodlands, and even backyards of houses in the foothills. Clearly larger than the sparrows it often flocks with, it has an orange-tinged butt, as if it sat in pumpkin-colored paint and couldn't quite wash it off.

What's in the Bushes?

California towhees forage for seeds in dirt and leaf litter. They scratch the ground with a distinctive two-step hop: forward, then back, scratching away to expose food. They mostly eat seeds but will also eat grasshoppers and beetles. If you hear something moving under a bush, it may sound like something large but is more likely to be one of these little birds. They nest in shrubs too, including poison oak; they love eating that plant's white berries.

Where to See Them

Year-round, in brush from sea level to about five thousand feet. Common in suburban residential areas and large parks (Elysian Park, Baldwin Hills, Debs Park), but less so in smaller parks surrounded by lots of urban hardscape (MacArthur Park or Exposition Park). **Trips 1**, **4**, **9**, **11**, **13**, **15**, **18** and **19**.

Hops on ground, never in tree tops

Larger than most sparrows

lain brown with an undertail

Folk names once included brown chippy (based on the call), canyon bunting (based on the shape), and *la viejita*, the little old woman (based on the way it scolds).

Cooper's Hawk
Accipiter cooperii

Cooper's hawks, also called chicken hawks, are ambush predators, flying swiftly between trees, over hedges, and around buildings to surprise and catch prey—small birds like finches and starlings and larger ones like doves and pigeons. They often hunt around backyard feeders, where we've unwittingly established a simple urban food chain: small birds eat birdseed, Cooper's hawks eat small birds.

Unlike the more familiar red-tailed hawk, which often soars on broad, stable wings, the Cooper's hawk is an accipiter—less a hang glider than an aerodynamic stealth plane. Accipiters aren't great gliders; they're built for speed and cornering, with slender bodies, long tails, and short wings.

Cooper's hawks were considered scarce and declining as recently as the 1970s, but their numbers in urban and suburban areas have rebounded thanks to diminished use of some of our worst pesticides, planting of more tall trees for them to nest in, stronger populations of the sparrows and doves they eat, and the fact that we no longer routinely harass and shoot them.

Both adult male and female Cooper's hawks are blue-gray above and reddish below, with a tail banded by wide, dark stripes. Juveniles are brown above, with light and reddish-brown stripes below.

Slim, mid-sized hawk

Expected in trees and yards (not soaring)

Long tail, with alternating gray and brown bands

Cooper's hawks can be very defensive around their nests, sometimes even diving at humans. Hawk researchers wear protective helmets when doing field work.

A look-alike species is the smaller, more square-tailed sharp-shinned hawk—a fairly common visitor from October to March. It too is a bird-hunting accipiter, and if either of these hawks is nearby, all smaller birds dive for cover.

Where to See Them

Widespread in areas with trees, from middle elevations in the mountains down through foothill canyons and suburban areas; also, common today in the urban core as long as there are enough trees. Present year-round, but there are more of them from September through March because of migrants passing through. Possible at all the sites, including **1**, **3**, **14**, **16**, and **20**.

A side effect of the insecticide DDT is that it thins bird egg shells, causing them to break during incubation. When DDT was widely used, many bird species declined, including brown pelicans, bald eagles, peregrine falcons, and Cooper's hawks. After the United States banned the use of DDT in 1972, all these species made dramatic comebacks.

Crows and Ravens

It's easy to confuse the American crow with its rowdier, more robust cousin, the common raven. Both are all-black, impressively smart, and able to find and eat a huge variety of foods—from worms to acorns to birds' eggs to lizards. In Los Angeles, people used to shoot both as farm pests, but as city has replaced farmland, we've grown more tolerant. Crows can be seen everywhere in urban Los Angeles. Ravens are usually spotted in large parks, mountains, and deserts.

These birds gather in ominous-sounding groups: a murder of crows and a conspiracy of ravens.

Here, There, (Almost) Everywhere

The expanding city and all the trees we've planted in it have helped crow populations flourish. They like trees for nesting, nighttime roosting, and food (nuts, fruits). They also really like dumpsters, and trash in general. Our society provides everything they need, which is one reason you see them from the beach up into the foothills. Ravens aren't as common in the lowlands, but as you climb into the mountains, they become more prominent, especially in picnic areas.

Smart, Smarter, Smartest

Crows and ravens are super smart. They can use tools and recognize not just the faces of people they like and don't like but even the cars those individuals drive. They know how

American Crow
Corvus brachyrhynchos

Calls are a higher-pitched *caw caw*

Smaller bill than raven

Slimmer, more sleek profile

Common Raven
Corvus corax

Overall larger size

Large bill

Shaggy throat

Calls are deep croaks

? Crow or Raven?

	Crows	Ravens
SIZE	wingspan about 3 feet	wingspan about 4 feet
TAIL (in flight)	square or slightly rounded	diamond shaped or very rounded
VOICE	caww, caww	kr-r-ruck and lots of other croaks and knocks
BILL	straighter and more slender than raven's	thicker than a crow's, hooked at tip
WINGS (in flight)	usually five broad feather "fingers" at outer tips	often show four long, thin feather "fingers" at outer tips
FLIGHT	flaps from place to place	soars in circles like a hawk
HABITAT	more urban inhabiting (cities, fields, and the coast)	generally more in mountains and deserts, sometimes large urban parks

to crack nuts by letting cars drive over them and can use traffic signals to figure out which cars are coming next. Some scientists believe they're as good at problem solving as chimpanzees. Our estimates of their intelligence rise higher with each study.

Where to See Them
Year-round, throughout the urban lowlands as well as open oak woodlands and wooded streams. They love dumps and parks. Work on your crow versus raven identification skills on **Trips 9**, **11**, **15**, and **20**.

Glossy, iridescent, speckled feathers

Pot-bellied, with straight, spikey bill

Often in noisy flocks

▼ Once starlings move in, native birds stop using tree cavities for nesting.

European Starling

Sturnus vulgaris

The starling loves cities—in Los Angeles you can see them in large groups on park lawns or perched on utility lines. It also loves farmland and can be a serious pest. Native to Europe, starlings are perhaps the most abundant and most invasive of all our non-native bird species (the house sparrow also competes for this title).

All 200 million starlings nationwide are descendants of one hundred individuals released in New York City in the 1890s by people who wanted all the birds mentioned by Shakespeare to live in North America. It was a horrible idea. They spread from Central Park, eating crops and driving out native species. As recently as the 1960s, spotting one in Los Angeles was rare, but now they're everywhere.

Nest Hogs

Starlings nest in holes, aggressively bullying native birds out of tree cavities. Bluebirds, purple martins, and multiple species of swallows have been especially hard hit by star-

A large flock of starlings is called a murmuration, because of the low, continuous sound produced by the birds' beating wings. Winter flocks spin like speeding black storm clouds, with many thousands of birds twisting and turning in sync.

lings stealing their nests. A good way to help bluebirds and other native species is to install nest boxes designed with entrances too small for starlings to fit through.

The Starling Changes Its Spots

The starling is chunky, with a straight, short beak and a short tail. It waddles on the ground, looking intently left and right, ready to stab its beak at an insect or a choice seed. In fall, the tips of its feathers show bright white dots, giving it a speckled look. As fall turns to spring, those tips wear away, leaving behind all-dark feathers. When breeding season approaches,

91

Where to See Them

Throughout the LA region, in urban and suburban areas, ranches, and open fields; starlings generally avoid deep woodlands. Flocks perch on wires, power poles and in trees; they mostly feed on the ground but take fruits in trees and shrubs. Your best chance at a local murmuration is present year-round along the San Gabriel River near El Monte. Typical sites are **3**, **7**, **10**, **12**, **19**, and **24**.

its bill brightens to a glowing yellow. Direct sunlight brings out its feathers' iridescent green and purple sheen—the overall effect is of a pot-bellied but snappy dresser.

Great Blue Heron

Ardea herodias

The familiar and eye-catching great blue heron stands nearly four feet tall and has a six-foot wingspan. Its thin, graceful neck and long legs give it a ballerina look, but its stout, dagger-like bill means business—these herons hunt a variety of food, including fish, frogs, and crayfish in the LA River. They'll also devour lizards, snakes, mice, birds, grasshoppers, and dragonflies. Sometimes you'll even see them hunting on lawns or golf courses, sneaking up on unwary pocket gophers. It usually manages to swallow a sizeable catch, but occasionally its eyes are bigger than its stomach—herons have been

At the end of the nineteenth century, this bird and other herons and egrets were killed not for food or eggs but to supply feathers for ladies' hats. The Audubon Society was created in part by women activists to regulate the feather trade and bring the birds back from near-extinction. In the case of the great blue heron, they were very successful.

Dark cap

Heavy straight beak

Tall gray waterbird with neck often in S position

Long legs

known to try swallowing fish so big they choke to death. Unless it's nesting season, they're usually solitary.

Where to See Them

Often seen along the LA River and around lakes, ponds, and river channels. Small nesting colonies, called heronries, occur in tall pines, eucalyptus, and other trees at places like Silver Lake, Marina del Rey, Malibu Lagoon, Legg Lake, and the Sepulveda Basin. Some nests are over four feet wide and get used several years in a row.

They're also found in coastal estuaries, sometimes perched on rafts of matted kelp. Expected many places, especially **Trips 3**, **5**, **10**, **18**, and **22**.

Great Horned Owl

Bubo virginianus

Eleven species of owls have been observed in LA County, but the great horned owl is our largest and most common. We most often detect it by its hooting call, delivered from atop a utility pole or tall tree in parks like Elysian and Griffith, from dusk to the earliest hint of dawn. If you hear one when there's still a bit of light left, try spotting it—their large size and distinctive silhouette make them easy to identify.

Hearing and Hooting

Great horned owls are mottled gray-brown, with black barring through their plumage and a reddish-brown face setting off yellow eyes. Feather tufts on each side of the forehead, which may help owls recognize each other, give them a cat-like silhouette, but the tufts aren't ears. Their real ears are hidden and placed in just the right spot on their heads so that their wide faces can act like a satellite dish to focus sound into them. For an owl, good hearing means good hunting.

Great horned owls nest in trees and cliff ledges, often taking over old hawk nests. They nest early in the year. Both males and females hoot, but the male's hooting is deeper, even though he is smaller, and usually consists of

Ear tufts

Large, 4.5-foot wingspan

Mottled brown color above and below

You'll occasionally spot a great horned owl in the daytime—often because they are being mobbed by scrub-jays or other smaller birds. It can be comical to watch a flock of small songbirds gathering around a perched owl to scold and fuss until it gets fed up and leaves.

four notes. The female's higher-pitched call has five to seven notes. Adults and especially young birds also give eerie shrieking calls.

See Food

The great horned owl's diet is diverse, including rodents, other small mammals, birds, reptiles, and large insects. Jerusalem crickets are common small prey, but they can also eat skunks, geese, and hawks. Although they occasionally prey on cats and small dogs, it's very rare.

Like other birds of prey, owls can't pass bone fragments through their digestive tract so they cough them up in a compact gray wad called a pellet, only digesting the tastiest bits of dinner. You can find pellets on the ground under roost trees and learn a lot about the owl's diet by picking them apart. A pellet is mostly fur, like a tightly packed lint ball peppered with harder fragments. You might find a mouse's jaw with the teeth still intact or perhaps pieces that look like bits of plastic but are actually leftover insect parts.

Where to See Them

Great horned owls have experienced some local declines from West Nile Virus but are still relatively common. They use a wide variety of habitats but especially like tall trees with adjacent open fields, chaparral, or open woodlands. Possibilities include **Trips 1**, **2**, **8**, **9**, **16**, and **17**.

Hooded Oriole

Icterus cucullatus

Orange hood and body

Black face and chin

Overall slim, streamlined shape

A flashy yellow-and-black harbinger of spring, the hooded oriole went from an oasis specialist in Palm Springs to a content LA urbanite. There are probably more hooded orioles in Los Angeles now than there ever were pre-irrigation and palm trees.

The male is a glamorous yellow, with a contrasting black throat and face, plus matching black back, wings, and tail. Two white bars on each wing add even more flash. Young birds and females are olive-green above and pale yellow below, with dusky wings and tail.

Urbanization has been good for the hooded oriole. They can drink nectar from the ornamental trees we plant and gather nesting material from fan palms.

Sugar and Fiber

Although they eat insects and berries, much of an oriole's diet is nectar. They're fond of ornamental trees such as coral trees and also visit hummingbird feeders. They weave their pouch-like nests from palm fibers and suspend the nest from the underside of palm fronds. However, because they were here before we planted exotic palms, they can also nest in any tree or shrub with large leaves and a dense canopy, such as stream-side sycamores—the key requirement is plant fibers for weaving.

Women and Children Last

Hooded orioles are here in summer only, and migrate to subtropical climates during our brief, cool winters. Adult males arrive first in spring (as early as the first week of March) and are the first to leave in fall (late August, early September). Females leave next, and hatch-year birds (juveniles) go last. On their first trip south, juveniles are on their own, with a built-in knowledge of the migratory path.

Where to See Them

In summer, hooded orioles are found in city parks and residential areas (from sea level to about 2,500 feet), usually not far from palm trees. Migrating birds (heading north in March–April and south in July–September) can occur more widely through the region. **Trips 4**, **8**, **11**, **12**, and **21** provide chances to see this showy migrant.

House Finch

Haemorhous mexicanus

Named for their familiar presence around our homes and their habit of nesting on window ledges, eaves, patio light fixtures, and planters, house finches are probably the most abundant native bird species in the LA region. Few birds sound more cheerful. For a small fry, it can really belt it out.

Los Angeles is home to many invasive species, but it's the origin for this one, now introduced across the country. These western US birds were once imported to New York and sold in pet stores as "Hollywood finches." Escaped birds have since multiplied and are now spreading back towards California.

You Are What You Eat

Like other birds that spend most of their time on the ground, all finches have a short, cone-shaped beak, good for crushing seeds. (Insect-eaters like warblers are the same body size but have thinner, more needle-like bills—think dagger, not hammer.) House finches are mostly streaked gray-brown, but the males

Red head (males)

Sparrow-sized brown body

Red rump shows in flight

scarlet. Birds can't produce yellow and red pigments on their own; the pigments come from carotenoids, which are derived from plants. Variations in finch color reflect variations in their food: the more pigment in the food, the redder the male, and the redder the male, the more likely females will be attracted to him.

Where to See Them

House finches are found year-round throughout the lowlands and foothills (to about 6,000 feet), in both natural and urban habitats. Possible on all trips, including **6**, **7**, **11**, and **24**—most easily seen on **Trip 7** at the seed feeders in the Museum's Nature Gardens.

show red on the throat and chest, forehead, eyebrow, and rump. Females have no red plumage, and young males are in between.

The red color of the males is actually highly variable and can range from pale mustard-yellow through orange to deep

House Sparrow

Passer domesticus

Brown cap with gray crown

Black bib in males; plain brown in females

Plump, plain gray belly

This is the stout little bird that steals your French fries at outdoor eateries. House sparrows should eat grains and seeds and catch insects to feed to their young, but in cities they mostly eat discarded human food.

Males look a bit like aging bank robbers, with a gray crown and black face mask. Both males and females are mostly streaky brown. They're often found hopping in the dirt or perched on the top of a chain link fence.

They're at Home Now

House sparrows were introduced from Europe into eastern North America in 1851. They were released in part for their perceived ecological services—as insect control when horses were the dominant mode of transportation—as well as for sentimental reasons, since nineteenth century European immigrants wanted to be surrounded by familiar species. They spread to the LA region by about 1900 and are now found here year-round. Today, house sparrows may be doing better in the United States than in Europe, where populations have recently declined.

Where to See Them

Look for them almost any place you find people—from the dense urban core to suburbs, shopping malls, parks, rural ranch yards, and coastal piers and wharves. There are even individuals that live much of their lives inside buildings like Home Depot, Costco, and terminals at LAX. You're not likely to find them in chaparral, oak woodlands, or mountain forests. Reliable spots are **Trips 3**, **7**, **10**, **12**, and **24** and outside any fast food restaurant.

> When house sparrows first came to America, they had an unusual food source. They would pick out undigested grains from horse poop—which was abundant on every street back then.

Hummingbirds

Allen's Hummingbird

Selasphorus sasin

Males have orange-red throat flashes

Sounds include a sharp *tink*

Back is a mix of green and cinnamon

Anna's Hummingbird

Calypte anna

Song is high and shrill, with whistles and chips

Males have magenta (not purple or orange-red) throat flashes

Plain green back (no red mixed in)

97

▲ Two baby hummingbirds in their fluffy, stretchy nest.

Zipping and darting, looping and probing, the hummingbirds are familiar friends in urban gardens. Start by learning the two most common. The Allen's hummingbird is the red-and-green one. Males are more cinnamon-red than the females, flashing a vermilion throat patch as they defend a choice blossom or feeder, ready to take on any challengers. Anna's has a plain belly, and in the males, a magenta throat patch.

Originally Allen's hummingbird was limited to the Channel Islands and the Palos Verdes Peninsula, but as houses, yards, and lush landscaping change the plant palette of Southern California, they continue to spread inland, inhabiting new regions every year, overlapping with and sometimes displacing other hummingbird species.

Jelly Beans, Spider Silk, Bugs for Brunch

A hummingbird is a marvel of movement. By beating their wings around fifty times per second, they can fly sideways, straight up, straight down, backwards, and even upside down. They can also hover in place by beating their wings in a figure-eight pattern. At the peak of activity, a hummingbird's heart beats over a thousand times a minute.

Mothers build nests out of lichen and soft plant fuzz, adding spiderwebs so the nest can stretch with her growing babies. Each egg is smaller than a jellybean. Through it all, the female is on her own—males don't help incubate eggs or raise young.

Everybody knows hummingbirds love sugar water. Few realize that a fair amount of their diet is insects as well. Hummingbirds coming regularly to a feeder still need to forage in the wild—bug protein keeps them healthy.

Magic Colors

Thanks to their dazzling feathers, male hummingbirds are even more beautiful than the flowers they feed on. The iridescent colors depend on the angle of the light, so brilliant red and green feathers can turn dull or black a microsecond later as the bird moves, then flash out again like an iridescent lighthouse.

Where to See Them

Like most hummingbirds in our area, Anna's and Allen's hummingbirds feed on cape honeysuckle, various kinds of eucalyptus, bottlebrush, and many other flowers. Reliable sites for Allen's—the one many visiting birdwatchers want to see—include **Trips 12**, **21**, and **25**. To see Anna's, try **Trips 1**, **3**, **6**, **8**, **9**, and most others. See both species at the hummingbird feeders in the Nature Gardens (**Trip 7**).

Green head in males (females are mottled brown)

Yellow bill

Orange feet

Mallard

Anas platyrhynchus

This is the most familiar of our urban ducks—it's a rare park lake that doesn't have mallards on it. They are so tolerant of people in urban areas that they even check out backyard ponds and pools—sometimes nesting in inappropriate places, like under hedges or in the ornamental pools at the Getty Center. A world map of mallards reveals that, except for the Arctic, Antarctic, and super high elevations, they'll live pretty much anywhere—from Disneyland to the Notre Dame Cathedral.

Their success comes in part from their ability to make lots of babies. A single hen (female ducks are called hens; males are called drakes) can lay up to thirteen eggs. The downy young are mobile right after hatching. They look like fuzzy yellow Easter chicks with brown stripes, swimming in a line after mom and sometimes catching a ride on her back. Their diet is also very diverse—snails, worms, seeds, and plant roots.

The mallard is one of our dabbling ducks or puddle ducks. It feeds by tipping its butt up in the air and grazing on underwater plants. In contrast, diving ducks feed by swimming under the water.

Mallards have long been domesticated and are the source for many domestic breeds. These are the ducks you see hanging, plucked, in Chinatown markets—they're highly prized for eating. The appearance of different breeds is astoundingly variable; feral domestic birds have interbred with wild birds, resulting in many color variations (all-black, light tan, all-white, etc.) and many sizes.

A Duck Eclipse

Feathers get battered over time and need to be replaced. Birds replace their feathers in a process called molting. Mallards undergo a major molt in the late summer—males lose their conspicuous green head and neck, deep reddish breast, and light gray body, and take on a duller, more female-like plumage. Any male duck in this phase (no matter the species) is said to be in eclipse plumage. Male mallards in their eclipse plumage still have a yellow bill and an iridescent blue patch on the wing bordered by white (this patch is called the speculum).

Shortly after replacing their body feathers, mallards also replace the primary feathers of their wings, rendering the ducks flightless for a few weeks. In the fall, males regain their showy, green-headed glory in preparation for their winter courtship and spring breeding season.

Where to See Them

Mallards can be found on any park lake, along the length of the Los Angeles and San Gabriel Rivers, and in other small wetlands throughout the area. They're present year-round and the most common breeding duck species here. **Trips 3**, **5**, **8**, **10**, **21**, and **23** often have mallards.

Mourning Dove

Zenaida macroura

Plain brown head and neck (no black band)

Overall pinky-tan color

Long tail

These are real survivors. Despite being food for everything from coyotes to Cooper's hawks, this long-tailed, small-headed, gray-tan dove is found pretty much everywhere. There may be over 350 million of them in North America.

Mourning doves live in a variety of habitats, from the urban core to grasslands, mountain forests, and canyon woodlands. However, they avoid areas with continuous shrub cover, such as chaparral, because they need open ground for foraging.

Many people misremember the name as *morning* dove, thinking perhaps it's an early riser. Instead, *mourning* refers to their call, which can sound sad.

Nests 101

Museum ornithologist Kimball Garrett says a mourning dove's nest "is a pathetic affair"—just a platform of twigs and sticks so spare you can see through it. They often build in planters and hanging pots in backyards, but also in shrubs, low in trees, and sometimes even directly on the ground. Like all of our pigeons and doves, they lay two white eggs.

For the first week after the babies hatch, parents feed them a kind of liquid produced in a part of their throat called the crop. Like human milk, "crop milk" is rich in protein. Later, parents switch over to sharing seeds, regurgitating partially digested food until the young grow feathers and can forage on their own.

Los Angeles's Changing Coo-Scape

When we think about the LA soundscape, in addition to helicopters and the next-door neighbor's music, mourning doves definitely play a part. From Silver Lake to Long Beach, Azusa to Tarzana, once you learn to recognize it, you can easily hear their five-part *cooWOO coo, coo coo* (you may also hear a more inconsistent *coo CWoo cu*, which comes from the Eurasian collared-dove, a relative newcomer not found in Los Angeles until 2001). A group of mourning doves taking flight from the ground creates a sort of whinny or squeaky door sound, caused by the shape of their wing feathers.

Where to See Them

Throughout the LA area, from sea level to the mountains, and from coastal woodlands to desert scrub to the city's urban core. They feed on the ground and readily come to seed feeders (or the seeds on the ground below). Check the feeders in the Museum's Nature Gardens on **Trip 7**. Other easy places to study them include **Trips 3**, **11**, **21**, and **24**.

Northern Mockingbird

Mimus polyglottos

Edge of tail and wings flash white in flight

Gray above, pale below

Long tail

▲ The mockingbird's white wing flash.

This sing-all-night bird is common in parks, neighborhoods, and the dense urban core. More than just a pretty voice, the northern mockingbird is also fierce. It's known to scold, chase, and dive-bomb crows, hawks, jays, cats, and even people.

While in general this is a slender, light gray bird without much obvious color or decoration, its wings do show a large patch of white when it's in flight, and the blackish tail is broadly edged with white as well. The tail flash is quite conspicuous when a mockingbird takes flight or lands. Of course, long before you notice the tail, you'll usually be alerted to its presence by its loud and varied calls.

Car Alarm Mimic

Depending on time of year and location, both females and males sing. In building their songbook, northern mockingbirds copy simple calls from other birds and, in the city, other sounds like car alarms. The mimicked phrases are usually repeated three times (sometimes more, sometimes less) before the singer moves on to the next phrase. A song can go on for many minutes or even hours, a source of consternation for some LA residents who value sleep—territorial males will sing through much of the night in spring and summer.

Where to See Them

Found year-round throughout the lowland and urban parts of the LA region (rarely above 4,000 feet in elevation). Found on almost all trips including **6**, **7**, **12**, **13**, **21**, and **24**.

Rock Pigeon

Columba livia

Found in cities all over the world, the familiar park and street pigeon is called rock pigeon or rock dove in bird books, while less charitable people call them sky rats. They're at home from the breakwaters of LA harbors through the densest urban areas to towns and ranches on the rural fringes of Los Angeles. Some find them a nuisance, but this bird has amazing stories to tell.

The most basic rock pigeons are gray with a white rump, with black bars on the upper wing, white underwings, a black tail tip, and green iridescence on the head and chest. But there are many variations on this theme, in large part because hobbyists who breed pigeons love different colors and patterns.

In flight, they raise their wings on the upstroke into an exaggerated V much deeper than most birds do. On take-off, their wings even clap together on the upstroke, which

Usually gray with dark wings

Often has shiny green and purple neck patch

Walks with head-jerking motion

Contrary to urban myth, feeding a pigeon popcorn, rice, or Alka-Seltzer tablets won't make it explode. Whatever a pigeon can't digest it will just spit back up. Be nice to pigeons. We don't encourage feeding them, but if you must, feed them bird seed.

might serve to alert other birds in the flock of potential danger, as well as disorient nearby predators.

A History of Heroics

Pigeons are capable of finding their way home over extremely long distances, sometimes greater than one thousand miles. Scientists are still researching how they do it, but they seem to use many senses, including vision, smell, low-frequency hearing, and assessing the Earth's magnetic field.

During World War II, homing pigeons were placed on every bomber and reconnaissance aircraft used by the United Kingdom's Royal Air Force. If a plane crashed, the pigeons were released to carry the coordinates of the crashed plane back to their home base so search and rescue missions could be sent

directly to the crash sites. These "war birds" are credited with saving thousands of servicemen's lives.

Cliffs, Bridges, Poles

Rock pigeons shun vegetation and prefer perching on hardscape—within their native range in North Africa and Europe they lived on cliffs. Cities, filled with bridges, railings, utility poles, wires, and statues, are ideal for them. They nest on building ledges and bridges—though if cliffs are available, like those on the Palos Verdes Peninsula, they'll nest there too.

Where to See Them

Abundant and familiar, pigeons are found throughout urbanized areas. You're not likely to find them in natural woodland or chaparral habitats, but where there's a clear human footprint on the landscape, these pigeons are likely present.

Humans domesticated pigeons over 5,000 years ago. Centuries of breeding for racing, homing, tumbling (backwards somersaults in the air!), and more have resulted in the wide variety of reddish, black, white, and patchy-colored (or *pied*) plumage you find on urban pigeons today.

Large gull with dark gray back and white head and belly

Most common along the coast

Pink (not yellow or green) legs

Western Gull

Larus occidentalis

This large, dark-backed, pink-legged seagull has learned to follow humans inland away from its seaside habitat. Traditionally, western gulls bred only on the Channel Islands (and in very small numbers in our coastal harbors), but in the past thirty years they've become familiar throughout the LA Basin, and even into the San Fernando and San Gabriel Valleys.

It's all about food. Western gulls feed on marine life, whether live or dead. But to a good scavenger, a leftover chunk of peanut butter sandwich is as good as a dead crab. Like other local animals, western gulls have learned the formula: people = trash = food. As a result, they congregate at landfills and schoolyards. Many western gulls also live along the LA River, often roosting on warehouse roofs.

New Year, New Look

There are nineteen species of gulls in LA County. Multiple species can sometimes be observed in a single flock. Hybrids create confusion and young gulls complicate things further. The western gull molts multiple times, resulting in new plumage and a new look from year to year. It also has two forms, one lighter and one a shade darker.

Where to See Them

Abundant along the Pacific coast and out to sea, the western gull can appear anywhere in the LA Basin, especially around large parking lots, open parks, schoolyards, and park lakes. You can almost always find them on **Trips 5**, **22**, **23**, **24**, and **25**.

The red spot on a gull's beak is a signal to other adults of breeding maturity.

▲ Smaller and paler than an adult western gull, the California gull has yellow-green legs (not pink) and is more common inland.

Longer tail than other area parrots

Flash of yellow on the wing

Bright green above and below

Yellow-chevroned Parakeet

Brotogeris chiriri

Parakeets are a type of parrot. We may not expect these exotic birds in the city, but they're here—and the yellow-chevroned parakeet seems to be thriving, from the tree outside your bedroom window to the high rise "parrot motel" palm trees lining our streets.

The yellow-chevroned parakeet is attractive and swift-flying, grass-green with a patch of yellow on each wing. A related species, the white-winged parakeet, sometimes gets mixed in with the same flock; as the name implies, it shows a flash of white in addition to the yellow patch. Both are just a bit larger and heavier than the common domestic budgie and quite a bit smaller than other wild parrots living locally, which have a harsher call, a shorter, squared-off tail, and other feather colors and patterns.

Parakeet flocks keep up a frequent, scratchy chattering, and in flight their loud call is an easy-to-learn *chreet chreet*. Listen for it and you'll soon realize how many are criss-crossing the LA skyways.

Feels Like Home

Over thirty species of parrot have been seen flying around the LA Basin. All are descendants of escaped pets. Twelve of these feral parrot species are now breeding here. They're supported by our abundant and diverse ornamental trees and shrubs, which provide seeds and nectar—notably the floss silk tree, which, like the parakeet, is from the Amazon region of South America. They also feed and roost in eucalyptus, coral trees, fruiting palms, ficus trees, and the dozens of other species that make up our urban jungle.

Where to See Them

Widespread throughout the LA Basin and in the San Fernando and San Gabriel Valleys. This is the parrot most often seen at the LA Civic Center, and noisy flocks flap around Echo Park, MacArthur Park, Huntington Gardens, Sepulveda Basin, Legg Lake, and many other areas, including **Trips 7**, **12**, **19**, and **21**.

Nesting behavior is hard to study because these birds are secretive. Even in the wild, very little is known about their nesting biology. If you know anybody looking for a research project, Los Angeles might be a good place to start one.

Insects and Spiders

Antennae are hockey stick shaped and end in small knobs

Highly veined wing with hundreds of cells

Adults are up to 2 inches long

Long, slender body

Juveniles are up to half an inch long

Large mandibles

Antlion

Myrmeleon species

Antlions aren't the easiest insects to identify or spot, but once you know where and what to look for, you could be recognizing them in no time. Walking along trails, riverbanks, or other open sandy areas, you may find evidence of their larvae. In summer, adults are attracted to lights at night.

Damselfly Look-alikes

Adult antlions are sometimes confused for damselflies, the dragonfly's slender, petite cousin. However, they're easy to tell apart. Damselflies have finely veined, gossamer wings—antlion wings have thick veins, which form hundreds of tiny cells that look like miniature windows. Damselflies have short, needle-like antennae—antlions have long curved antennae with small knobs on the ends,

Some antlion larvae are called doodlebugs. The winding trails they leave while looking for a spot to build their conical traps look like someone has been doodling in the sand.

like little hockey sticks. Finally, damselflies are fast-moving predators, while winged antlions feed on pollen and nectar from flowers.

Lion of the Insect World

Immature antlions are small, soft-bodied insects with gigantic, tong-like mouthparts. They dig conical pits in sandy soil and hide at the bottom with their mouthparts barely concealed by a fine layer of sand. Unsuspecting insects—often ants—trek through the sand and stumble into these deathtraps. If the ant falls to the bottom of the pit, the antlion swiftly makes a meal of it, using its mega-mandibles as spears then sucking the body fluids out. If the ant falls only part-way in and tries to escape, sand cascades down the sides of the pit, alerting the antlion, who then flicks sand grains towards the ant in an attempt to make it fall to the bottom. Sometimes the ant escapes—sometimes it becomes lunch.

Where to See Them

Their conical traps are most easily seen along sandy trails on **Trips 1**, **13**, **15**, and **17**. Adults can also be found coming to porch lights at night.

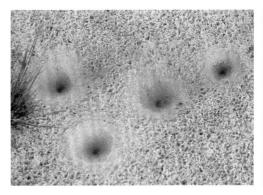

▲ Each of these small conical sand traps belongs to a different antlion larva.

Argentine Ant

Linepithema humile

This is the ant that invades picnics, dishes of pet food, and sometimes kitchens across the LA Basin. In summer and fall, these ants make their way indoors seeking water, food, and more comfortable temperatures.

Argentine ants are our most common urban ant by far. Introduced to North America in the late 1800s from northern Argentina, they're well adapted to our climate. Helped by human alterations to the environment, they've displaced native ants like harvester ants, the preferred food of local horned lizards, who won't go near an Argentine ant buffet. As harvester ants are driven away, so too are horned lizards.

Ant Supercolony

Unlike other ant species, Argentine ant colonies in California show little aggression toward each other. This gives them an edge—instead of fighting amongst themselves, they spend their time gathering food or fighting with native ants. Scientists have dubbed the colony in California a supercolony—with all the ants from San Diego to Northern California part of the same giant group. This has allowed them to outcompete and displace other ant species.

Where to See Them

Find these ants anywhere, anytime! There are almost certainly Argentine ants within a one hundred-foot radius of you right now. They can also easily be observed on **Trips 7**, **12**, and **19**, and along any grass-lined sidewalk.

Argentine ants herd scale insects and aphids much like humans herd dairy cows. The ants protect the aphids so they can feast on the sugary secretions known as honeydew produced by these plant pests.

Small (most are about 0.1 inches long), with elbow-shaped antennae

Slender body

Light to medium brown (can look black if not close)

Convergent Ladybug

Hippodamia convergens

Crawling amongst the spinach in community gardens, chewing on the pesky aphids threatening your roses, or overwintering in our local mountains, this charismatic insect is often a gateway bug for the insect phobic.

The convergent ladybug fits the ladybug archetype—an iconic reddish orange beetle with black spots on their elytra. The number of spots varies, but it's usually thirteen.

The best way to identify it is to look at the *pronotum*, the shield-like covering above the head. It's black with a white border and two white lines that are about to converge—hence the descriptive scientific name.

Small Insect, BIG Appetite

Few insects inspire warm, fuzzy feelings in humans the way ladybugs, sometimes known as lady beetles or ladybird beetles, do. But to an aphid or other small soft-bodied insect, ladybugs are terrifying killers. Both adult and young ladybugs are voracious predators. Immature ladybugs are soft bodied and elongate—some people think they look like miniature alligators, and they certainly act the part. Ladybug larvae can eat thirty to fifty aphids a day—you're welcome, gardeners!

When days get shorter and colder, and aphids are in short supply, convergent ladybugs head for the hills to overwinter and wait for food to return.

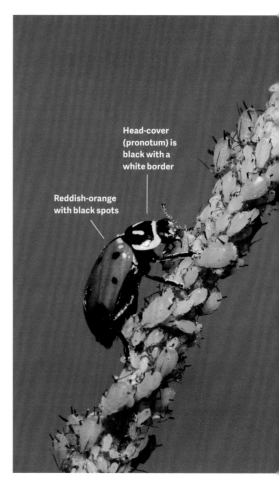

Head-cover (pronotum) is black with a white border

Reddish-orange with black spots

How to Get the Ladies

Adult ladybugs are sold in nurseries to help gardeners control pests. However, they have a habit of flying away without eating much. Scientists have found it takes two applications of 1,500 ladybugs spaced a week apart to control the aphids on one infested rosebush!

Encouraging ladybugs to show up in your yard by choice is better than buying them, but they won't show up if there's no food. Try creating a companion planting, a group of plants where you won't mind some pest insects moving in to tempt beneficial bugs to your garden. Plants to try include yarrow, cilantro, cosmos, and marigolds. Always skip pesticides—they kill good bugs as well as pests.

Fifty-five species of ladybugs have been found in LA County. Less common than the convergent ladybug, but easy to identify, is a black ladybug with two red spots, the twice-struck ladybug.

The red and black color of adult ladybugs is a warning signal—don't eat me, I'm toxic! If disturbed they release a yellow liquid from their leg joints which is extremely bitter and distasteful to many would-be predators. If you get it on your hands, be sure to wash before eating.

▲ Immature ladybugs are shaped differently than adults but they still have warning coloration to warn would-be predators of their toxic chemicals and bad taste.

Where to See Them

In spring through fall, find them in almost any vegetable garden—try the Erika J. Glazer Family Edible Garden on **Trip 7**. For a real spectacle, head to higher elevations in winter and early spring to find them overwintering along the trails of **Trips 16** and **17**.

Golden Velvet Ant

Dasymutilla sackenii

This velvety-looking insect is hard to spot, but if you're lucky enough to find one, it's hard to ignore. It's not actually an ant at all, but a type of wasp (ants and wasps are closely related in the insect group Hymenoptera). There are a number of species of velvet ant in our region—ranging in color from bright red, to orange, to the golden velvet ant's white or pale yellow. They look like white pom-poms made of dandelion fluff.

Wingless Females and Winged Males

Female velvet ants are wingless and very fuzzy, resembling large ants. Males are smaller, have a black stripe on their abdomen, and have wings, which make them look more waspish. When confined, some female velvet ants will make a squeaking sound. If you've caught one in your hand and you hear this, it's a good idea to drop it immediately. Female velvet ants can pack a strong punch with their stingers—some species are referred to as cow killers. Look but don't touch!

Parasites of Other Wasps

Scientists have observed adult velvet ants sipping nectar from flowers, but immature wasps choose more protein-filled foods. Female velvet ants lay their eggs in the burrows of other ground-nesting wasps. They're the perfect spot—hidden from other predators and filled with food. The female enters the nest and lays her eggs on the developing larva or pupa. When the velvet ant hatches, it has fresh meat to eat!

Where to See Them

Velvet ants can be found in dry, sandy areas. Foothills surrounding the LA Basin and the surrounding deserts are good places to spot them. Females can be seen scurrying around on the ground; males are winged and rarely seen. Look for them on **Trips 1** and **13**.

Short antennae

Can be nearly three inches long

Gray/brown body with white and black markings

Gray Bird Grasshopper

Schistocerca nitens

The gray bird grasshopper is the largest grasshopper in our area, sometimes growing to almost three inches long. As the name implies, it's mostly gray, with mottled brown/black and white markings. This allows them to hide in plain sight, camouflaged against gray-brown soils (as nymphs, gray bird grasshoppers are bright green for hiding in vegetation).

Super Jumpers

Although this species has been known to fly up to three hundred miles over oceans (no wonder they are found on the Channel Islands), grasshoppers are generally better known for their jumping ability. With their modified hind legs—entomologists call them saltatorial legs—most can jump about twenty times their body length. This would be the equivalent of a six-foot-tall human hopping a whole football field in three jumps! One reason grasshoppers can jump so far is their specialized knee joints, which act like catapults and propel them forward.

Where to See Them

All over Los Angeles, particularly in summer. You'll sometimes spot a female laying eggs in the gravelly dirt paths in the Museum's Nature Gardens—she digs her abdomen in and sits there until all her eggs are deposited. Look for adults, nymphs, and egg-laying females on **Trips 7** and **12**.

Grasshoppers make their singing sounds by rubbing their hind legs against their forewings.

Black bullseye

Green thorax

Big wings outstretched when it's at rest; about 3-inch wingspan

Green Darner

Anax junius

As they dart along the banks of the San Gabriel River or sit on reeds at Echo Park Lake, these large dragonflies are hard to miss. Although they can be seen year round, they are most common spring through fall, when their migration brings large numbers to our area.

This insect belongs to a group of large dragonflies called darners, named for their resemblance to a darning needle. One of the largest dragonflies in our area, they have a three-inch-long body and a wingspan of up to four inches—similar in length and wingspan to some hummingbirds.

They also have a bright green thorax and huge eyes. These eyes take up most of the head and give the dragonfly nearly 360-degree vision. Males have bright blue abdomens, whereas females are a purplish gray. Unlike some dragonflies, green darners have clear wings.

When mating, a male dragonfly uses the claspers at the end of his abdomen to hold the female behind her head. She then arches her abdomen up to his, producing the wheel position you sometimes see dragonflies flying around in.

Dragon of the Air, Lion of the Deep

Dragonflies are amazing predators, both as winged adults and aquatic larvae. The fast-moving larvae are able to escape their own would-be predators by jet propelling water from their hind end. They can also move slowly, particularly when stalking prey like small fish, tadpoles, or other dragonflies. As adults they

Female dragonflies have been observed trying to lay their eggs on cars. The shiny finish of some automobiles can be mistaken for the surface of a pond.

hunt on the wing, using their spiny legs to capture and hold soft-bodied flying insects like mosquitoes. Then their large, crushing mandibles help them kill and break down their prey.

Where to See Them

Most easily spotted on **Trips 1**, **5**, **7**, **10**, and **21** on warm sunny days between April and November. Look for molted exuvia around the water's edge at sites **7** and **21**.

▲ It takes a few hours for an adult dragonfly to molt, inflate its wings, and harden its exoskeleton.

Green Fruit Beetle

Cotinis mutabilis

The clumsy, haphazard flight of green fruit beetles often finds them colliding with people, buildings, or cars. You can find them just about anywhere, but gardens and orchards are the easiest places to spot one. Look for their grubs (grubs are to beetles, as caterpillars are to butterflies) in a backyard compost bin, and the adults around ripe fruit.

There's no need to fear these chunky flying tanks, with their velvety green wings, golden sides, and shiny green underbellies. They cannot sting or bite us, and they are neither poisonous nor venomous. The worst they can do

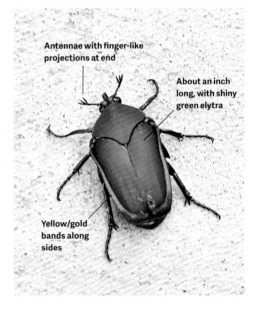

Antennae with finger-like projections at end

About an inch long, with shiny green elytra

Yellow/gold bands along sides

is chew on the fruit in our garden. Many people confuse them with the Japanese Beetle, *Popillia japonica*, a common East Coast agricultural pest. In comparison, green fruit beetles are larger, much less damaging to crops, and have green rather than copper-colored elytra.

Peaches and Pears

Green fruit beetles moved into the LA Basin in the 1960s from New Mexico and Arizona. They eat fruit—cactus pears in the wild and backyard fruits in cities. Adults have a horn-like projection beneath their head to help them cut into their fruit of choice—peaches, nectarines, and figs are particular favorites.

In grub form, green fruit beetles are sometimes called crawly backs because they travel through the soil upside down. They have a series of short bristles on the back of the thorax that help them grip the ground to move forward. If you find one in your compost bin, pick it up and gently rub the area behind its head to feel the bristles. This won't hurt them, and they won't hurt you either.

Where to See Them

Look for these beetles close to where fruit trees grow in the summer months. Most likely to be seen on **Trips 10**, **11**, and **12**.

Jerusalem Cricket

Family Stenopelmatidae

Although primarily nocturnal, Jerusalem crickets are sometimes seen in the daytime after getting stranded during a nighttime foray. They can also be found taking cover under old boards or downed logs.

Not a True Cricket

Unlike the cricket under your refrigerator who chirps at 2 a.m., Jerusalem crickets can't sing. True crickets rub their wings together to produce their songs, but Jerusalem crickets are wingless. They have a high domed head reminiscent of a human skull, a shiny brown exoskeleton, and large biting mouthparts. Their six robust, spiked legs are modified for digging in soil, which is where you'll find them most of the year. Their biting mandibles are ideal for cutting through underground roots and tubers, which sometimes includes gardeners' potatoes—hence the common name potato bug.

Nothing to Fear

The unmistakable visage and large size of Jerusalem crickets has inspired fear in various cultures. The Navajo named them *skull insect*

High domed head

Big, up to 3 inches long

Ringed abdomen

Thick, strong legs for digging

Jerusalem crickets aren't well studied in our region. The species are hard to tell apart by looks alone, so researchers analyze their mating drumming songs or sequence their DNA.

and believed they were deadly venomous. In reality, they aren't venomous and can't kill you. They can bite, but usually don't—we don't smell or taste like their food.

In Spanish, they're called *niños de la tierra* or children of the Earth, and folklore says they can cry like a baby. Scientists haven't recorded this behavior, but they have observed drumming communication. Using their abdomens as a drum stick, they beat the ground and send vibrations to each other through the soil.

Where to See Them

Look for Jerusalem crickets while doing garden work, after heavy rains, and along trails in natural areas. Most likely to be seen on **Trips 14**, **16**, and **17**.

Marine Blue Butterfly

Leptotes marina

Wingspan about one inch

Pale brown and white underwing patterns

Wings often have two small black spots on outer edge

Find marine blues hovering over flowers right outside City Hall, in backyards all over town, or in a local park—notably, it's the most common blue butterfly in Griffith Park. Although it's active February through November, it's most commonly seen darting from flower to flower on warm, sunny days.

The Plight of the Picky Eater

Luckily, marine blue caterpillars aren't picky eaters. Two other locals, the El Segundo blue butterfly and the Palos Verdes blue butterfly, have caterpillars that eat only one species of plant. As Los Angeles grows, habitat for these host plants disappears, and with few host plants, both species have ended up on the U.S. Fish and Wildlife Service's endangered species list.

Marine blues, however, eat many native plants found throughout Los Angeles, including common deerweed, milkvetch, and sweet peas. Increasingly, they've also been enjoying plumbago, an ornamental from South Africa. Lucky for them, this flowering shrub with sticky, purple blooms is all over the city,

▲ This marine blue couldn't spot the camouflaged predator in this flower. Can you?

▲ Marine blue caterpillars come in a variety of colors, depending on the plants they eat. They range from green to brown, to this spectacular pink.

purposefully planted next to front porches, in alleyways, along the LA River, and on many freeway embankments.

Ants and the Caterpillars that Love Them

Marine blue caterpillars are among many species of blue butterfly with a special relationship to ants. Here's how it works: an ant strokes the caterpillar with its antennae (called antennation), and, from two special tubes near its head, the caterpillar produces drops of a sugar and protein-laced liquid it produces specifically for the ants. In return, the ants protect the caterpillars from predators and parasitic insects.

Where to See Them

These butterflies can be easily spotted on warm sunny days March through October. Check out **Trips 7**, **9**, and **21** for your best chance to see them.

Monarch Butterfly

Danaus plexippus

You can find monarchs fluttering at a fifth story window box downtown, visiting flowers at your local plant nursery, or just winging it along your neighborhood street. During winter months they form colonies of thousands in trees along the coast. You might see them on eucalyptus in the Pacific Palisades or Malibu, but for really impressive roostings, head up to Pismo Beach State Park.

Toxic Wings from Toxic Leaves

The monarchs' orange and black alternating stripes are warning colors to potential predators that they won't taste good. As caterpillars, they pick up toxins from the milkweed plants

Black and orange warning coloration

White spots along black wing borders

Males have black pheromone pouches on hind wings

▲ When roosting, monarchs hold onto trees upside down using the small claws on the end of their feet.

they eat. The toxins don't harm the caterpillars but protect them and the adults they become from being eaten. Young birds that haven't learned the lesson yet spit out monarchs after the first few chomps.

Winter Beach Bums

Monarchs are perhaps most famous for their long migration south to Mexico. But our monarchs don't make that trip. They don't need to. Los Angeles winters are mild and food is available year round. Instead they choose one of two options. Either they head to the beach to meet up with hundreds, if not thousands, of their kin and roost in trees through the winter months. Or they stick around in backyards where milkweed is still growing. Historically, the native milkweeds in our area would go dormant in the winter months—dropping their leaves until spring. When Angelenos started planting tropical milkweed, monarchs were able to stay inland through the winter and continue laying eggs on fresh leaves. Some people

Many monarchs overwinter in eucalyptus groves. Before eucalyptus was introduced to California, they mostly used pines and cypress and sometimes still do today.

▲ A monarch caterpillar with its warning colors.

worry that non-native milkweed disrupts monarch seasonality, and could harbor protozoan parasites that infect monarchs, so they prune back the plant over winter months.

WEST COAST MIGRATION

Some West Coast monarchs do migrate. In the spring after the butterflies have overwintered up and down the California coast, some fly up to the Sierra Nevada or Central Valley and lay eggs. Their offspring head further north and east into Oregon, Washington, Idaho, Colorado, or Nevada. At the end of the summer, the great-grandchildren of the overwintering monarchs return south to hang out along our California coastline. A few even head south through Arizona and into Mexico to join the East Coast butterflies.

Loss of milkweed in its spring through fall range, use of pesticides, and loss of overwintering habitat in Mexico threatens the eastern population of monarchs. Our western population is constantly changing, but despite yearly fluctuations in their numbers, scientists believe the overall population is on the decline too. Groups like the Xerces Society are working to ensure that West Coast monarchs are protected, and in urban California, their numbers may be higher thanks to increased wildlife-friendly landscaping.

TAG YOU'RE IT

Community science projects like Monarch Alert (monarchalert.calpoly.edu) help track monarch movements by tagging adults. Any-

You can tell male and female monarchs apart by looking at their hind wings. Males have a small black pouch on each of their hind wings, which stores pheromones, chemicals used to attract a mate.

one can be trained to catch the butterflies and attach the small circular stickers to their hind wings. When butterflies with a tag are recovered, people call in their findings to the project and help scientists understand where West Coast monarchs spend the winter.

Where to See Them

Monarch butterflies are most easily found in the spring, summer, and fall. Look for their caterpillars on milkweed plants, and for adults flying around on **Trips 7** and **12**. In winter, go north to one of the Central California overwintering sites.

Praying Mantis

Family Mantidae

These charismatic insects appear all over Los Angeles in summer and fall—clinging to screen doors, cruising along sidewalks, or hunting insects in your garden. In winter when it's too cold to find the adults, you can still find their egg cases, called *oothecas,* attached to twigs, downed logs, and the sides of buildings. The loaf-shaped papery masses are a great sign for gardeners opting for organic pest control.

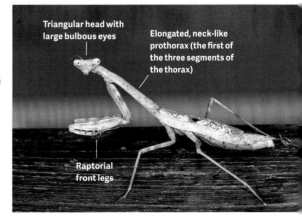

Triangular head with large bulbous eyes

Elongated, neck-like prothorax (the first of the three segments of the thorax)

Raptorial front legs

▲ European mantis in defensive posture.

Warning Wings and Lethal Legs

From the tiniest, newly-hatched mantids, to the large green- or brown-colored adults, these insects are unmistakable. Their modified front legs are perfect for capturing and manipulating prey. They hold these legs together in front of them, a posture that looks like praying and gives them their common name.

Ever noticed how they tilt their head when looking at you? Their triangular heads have two large compound eyes made up of hundreds of individual lenses, ideal for detecting prey and tracking movement. Adults have leathery front wings that protect their flying wings. Some local mantids can use these wings to clumsily fly. Some also have warning coloration and eye-spots on the hind wings. When threatened, they rear up on their hind legs, raise their front legs, and show off the shocking patterns on their wings—keep away, I'm dangerous!

A Patient Predator

Mantids are legendary predators. They sit and wait for their prey of choice—crickets, grasshoppers, or flies—and pick off the food as it walks or flies by.

Mantids are no strangers to cannibalism. When young mantids hatch out of their egg

Los Angeles has seven species of mantids. Four of them—European, Chinese, Carolina, and Mediterranean mantids—are introduced species. The other three are the California, bordered, and agile ground mantis.

cases, they must find food small enough to chew. Tiny flies and immature insects are good, but siblings also work. If you ever take an egg case inside for observation, be sure to let the immature mantids out immediately after hatching or you'll end up with a few very large babies.

Cannibalism often features in tales of mantis mating. Although females have been observed decapitating their male companions after mating, it's not the rule. One study found that males escaped 83 percent of the time.

Where to See Them

Start looking for immature mantids in the spring and large adults later into the summer. They are most likely to be found on **Trips 7**, **11**, **12**, and **15**.

Stink Beetle

Family Tenebrionidae

Stink beetles, or darkling beetles, can be seen crawling across almost any hiking trail in our natural areas. Because they can't fly—their shield-like front wings are fused together—they have to walk everywhere. Usually they're out searching for food. Well adapted to dry climates, they don't need to search for water because they can get all the water they need from the plants they eat.

▲ A stink beetle in defensive posture. Watch out!

Chemical Defense on the Menu

If a stink beetle is disturbed, it has a few ways to escape trouble. Some species freeze and play dead—laying on their backs with all six legs stuck in the air. Some choose a more aggressive strategy: turning their backs to the danger, they raise their rear ends and eject a dark brown, unpleasant-smelling substance from the tip of their abdomens. Even a hungry coyote won't make a meal of something so foul.

Some animals have figured out how to deal with the bad smell. Skunks grab the beetles and roll them on the ground until they expel all of the unpleasant chemicals. Grasshopper mice take the beetles and bury their hind ends in the sand. The mouse then delivers a death-blow to the head and eats its prey in peace.

Where to See Them

Expect to cross paths with these charismatic travelers on any of your foothill hikes, such as **Trips 1**, **2**, **4**, **8**, **9**, **11**, **16**, and **25**. If you see one in loose dirt, check out its tracks and see where it has been.

Shiny black body; can be up to two inches long

Fused elytra

Bead-like antenna

Stripe-eyed Flower Fly

Eristalinus taeniops

Striped abdomen

One set of wings (like all flies)

Large striped eyes

Flitting from flower to flower in Eagle Rock backyards or in the Museum's Nature Gardens, this fly is a beautiful garden inhabitant. Look closely—what you thought was a bee, with distinctive alternating bands of yellow and brown, is actually a pollinating fly!

Hovering Like a Hummingbird

The family Syrphidae, also known as drone flies or hoverflies, are relatively easy to identify. If you see an insect with huge eyes hovering over flowers in your garden, chances are you have just spotted a flower fly. The stripe-eyed flower fly is the flashiest of our local hoverflies, with patterned eyes and a large body about the size of a honey bee. At a distance, many mistake these flies for bees, but when you're close enough, the mimicry is obvious. Honey bees have hairy bodies and dark brown eyes— the stripe-eyed flower fly has a smooth body and bigger, patterned eyes. Bees also have four wings as opposed to a fly's two, but that's almost impossible to tell when it's flying or at a distance.

Another California Transplant

The stripe-eyed flower fly was first recorded in California in 2006 at the Fullerton Arboretum in Orange County. It's originally from Southern Europe, Africa, and the Middle East, and scientists aren't exactly sure how it got here. As with other introduced species, scientists monitor the effects they have on native flora and fauna—to date, no ill effects have been recorded in California.

There are more than thirty-five species of flower flies found in LA County. Most of these mimic bees or wasps.

Where to See Them

Look for stripe-eyed flower flies hovering near flowering plants, where they collect nectar and pollinate flowers in the process. Larvae are aquatic, so look for them in standing water. The adults can be found on blooming flowers in pocket parks along the LA River (**Trip 10**), and blooming buckwheats on **Trip 7** are an especially likely spot to observe this newcomer.

Males have enlarged pedipalps

Large hairy body

Tarantula

Family Theraphosidae

Tarantulas are a thrilling yet rare sight in Southern California. You'll see them most commonly in fall, when male spiders are out looking for mates. They clamber along hiking trails, cross roads, and sometimes walk into homes adjacent to natural areas.

Big Fangs, Weak Venom

These large, hairy spiders sometimes appear to have ten legs. However, the first pair of appendages aren't legs at all; they're sensory organs called pedipalps. Mature males have particularly long pedipalps with enlarged tips that look a bit like they're wearing extra-warm mittens. In the fall, males use them to store and transfer sperm while mating.

Tarantulas also have large fangs to deliver venom, which subdues their prey—crickets, grasshoppers, and other small insects. Our local species aren't a threat to humans. Their venom is mild, and it's very hard to provoke them to bite.

Spider Welcome Mat

Tarantulas are delicate creatures and vulnerable to predators. Once they build their underground burrows, they mostly stay inside. Immature males and female tarantulas are very rarely seen outside, but like all creatures, they must eat. To stay as risk-free as possible, they spin a silken "doormat" around their burrow entrance. When an unsuspecting insect—or other small creature—stumbles onto the silk, vibrations alert the tarantula. Quick as a flash they come out to subdue their prey, then take the food back into the burrow and eat in safety.

When it reaches about 6–7 years old, a male tarantula makes its final molt and is ready to reproduce. His only objective is to find a mate, so he wanders around in search of a female's burrow. When he finds one, he'll tap gently on the silken doormat to let her know he's there. If she's receptive, she'll come out and receive his sperm packet, which he deposits on the silk for her. As with some other spider species, females have been reported to attack males after mating, making a meal of them.

Hair in Your Eye

Though their venom is too weak to threaten large predators, tarantulas do have a defense strategy. When a coyote or rodent gets too close, they use their back legs to kick off abdominal hairs—arachnologists (spider scientists) call them urticating hairs—and throw them like darts. The hairs are barbed and irritating, particularly when they land in the eyes, nose, or mouth. Some caterpillars and many plant species, such as stinging nettle, also have urticating hairs for defense.

Where to See Them

Tarantulas aren't easy to find, but the best time to see them is in the fall from September to October, when males are out looking for a mate. They may be seen crawling over roads, trails, and across sandy washes. Look for them on **Trips 1**, **2**, **4**, **15**, and **16**.

Tarantula Hawk Wasp

Pepsis species

These wasps, also known as pepsis wasps, aren't often seen in the middle of the city, though they can be spotted in areas that have native flowering shrubs, including along the LA River and in the Museum's Nature Gardens. More likely, you'll see them moving from flower to flower in native shrubland. If you follow their flight, you may see them flying low over the ground looking for their burrows. If you're really lucky, you might spot a female stalking her tarantula prey.

A large insect with a steely-blue exoskeleton and bright orange wings, the tarantula wasp eats nectar and is not interested in stinging humans (though it will defend itself if you threaten it, so look but don't touch). Males and females are almost identical in size, shape, and color, but females have curled antennae.

Tarantulas in the Nursery

When a female tarantula hawk wasp is ready to lay eggs, she digs or finds an underground burrow to use as a nursery. And she stocks the pantry by hunting and capturing fresh tarantula meat for her larvae to eat.

Orange wings

Up to two inches long

Steely-blue body and legs

Orange antennae (if tightly curls, it's a female)

Tarantula hawk wasps pack a ferocious sting—the most powerful in North America. According to the Schmidt Sting Pain Index, it's "blinding, fierce, [and] shockingly electric. A running hair dryer has been dropped into your bubble bath (if you get stung by one you might as well lie down and scream)."

To successfully battle a tarantula, she must sting the spider's underbelly, paralyzing but not killing it. She then drags the incapacitated arachnid into the burrow and deposits an egg. When the egg hatches, the larva burrows into the paralyzed spider body and stays there feasting on fresh meat until it develops into an adult.

Where to See Them

Look for tarantula hawk wasps on warm, sunny days in large open spaces with native vegetation, like Griffith Park, other parks in the Santa Monica and San Gabriel Mountains, and sometimes in urban spaces growing appropriate plants—most likely on **Trips 1**, **2**, **15**, and **20**.

Ten-lined June Beetle

Polyphylla decemlineata

Attracted to porch lights in Altadena, lanterns at San Gabriel Mountain campsites, or screen doors of Hollywood homes, this nocturnal scarab beetle (of the family Scarabaeidae) stops people in its tracks wherever it goes. It's part of a group of beetles known as June bugs, and emerges in summer, allowing lucky Angelenos to enjoy its colorful pattern and clumsy flight for a few short months.

Beetle Bodies

Ten-lined June beetles are large (about the size of a big peanut), hairy, and brown. They get the first part of their name from the ten bold white stripes that pattern their elytra. Males and females look similar but with different antennae. Males' specialized antennae are enlarged at the end with a number of plates, which can be held flattened together or extended like a hand with the fingers spread out. Male beetles use these extra sensitive antennae to find mates. When a female wants to announce she's ready for mating, she settles in a tree and

Males have large fan-like antennae

Brown body about an inch long

White line patterns on thorax and wings

When disturbed, ten-lined June beetles hiss by rubbing their abdomen against the edges of their wing coverings.

releases a special chemical pheromone. Sometimes these pheromones can attract swarms of ready-to-mate males.

Where to See Them

Look for these beetles in late spring through early fall, particularly on **Trips 16** and **17**. If you live near Griffith Park or the Verdugo Mountains and hear something clumsily bumping into your window screen at night, this beetle might be paying you a visit.

Valley Carpenter Bee

Xylocopa varipuncta

Uniform body color; black females, tan males

Naked abdomen

Big! Up to about an inch long

Buzzing from flower to flower on a warm, sunny day, valley carpenter bees can be seen in our local foothills or down in the lowlands—from Burbank backyards to Paramount parks. Because they're about the size of a pecan and have a loud buzz, they're often mistaken for bumble bees. However, carpenter bees are solid in color—females are black and have a "naked" shiny abdomen, whereas males are tan with a "fuzzy" abdomen—bumble bees usually have distinctive bands of black and yellow-white on their bodies and are hairy nearly all over.

Carpenter Bee Nurseries

There are three species of carpenter bees in Southern California, and all of them feed on nectar and pollen collected from flowers. They get their carpenter name from their habit of tunneling into wood when nesting. After a female carpenter bee bores a tunnel into wood, she deposits an egg and a ball of pollen and nectar then seals it off in a small cell with a partition made of sawdust. She may make five or six cells in a tunnel, one in front of the next, each about an inch long. One cell takes about a day to construct. When she's finished, she

The dense hairs on a carpenter bee's legs hold an electrostatic charge. When they enter a flower, pollen is attracted to their legs—just like when you stick a balloon to the wall by first rubbing it on your head.

▲ Because of their extra fuzzy bodies, male carpenter bees are also called teddy bear bees.

seals up the entrance with more sawdust. Six to eight weeks later, the eggs hatch—usually in spring—and the larvae eat the nectar and pollen before pupating and eventually emerging as young adults.

Carpenter bee nests can be found in telephone poles, old stumps, and brush piles, but also in living wood—they prefer redwood, cedar, cypress, and pine, but will also use eucalyptus.

Solitary Bees Don't Sting Easily

Many people fear carpenter bees because they're large and their buzz is formidable. But these solitary bees rarely sting. You're more likely to be stung by a honey bee. Because they are social and live in a hive with their relatives, honey bees defend each other and can be aggressive when disturbed. Carpenter bees don't form hives, so they're extremely docile and not apt to sting. Also, only female bees can sting (an insect stinger is a modified ovipositor, which is an egg-laying organ). Some male bees are known to feign stinging by pumping their abdomen in a stinging motion, but all male bees lack stingers and can't hurt you.

Where to See Them

Valley carpenter bees can be seen buzzing around well-flowered areas in urban and suburban Los Angeles and up into the foothills. Look for them on **Trips 7**, **11**, **12**, and **21**.

Western Giant Swallowtail

Papilio rumiko

The largest butterfly in our area, western giant swallowtails are usually seen in solitary flight, searching for food, a mate, or places to rest or lay eggs. They are mostly black or dark brown with yellow bands extending across the upper parts of the front and hind wings (their underwings are pale yellow).

Big (up to 6.25-inch wingspan) and mostly black

Distinctive yellow stripe across wings

One "tail" on each hind wing

Because of the destruction they can cause in citrus groves—attacking like an aggressive dog that won't let go of a bone—this butterfly's common name is orange dog or orange puppy.

▲ A western giant swallowtail caterpillar with its osmeterium extended.

How to Fool Predators

Some butterflies in the swallowtail family have tail-like projections at the end of each hind wing, similar to the long, forked tails of swallows. These tails help keep them safe from birds and other predators. Sometimes you'll see tails torn or missing—better to lose a small part of your wing than any part of your head, thorax, or abdomen where all your critical organs are located.

After hatching, western giant swallowtail caterpillars have excellent camouflage and are easily mistaken for bird droppings. Later stages grow up to an inch long, with dark eyespots.

They can look like small snakes, a mimicry that is even more dramatic when the caterpillars are disturbed. A forked-orange organ (the *osmeterium*) inflates party-blower style from just behind the head, resembling a snake's forked tongue. Inflated with fluid, it also emits an odor that's not unpleasant to humans but is a deterrent for some species of ants and spiders.

Where to See Them

Look for this butterfly anywhere close to citrus trees. Most easily spotted on **Trips 7** and **12**, but you could also see it flying down your neighborhood street seeking local gardens.

Widow Spiders

Brown Widow
Latrodectus geometricus

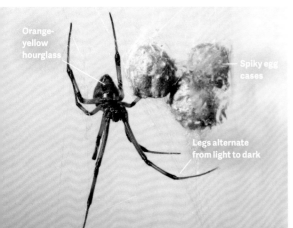

Orange-yellow hourglass

Spiky egg cases

Legs alternate from light to dark

Western Black Widow
Latrodectus hesperus

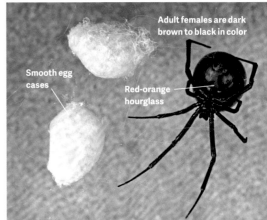

Adult females are dark brown to black in color

Smooth egg cases

Red-orange hourglass

Black widow spiders and their haphazard webs used to be found throughout the LA Basin in rural and urban areas alike. They could be found inside sprinkler boxes, under woodpiles, in corners of garages, and under patio furniture. However, these spiders aren't as common as they used to be. Today, the introduced brown widow spider is quickly taking over in urban areas, and black widows are mostly found on the urban edges and in less developed areas.

The first brown widows in California were found in 2002 by community scientists participating in the Museum's LA Spider Survey. Those spiders were found at Van Deene Avenue Elementary School in Torrance, but now brown widows are found across the LA Basin. This turf takeover happened incredibly quickly.

The Hourglass and the Egg Sac

Adult female black widows are hard to mistake for other spiders. Large and shiny black, they have the telltale red hourglass pattern on the underside of their abdomen. Brown widows are mottled brown, have banded legs, and have an orange hourglass. Males of both widows are much smaller and thinner.

The easiest way to identify the widows in your yard is to look at their round egg sacs. If the sac is smooth, it was laid by a black widow; if it is spiky, it's the work of a brown widow.

Watch Where You Put Your Hands

Black widow venom is lethal to crickets and other ground-dwelling insects the widow eats. It's also a potent neurotoxin for humans—black widow bites are very unlikely to kill a healthy adult, but their bites can be painful. That said, bites to people are incredibly rare—black widows are very shy and tend to only bite when being pinched or crushed. Black widow bites are most frequent when people reach into areas under rocks, wood piles, or abandoned plant pots without looking. Brown widows are even more timid than black widows. Both are active mostly at night and hide during the day.

Where to See Them

You can find brown widows and their egg sacs in garage corners, irrigation boxes, and in cracks in walls in most urban areas of the LA Basin. Black widows like the same kinds of spots but now are uncommon in urban areas. Look amongst brush and rock piles in the drier, more rural habitats surrounding the LA Basin, such as **Trips 9** and **15**. Be cautious when looking for this species that you don't hurt the spider, damage its habitat, or cause it to bite in a last-ditch effort to protect itself.

Perched attractively on stucco walls across the city or flying into homes at night, this moth

False widow spiders are similar in size, shape, and color to black widows, but they have no hourglass pattern and their venom is harmless to humans.

White-Lined Sphinx Moth

Hyles lineata

is one of the most commonly photographed in our region, in part because it's so large and colorful. White-lined sphinx moths have aerodynamic, torpedo-shaped bodies, a three-inch wingspan, and a bold white stripe along the front wing.

Mystery of the Sphinx

The sphinx name refers to caterpillar behavior—when disturbed or threatened, they lift up their front end and tuck their head under, resembling the Egyptian sphinx. Fully-grown, a white-lined sphinx moth caterpillar can be over three inches long, often dark green or black with yellow markings along the body. It also has a horn on the end of its abdomen, which is a harmless spine and doesn't sting.

Where to See Them

Caterpillars can be found swarming over plants of all sorts, particularly during super bloom events. However, they are well-camouflaged and surprisingly hard to spot. Adults are nectar feeders—look for one hovering over flowers, drinking nectar with its long proboscis. They frequent flower-filled urban gardens, so try finding one on **Trip 7** or **12**.

White lines on the wing veins

Narrow wings

Stout hairy body

The white-lined sphinx moth is a strong flier that looks uncannily like a hummingbird as it hovers mid-air over flowers. Sometimes during cool mornings in early summer, you can spot large groups drinking nectar from flowering landscape plants like lantana.

▼ White-lined sphinx moth caterpillar.

Yellow Garden Spider

Argiope aurantia

In late summer and fall, yellow garden spiders and their impressive webs begin to get noticed all over town. The spiders were there all year, but eggs and spiderlings (baby spiders) are easily overlooked. Eggs, laid in fall, are well camouflaged. Spiderlings, which hatch out in spring, are about the size of a pinhead. However, the large adult spiders that skillfully string their webs between bushes in Highland Park backyards, downtown Los Angeles parks, and schoolyards all over town are showstoppers.

The yellow garden spider is a type of orb weaver, the common name for spiders in the family Araneidae, and it's one of the showiest orb-weavers in Los Angeles. Its size and the jagged-yellow markings on its abdomen make it hard to miss. An adult female can have a leg-span as wide as a tennis ball. When she's ready to lay an egg case, her abdomen swells and looks like a ripe grape. Males are much smaller.

Black and yellow markings

Female bodies can be up to 1 inch, with leg to leg spread of 2.5 inches

Web often has zigzag "writing"

The Writing Is in the Web

Orb weaver webs are iconic—composed of many spokes connected by a spiral of silk. Yellow garden spiders further embellish their webs with designs called *stabilimenta*. The zig-zag webbing often aligns with the spider's legs as she sits on the center of her web. There's a lot of debate about the function of stabilimenta, and some scientists think this web design might help camouflage the spider.

Many orb weaver spiders will take down their webs and rebuild them each day. To save energy, they eat the old silk. This makes orb weaver webs look clean, lacking the build-up of dead insects seen in other spiders' webs. The yellow garden spider is a meticulous house cleaner, consuming the center of the web each evening, then rebuilding in the morning.

Community scientists participating in the Museum's LA Spider Survey have found at least thirty-eight species of orb weaver spiders in Los Angeles.

Where to See Them

Look for these spiders at eye level in the fall when the adults build their large webs between trees or bushes. Easiest to spot on **Trips 3** and **21**.

129

Mammals

Bats

Western Mastiff Bat

Eumops perotis

Chocolate brown fur

Large ears that join across the forehead

Wingspan up to 22 inches

Canyon Bat

Parastrellus hesperus

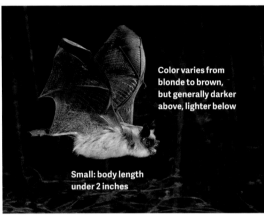

Color varies from blonde to brown, but generally darker above, lighter below

Small: body length under 2 inches

Los Angeles County is home to twenty species of bats, including the largest bat in North America, the western mastiff, and the smallest, the canyon bat. These nighttime fliers are most commonly observed in foothill, mountain, and desert areas. In summer and fall, you can see them foraging at football stadiums and golf courses where the bright lights attract large numbers of flying insects, or dipping low over Echo Park Lake and the LA River.

A typical bat eats its own body weight in insects each night, catching up to one thousand mosquitoes an hour.

Catching Food in the Dark

Contrary to legend, bats actually have good vision. Some species can see colors and UV light. But they hunt at night because that's when their food comes out. Most bats use echolocation, which works like sonar in a submarine, to catch insects. The bat sends out very fast, high-pitched clicks, from twenty per second while cruising slowly (called search phase calls) to two hundred per second (called a feeding buzz) when closing in on dinner. Timing the gap between when the sound leaves its mouth and when it bounces off a juicy moth and returns, helps the bat locate objects even in complete darkness.

Petite to XXL

The largest bat in the world is a kind of fruit bat with a wingspan of nearly six feet. The western mastiff bat isn't quite that large, but it is the biggest bat in North America. Its wings, from tip to tip, measure nearly two feet across, and its hunting clicks are audible to humans. Thought to be gone from Los Angeles, western mastiffs were detected in 2012 near Griffith Park. America's smallest bat, the canyon bat, can be found in Los Angeles too. Fully grown, it weighs about as much as a ripe grape.

Bats are the only mammals capable of true flight, but they are more similar to us than you might guess. The bones that make up a bat's wing are the same as the bones in our own arms and hands—only their bones are thinner and a membrane of skin connects the fingers to create a wing.

Where to See Them

Most bat hunting calls are too high pitched for us to hear, so experts use bat detectors when surveying night skies. The western mastiff bat is a unique exception and emits a low-pitched call within the range of human hearing. Canyon bats come out before dark (it belongs to a group called the vesper bats, named for evening prayers)—if you watch for them at twilight you can spot them without super-hearing or fancy equipment. Good places to try are **Trips 1**, **10**, **13**, **14**, and **17**.

Black Bear

Ursus americanus

Most Angelenos don't think of bears as their neighbors, but people living at the base of the San Gabriel Mountains know that bears come down from the high country to explore backyards and trashcans or sometimes take a lap in the pool. When around human developments, bears become nocturnal, so in our area, hikers don't often see them. In late summer and fall, watch for their large, seed-filled mounds of scat.

Woodland Triathletes

Despite their large size, black bears are quite adept at climbing trees and can run about thirty-five miles per hour, faster than the fastest human. As tourists in Yosemite have learned, they're also strong enough to peel back a car door or trunk in search of people food.

If you come upon a black bear in its habitat and it's just being a bear—eating, digging up termites, etc.—keep your distance and slowly leave the area. If a bear approaches you, you'll want to scare it off. Look big—if you're in a group, stand together and wave your arms. Talk loudly to the bear. This is usually enough to scare it away. Never play dead with a black bear—that is advice for grizzlies.

Usually 100–200 pounds in our area

Usually dark brown in our area

> "If [the bears] thrive, they will become a real attraction to the thousands of visitors who spend summers and weekends in the mountain playgrounds... Their comical, clownish appearance and actions are a never-ending source of amusement to youngsters and adults alike."
>
> —*California Department of Fish and Game biologist A. E. Burghduff, on the 1933 introduction of black bears to the Angeles and San Bernardino National Forests*

With our mild climate, only pregnant females hibernate in winter. They dig into hillsides and find spots under logs or the roots of large trees, in caves and rock crevices, and sometimes just in dense brush. Most remain active year-round.

In the Forest but Not on the Flag

The high, humped shoulder of the bear on California's state flag tells you it's not a black bear but a grizzly. Grizzly bears used to live here, and settlers adopted them as a symbol during their brief war for independence from Mexico. However, the grizzly bear has had more staying power on our flag than in our landscapes. Within fifty years of the Bear Flag Revolt, human activity made this icon scarce. The last California grizzly bear in the wild was seen in 1924.

The grizzly bear's disappearance created a job opening for the smaller and more adaptable black bear. They started spreading south from the southern Sierra Nevada, and their range expansion sped up in 1933 when state biologists introduced twenty-seven bears into the San Gabriel and San Bernardino Mountains. The biologists wanted to increase tourism and relocate pest bears out of Yosemite. Six bears were released near Big Bear Lake, a spot named for the vanished grizzly bears they would replace.

Where to See Them

Black bears are found throughout the mountains, but they're often nocturnal. You might get lucky and see a bear on **Trips 16** and **17**.

Bobcat

Lynx rufus

Short ear tufts atop pointed ears

Short bobbed tail (4–8 inches)

Medium-sized cat, with ruff of fur on sides of face

Bobcats are our in-between cats: smaller than a mountain lion but larger than a house cat. Tan above, lighter below, with scattered dark spots, tufted ears, and a short (bobbed), six-inch tail. More common than most people guess, the solitary bobcat is good at staying out of the way.

Rabbit on the Menu

Bobcats are stalkers, carefully sneaking up on a potential meal and then pouncing. Unlike coyotes or black bears, bobcats don't spend time in the produce aisle. Scientists call them *obligate carnivores,* which means they're meat eaters only, with a special skill at finding and catching rabbits, gophers, and ground squirrels. They'll eat smaller things (insects, mice, birds, and lizards) and bigger things (all the way up to deer), but rabbit-sized mammals are their specialty. Sadly, their emphasis on small prey and their meat-only diet makes them vulnerable to the rat poison some Angelenos use in their yards.

Typically very secretive, bobcats avoid contact with humans and are mostly nocturnal, resting in a den or under a dense bush during the day, then covering many miles at night. One animal may have multiple dens. These can be inside an old tree, in a hollow of a cliff, under a brush pile, or even along the edge of the freeway.

Hunted No More

Once hunted for its fur and persecuted in misguided predator control campaigns, the bobcat has since recovered across most of its range. It can be found now from Canada to Mexico and California to Maine. It shows a remarkable ability to fit into all sorts of habitats, including snowy high mountains, coastal habitat, wetlands, and the summer heat of Death Valley. It even thrives, generally unseen, in the middle of Griffith Park.

Where to See Them

Bobcats live in all wild habitats, from deserts to coastal scrub. Studies with camera traps prove they are more common than we might guess, and they can be observed in urban parks, including Griffith, Franklin Canyon, Elysian, and Debs. Sometimes they even venture down into neighborhoods near parks, such as Los Feliz and Silver Lake. Particular trips to try include **1**, **9**, **13**, **16**, and **17**.

> Like other cats, bobcats mark territory and share news through scent marking—their poop and urine tell other animals who's around, and what their dating status is.

Botta's Pocket Gopher

Thomomys bottae

You've seen evidence of this brown, rat-sized animal even if you've never seen the *Caddyshack* nemesis itself. From the top of Kenneth Hahn State Recreation Area to your local golf course, few large lawns are free of the dirt cones that tell us pocket gophers have been at work. If you do see one out of the hole, you'll note a big head, a stocky, tubular body, and a short, hairless tail.

Brown, torpedo-shaped body

Small eyes and ears

Large incisor teeth always exposed

The name *pocket gopher* comes from the fur-lined external cheek pouches where they store food. After they're done foraging, the gophers carry food back to storage areas and stow it for future meals.

▲ Different diggers dig differently. The California ground squirrel makes a clean hole and moves all the dirt away. The broad-footed mole makes volcano-shaped mounds that lack an obvious entrance hole. Pocket gopher mounds like this one are shaped like a handheld-fan, or a kidney bean, with a very obvious front door (sometimes the doorway is plugged up by dirt).

🔦 A rare glimpse of a pocket gopher completely out of its hole.

Tunnel Masters

Gophers are *fossorial,* which means they spend most of their lives underground. They dig an underground burrow system that includes tunnels, food storage areas, and a central nest area. And it's not just their houses that are hidden away—their grocery stores are too. If you ever see grasses or small plants being pulled down into the ground, that's the work of a pocket gopher feasting on roots or tubers just below the surface. Underground living is a good way to keep away from coyotes and red-tailed hawks, even if it makes gardeners and groundskeepers furious.

Most gophers have large, strong hands and claws for digging. Pocket gophers also have serious incisor teeth they use to bore their extensive tunnel systems. Their lips close behind their incisors, which prevents dirt from getting inside their mouths while excavating.

LIFE IN THE MOUNDS

Just because a field has mound after mound of dirt doesn't mean there's a gopher community underground. Unlike ground squirrels, pocket gophers are solitary animals, defending their territory against other gophers and making burrow systems that can be five thousand square feet, about the size of two tennis courts. Female pocket gophers typically have slightly smaller burrow systems, usually around three thousand square feet.

Most of the year, gophers strictly defend their territories, but during breeding season they may overlap. Neighboring territories are usually separated by a gopher-free buffer zone, which allows them to spend energy on tunneling instead of worrying about an encroaching neighbor.

Where to See Them

Throughout the basin and foothills where loose soil is present. Common in grassy yards, parks, and fields, including on **Trips 3**, **6**, **11**, and **18**.

California Ground Squirrel

Otospermophilus beecheyi

Usually observed on the ground

Mottled gray-brown fur

Tail about 70 percent the length of its body and relatively narrow

Sometimes, there's a whole community living under your feet. From vacant lots in Long Beach to San Gabriel Mountain woodlands, California ground squirrels build their underground dwellings in fields, along freeway edges, on brushy hills, and in open forest. They are colonial animals, which means they live in family groups ranging from a few squirrels to over one hundred.

Ground squirrel colonies live in a network of tunnels. Each tunnel can reach up to thirty-five feet long, and dive down as deep as thirty feet. They lead to nesting chambers where babies are born and cared for, food storage areas, and even underground bathrooms. Although colony members share this communal home, the adults are pretty independent and maintain their own entrances.

Ground Squirrels Are Good Neighbors

The ground squirrel's underground condo complex is used by many other species. Western toads and other amphibians seek shelter in the cool, humid tunnels. These houseguests will spend the majority of their lives in the burrows, enjoying the damp air and feasting on beetles, worms, and other small critters. Snakes also use them, both to find ground squirrel meals and for shelter.

Even when the squirrels have moved out, burrowing owls will enlarge tunnels to use as a home. Foxes and badgers will do the same, sometimes after making a meal of the original owner!

Dirt-colored Camouflage

The California ground squirrel is the color of dirt, which provides good camouflage against aerial predators such as hawks. It has speckled, grayish brown fur and a long tail. It might look a bit like two other common Southern California squirrels (the western gray and the eastern fox squirrels), but the ground squirrel is plain brown and has a slimmer, less showy tail. It also doesn't climb trees—the highest off the ground it might go is to perch on a fencepost, log, boulder, or tall bush when acting as lookout.

These squirrels feed during daylight, so you can see them all day long. Their diet includes grasses, grass seeds, and other vegetation (they can be a real terror in a garden), but also berries, acorns, mushrooms, bird eggs, insects, and even small animals like mice and voles.

The Lookout

Perched on a fence or tall rock, some squirrels stand guard while the others sun themselves or find food. The lookouts not only warn of potential predators but also say which ones are approaching. Rapidly repeated whistles and loud chattering means a coyote, fox, or other mammal is on the prowl. A single whistle let out while sprinting for cover means a winged predator like a red-tailed hawk is scanning from above. And slowly repeated, sporadic whistles mean a snake is in the area.

Where there are ground squirrels, there are often rattlesnakes. Although alarm calls announcing a coyote or hawk trigger squirrels to sprint for a burrow, their snake alarm call sparks the opposite response. Squirrels will start scanning for the predator, and once spotted, a squirrel will boldly approach, even within the snake's striking distance. Their confidence comes from their incredible ability to dodge strikes, and also because they have some resistance to rattlesnake venom. Nevertheless, rattlesnakes are major squirrel predators. They eat an especially large number of young squirrels, which have less snake experience and, because they are smaller, less resistance to the venom.

In addition to calling, squirrels approach rattlesnakes and tail flag (wave their tail in the air from side-to-side) to tell the snake "I see you" and warn other squirrels of the danger.

Ground squirrels will chew shed rattlesnake skin and then lick themselves or their pups to mask their squirrely scent—this way rattlesnakes can't smell them as easily.

Snakes strike less often at tail-flagging squirrels, and tail-flagging squirrels are more likely to dodge a strike. After tail flagging, snakes are also more likely to abandon an ambush site because the element of surprise is lost.

Where to See Them

Look for California ground squirrels in open fields. They like areas where the grass is short and the views are long so they can spot any approaching predators—they avoid areas with dense grass or lots of trees. Found on many of the listed trips, and especially likely on **Trips 1, 2**, **3**, **5**, **11**, and **18**.

Coyote

Canis latrans

Gray, or reddish gray

Neck and belly light colored

About the size of a medium-sized dog

Somebody encountering a solo coyote at night might mistake it for an escaped pet. On closer inspection, the coyote's narrow snout, pointed ears, buff-colored fur, and long and bushy tail all reveal that this is not Fido out for a midnight stroll. This is Los Angeles's ultimate survivor.

From Koreatown to the Hollywood Bowl, the nimble and quick-witted coyote can live in a lot of places, and scientists are just beginning to study them closely in the city's urban core. Their flexibility is partly because of their social structures and their wide-ranging diets. But it's also because they know how to make do with forgotten pieces of landscape. We rarely think about storm drains, power line rights of way, or railroad tracks, but these are all coyote highways, linking one island of habitat to another. There's a downside though—their wide-ranging behavior makes them vulnerable to cars.

Rabbit, Fruit, or Frogs

Coyotes can find a meal just about anywhere, eating rodents, rabbits, snakes, frogs, birds, insects, fish, roadkill, trash, fruit, seeds, grass, and even deer. They are among the most successful of our native urban explorers. But like bobcats, the coyote's preference for small mammals and ability to hunt in backyards makes it vulnerable to rat poison. And it's true—they do eat the occasional unsupervised pet, so be sure you don't let yours stray at night.

It takes a pack to raise a litter of coyote pups—mom, dad, and older siblings all help out. The resourceful coyote can successfully hunt alone, in pairs, or in packs up to ten. Packs are family groups, with the alpha pair (mom and dad) and several offspring, often from different litters. Coyotes will sometimes form even larger informal hunting groups to take down big prey.

How to Speak Coyote

Coyotes, like other members of the dog family, maintain social status through a variety of signals, including scent marking, body language, and vocalizations. Here's our version of. . .

Coyote 101:

A tentative, huffing woof is a cautionary note—"stay back, partner, until I figure out what you are."

A simple bark is an alarm, warning of a potential long-distance threat.

A *woo-oo-wow* call is a greeting to other coyotes.

A lone howl, called a herald bark, is like a formal hello. "This is who I am. This is what I'm doing here."

The whole pack joining in to *yip-yip-yippy-kai-aye* might be a way of asserting control over a home range, warning rival groups the territory is occupied.

As they fill the night with a canine chorus, it's no wonder coyotes are nicknamed the song dogs.

Where to See Them

Coyotes are present at almost all sites in the book, though less expected in the densest parts of the urban center. Hear or see them in Griffith Park (**Trip 9**), most commonly at sunrise, sunset, and after dark. Other good sites include **Trips 1**, **13**, **14**, and **20**.

137

Desert Bighorn Sheep

Ovis canadensis nelsoni

Smaller sweeping horns in females

Large, coiled horns in adult males

Tannish-brown bodies with a white rump

The desert bighorn sheep is the ace rock climber of the animal world, able to navigate sheer cliffs with casual ease. Once found in mountains throughout the American West, bighorn sheep numbers dropped to fewer than 20,000 animals due to overhunting, diseases brought in with domestic sheep, and habitat loss. The California Department of Fish and Wildlife has tracked bighorn since 1976—about four hundred bighorns live in our local mountains today. They are a desert subspecies, able to go weeks without water.

Head-Butting for Dominance

When two strong-willed people disagree, we say they butt heads. During the *rut* (fall breeding season), male bighorns really do butt heads, crashing into each other headfirst to establish dominance. They can be going as fast as twenty miles per hour when they hit. Why don't they get serious injuries (or at least bad headaches)? Inside the bones that make up the skull are a network of reinforcements and air-filled sinuses that protect their brains.

> Bighorn sheep duels can be heard a mile away and may last for hours.

Big Horns and Little Horns

Both male and female bighorn sheep are sandy brown, with a pale circle on their butts. They are heavier-bodied than a deer, and almost always seen on a hillside or ridge. Both male and female bighorn sheep have horns. Even young sheep have them, though at first theirs stick straight up like two baby carrots. Young males and females have horns that don't curve very far, but on dominant males, the horns sweep down and around into a full circle. Because a bighorn sheep's horns never stop growing, they are a rough indicator of age and sex. The heaviest adult male horns can weigh thirty pounds. Bighorn, indeed.

Threats Ancient and New

To avoid becoming a mountain lion's dinner, bighorn sheep stay in small groups for protection—the more eyes to keep watch, the better.

What's the difference between antlers and horns? Antlers are made of bone that grows from the *pedicel*, a bony extension of the skull. Antlers grow and are shed every year, usually only by males. Horns have a bony core that extends from the skull and an outer layer of keratin, the same material that makes your fingernails. Horns aren't shed—they grow throughout the animal's life.

the ewes and young in their own group. In summer, the groups come together for breeding then separate again in the fall.

These are sturdy, tough animals, willing to eat cactus (often bashing spines away with their horns) and able to navigate the most rugged, spectacular terrain, but they face threats we often don't think about. Herds of domestic sheep grazing in or near the bighorns' home territories is a problem. Not only is there a limited amount of grass and water, but bighorns can catch a kind of pneumonia from domestic sheep and cattle that can wipe out an entire herd in less than a few months.

Where to See Them

The best place to see them locally is around Mount Baldy. They migrate seasonally, moving lower down the mountainside in winter. For details see **Trip 17**.

They also prefer steep, open slopes that are hard for predators to traverse. For much of the year, males and females stay in separate groups. The rams stay in a bachelor herd and

Mountain Lion

Puma concolor

Adults are tawny brown with a lighter belly

Long tail

Prowling under the Hollywood sign, crossing eight-lane freeways, or hunting mule deer above Malibu, the mountain lion is the ghost among us. Though rarely seen, it's present in all our local mountains: Santa Monicas, Santa Susanas, Simi Hills, Verdugos, San Bernardinos, and San Gabriels.

Mountain lions, also called pumas or cougars, have the widest natural range of any large cat in the world. They live all the way from Alaska to Patagonia. Once found across the entire United States, overhunting of the cats and their main prey, deer, resulted in their extinction in eastern states. (The one exception is an endangered subspecies called the Florida panther that lives in the Everglades.)

Adults are solid tan with a long, black-tipped tail. Cubs have spots like a bobcat but always have a long tail. Cubs also have deep blue eyes for the first few months, then their eyes turn golden yellow and remain so through adulthood. They can grow up to eight feet long. Just about every naturalist hopes to see a mountain lion someday. It's a special treat. More likely you'll come across footprints or scat.

Tracking Big Cats

Hunted in California until 1990, the species is now protected, and the overall statewide population is recovering. Freeways chop up their ranges, however, making it hard for young animals to disperse, and hard for new animals to meet up and reproduce.

Scientists track mountain lions using radio and GPS collars, so we know where they go and roughly how many there are in the Santa Monica, Santa Susana, and Verdugo Mountains. This tracking helps biologists identify preferred travel routes and possible choke points where they can't easily get from point A to B. Tracking the pumas' movements allows scientists to study how an increasingly fragmented landscape affects the cats' population.

> Mountain lions can jump forty feet—more than the length of an RV.

This work shows us that wildlife crossings under and over local freeways would help a lot. Mountain lions need room to roam. The typical home range of an adult male is two hundred square miles (just under half the size of the entire city of Los Angeles), yet that's not always possible. P-22, the famed bachelor of Griffith Park, has a home range of just eight square miles, the smallest known home range of any mountain lion ever studied.

Dinner and Other Hazards

Ninety percent of a mountain lion's diet in the Santa Monica Mountains is mule deer, but they will eat anything from seals to wood-rats. Mountain lions living along the city/wilderness boundary have gotten sick from rat poison in their food. Other threats include mountain lions killing other mountain lions and vehicular collisions. The first results from not being able to move around and expand into vacant territories, the second from the threat of cars and motorcycles as they try to do so.

Where to See Them

In Southern California, urbanization has restricted mountain lions to less developed hills and mountains. If you hope to see one, spending time in prime habitat helps, but most sightings are a matter of luck. Places with the best probability include **Trips 1**, **2**, **16**, and **17**.

Mule Deer

Odocoileus hemionus

Large, mule-like ears

Whitish rump with a black tail

This swivel-eared, long-legged animal is a favorite mountain lion food and surprisingly capable of hiding in plain sight in our foothills and mountains. Sometimes they're more visible, like when they're eating flowers off Forest Lawn graves or trotting across a road in the San Gabriel Mountains. Sharp-eyed commuters have spotted them from the 405 in the Sepulveda Pass and next to the 2 Freeway in Glendale, and the deer that graze the lawns at the Jet Propulsion Laboratory had their own Twitter feed.

They're called mule deer because of the size and shape of their ears, which, like a mule's, are tall and active. A mule deer can hear well, see even better, and smell even better than that. With eyes on the side of its head, a

If they detect a predator, mule deer will often escape by *stotting*. Stotting is an unusual run, which involves jumping high off the ground with legs stiff and all four feet in the air. It probably has two purposes: telling the predator that it now lacks the element of surprise and signaling to other deer that there's a predator nearby.

▲ A male, or buck, shows off his antlers.

▲ Black tails and fawn spots on display.

deer can see 310 degrees around. If you were a deer, in one view you could see everything from behind your left ear all the way around in front of you and back around to behind your right ear.

Only male mule deer have antlers, which they shed each winter and start growing anew each spring. When growing, the antlers are covered in velvet, which is full of blood vessels that bring oxygen and nutrients to the growing bone beneath. They shed the velvet in late summer or early fall when their antlers reach full size. Males then use the antlers to battle and establish dominance. Dominant males breed more, contributing more of their genes to the next generation.

Baby deer, called fawns, can make a bleating sound like sheep and adults can bark and grunt, but on average these are silent animals. They eat vegetation, browsing twigs and leaves then digesting them in a multi-chambered stomach. Like a cow, a deer spends part of each day chewing cud—after it eats food it continues to spit it back up and chew it again to get all the nutrition possible. They also eat grass, weeds, acorns . . . and the prize flowers in homeowners' gardens.

Although they are seemingly widespread, there have been no formal studies conducted on mule deer in our area. Surprisingly, researchers don't truly understand the local population, despite their impact on vegetation and mountain lion diets.

Where to See Them

Forested and brushy areas of mountains, canyons, foothills, and their neighboring communities. Watch for them at dusk and dawn on **Trips 1**, **9**, **16**, and **17**.

· ·

If you find a shed antler, look for tooth marks. Squirrels, opossums, raccoons, mice, and other rodents chew on the sheds to get calcium, phosphorous, and salts.

Northern Raccoon

Procyon lotor

Brazen and widespread, the northern raccoon can be found poking its head out of storm drains, knocking over trashcans in your backyard, and photo-bombing camera traps in Griffith Park. They're so adaptable that researchers have found more of them in urban areas with human resources than in nearby natural areas where they'd have to work harder to find food and deal with competitors. Thanks to their bold curiosity, bandit face mask, and striped tail, most everybody knows them. Few animals are so easy to identify—and so fun to watch.

Crayfish, Clams, and Carrion

Raccoons swim well and spend time around water, where they seek out much of their food. In Los Angeles this means they like streams, ditches, runoff basins, culverts, and backyard ponds. They eat a good amount of aquatic life, including clams and non-native mini-lobster lookalikes called crayfish.

Out of the water, their wide menu includes grubs, worms, pet food, birdseed, trash, and even baby birds. They scavenge carrion and also make use of the fruit and vegetable side of the menu, including berries, walnuts, and wild grapes. It may seem mean, but they do earn their nickname—trash pandas.

Whiskers on their Fingers

Urban legend holds that raccoons wash their food before eating it. This behavior is tied more to their incredible sense of touch than to tidiness. Raccoons have extremely sensitive front paws covered in a rough, callused layer. When wet, this layer becomes softer and more sensitive, allowing a raccoon to carefully knead food, clean off grit, and check for any parts that might be bad to eat. This behavior gives the northern raccoon its scientific species name: *lotor* means washer. The digits on their front paws also have whiskers, modified hairs that connect to nerves, further increasing their sense of touch.

In the mud along a creek, raccoon tracks are among the easiest to learn because their back feet leave a very human-shaped track, sort of like a miniature human hand with long fingers and sharp claws.

Where to See Them

Raccoons live along streams and in heavy undergrowth in foothill and mountain regions, but they are very well adapted to life in the suburbs and city. Most trips offer a chance to see them; besides the LA River, consider **Trips 1**, **8**, **18**, and **21**.

There are only three species of raccoons in the world. In addition to the common northern raccoon, there's the crab-eating raccoon of Central America and northern South America, and the Cozumel raccoon, found only on the island of Cozumel in Mexico.

Banded, bushy tail

Gray-brown coat

Facial mask (dark eye patches on lighter face)

Striped Skunk

Mephitis mephitis

The striped skunk is famous for its black and white colors and the noxious spray it shoots from glands under its bushy tail. It can accurately aim this yellow stink spray for ten feet. Even if you've never seen one in your neighborhood, you know when it's around. If a skunk gets hit by a car, the street will carry the smell for many days afterwards.

Their black and white stripes are good examples of "aposematic coloration," which advertises their chemical defense. Potential predators learn to recognize and avoid animals with these warning markings, though some, like the great horned owl, aren't deterred and will eat them anyway. Some dogs also haven't learned to keep their distance—if yours comes home smelling like a skunk, you can find a number of remedies online.

The skunk is an opportunistic omnivore, meaning it likes to eat most anything, from insects to mice to crabs to bird eggs to fallen fruit. They're also famous lawn specialists, using their long curved claws to dig for below-ground grubs.

Pet Skunks?

In the nineteenth century, skunks were a popular way to help keep barns free of pests. They were also trapped for their fur. By the 1950s and 1960s pet skunks were a fad. Supposedly they could be housebroken (and their scent glands removed) and were quite affectionate. It's now illegal to have skunks as pets in California.

The scientific name for striped skunk, *Mephitis mephitis*, basically means "bad smell bad smell" in Latin.

Black body with a narrow white stripe on forehead

Big bushy tail can vary in amount of black and white

Often with two white stripes down body but sometimes has other patterns

Our other local skunk is the smaller and shyer western spotted skunk. Kitten-sized, with a white-and-black dots and dashes pattern, they mostly stay out of sight in forests and brushy chaparral.

Where to See Them

Skunks thrive in many parts of our natural and built environment, even finding shelter under people's houses and sheds. They're usually nocturnal and often found in edge habitats and urban waterways. It's most productive to look for them around dusk along the margins of fields, by golf courses, or around large parks.

Places to try include **Trips 11**, **19**, and **20**. A really reliable skunk viewing spot is **Trip 6**; just after sunset, skunks often descend from the hills in search of trash and dropped food among the grassy picnic areas. Prepare yourself for cuteness overload.

Tree Squirrels

Western gray squirrels are native to this area, but because of their dependence on forest habitat, they're largely absent from the LA Basin and much more likely to be found in our local foothills and mountains. Native to the eastern half of the United States, eastern fox squirrels have been part of the landscape since 1904, when they were released at the Sawtelle Veterans Home in West Los Angeles. Civil War veterans brought them to California to keep as pets and possibly for the soup pot. As happens, some pets escaped or were released. Today, with over seven thousand miles of overhead utility lines acting as superhighways in the sky, eastern fox squirrels are spreading across the LA Basin (at rates estimated up to 4.25 miles per year).

There's an overlap zone where the foothills meet the city—and it's here that the native western gray and the non-native eastern fox squirrel engage in a turf war. Gray squirrels are more sensitive to urban development than eastern fox squirrels due to their limited diet, habitat requirements (oak woodland or mixed coniferous forests and trees with branches that connect), shyness, and slower reproductive rate. The eastern fox squirrel may be winning the turf war because it's more aggressive, more adaptable to disturbed landscapes, and less afraid of humans.

Telling the two apart is easy. The western gray squirrel is typically larger and gray with a pure white belly. Eastern fox squirrels are gray-brown above with an orange-to-rusty brown belly—its bushy gray tail has orange highlights.

Help Museum scientists study the changing distributions of native and introduced squirrels by submitting photos to the Southern California Squirrel Survey (nhm.org/squirrelsurvey).

Western Gray Squirrel

Sciurus griseus

Tail about the same length as body and very bushy

Usually in forested areas, in or near trees

Large, mostly gray with a white belly

Eastern Fox Squirrel

Sciurus niger

Tail about the same length as body and very bushy with reddish-brown highlights

Usually in urban areas where there are trees and powerlines

Brownish-gray, with a brownish-orange belly

Where there are tree squirrels, there are also squirrel nests, called dreys. A drey can be a hard-to-find leaf-filled cavity in a hollow tree, or an easier-to-spot dense clump of leaves and intertwined twigs tucked between tree branches.

Health(y) Nuts and Junk Food

Western grays use the forest as their grocery store—they eat acorns, seeds, pine nuts, green vegetation (like buds, young stems, and leaves), fruit, and mushrooms. When food is abundant they collect the surplus and store it for later when times might be hard. They bury the acorns and nuts a couple inches deep and find them later by smell.

They also eat mushrooms, and their absolute favorite is truffles. In fall and spring, truffles, the same kind chefs pay thousands of dollars for per pound, can make up more than half of a western gray squirrel's diet.

The eastern fox squirrel is a generalist that survives on whatever food is available: fruit, Fig Newtons, French fries, or fairy ring mushrooms. It's a raider of yards, trashcans, and bird feeders. Once, Museum scientists caught them on a Nature Gardens camera trap eating a slice of pizza. A more natural, healthy diet includes acorns, seeds, pine nuts, flower buds, insects, and bird eggs.

How to Speak Squirrel

Western gray squirrels and eastern fox squirrels can be loud. And to drive home their message, they will often also wave their big, bushy tails. Squirrels have multiple calls and also multiple types of tail flags, but the most common are alarm signals. Alarm calls include *kuks* and *quaas*. The *kuks* are repeated and, typically, the squirrel is flicking or flagging its tail. Other squirrels that hear or see these alarm signals learn a predator could be nearby, and the predators learn that they have been detected. With the element of surprise gone, some predators may simply give up.

Where to See Them

In Griffith Park and the rest of the Santa Monica Mountains, look for western gray squirrels in areas with lots of trees (though they're absent in the section between the 101 and 405 freeways). Your best chance is to watch while hiking in the San Gabriel Mountains, and in the pine trees of adjacent foothill communities. **Trips 15, 16, 17,** and **18** provide good opportunities.

Eastern fox squirrels are a common part of our daily wildlife experience, found on college campuses, cemeteries, large urban parks, as well as many neighborhoods with tree-lined streets and overhead utility lines. They can be seen on many of the field excursions, including **Trips 3, 7,** and **21.**

Virginia Opossum

Didelphis virginiana

With its off-pink tail, scruffy fur, and wide-load waddle, the Virginia opossum will never win the animal beauty contest. It's another city animal with a broad diet that includes insects, worms, fruit, pet food, garbage, and carrion.

Unlike skunks and racoons, they don't dig much, so cause less damage to yards and houses—some gardeners love opossums for their ability to eat pesky snails and slugs. Whether eating dog food from an unattended

Gray-brown coat, with a white face

Cat-sized

Long, mostly hairless tail a little over half the length of the body

that smells like death and decay. The opossum will remain motionless in this semi-catatonic state for minutes or hours, hoping to convince a would-be predator that it's too diseased or decomposed to eat.

Another special attribute is the opossum's prehensile tail. It can grasp like a monkey's tail and help the animal climb. They sometimes wrap their tails around leaves and other debris to carry the material home.

As the name reveals, the Virginia opossum isn't native here. It was brought to California by people who kept them as oddities and pets. The first opossum was recorded in LA County in 1906. It has become widespread on the West Coast from as far north as British Columbia down into Baja California.

Opossums are somewhat resistant to snakebites and rabies. Scientists are studying their blood for use in snakebite antivenom.

bowl, tightrope-walking along power lines, or pretending to be dead, the opossum has shown a remarkable ability to adapt to urban Los Angeles.

About the size of a house cat but with a pointed snout and long, naked tail, the opossum is sometimes mistaken for a large rat. Not only is it not a rodent, it is not like any other animal in this book.

North America's Only Marsupial

The Virginia opossum makes it into the record books several ways. It's North America's only native marsupial, a group of mammals with a pouch (or marsupium) where their babies develop after they're born. Familiar marsupials include Australia's kangaroos and koalas.

It can claim another first-place ribbon for its fifty teeth—more than any North American mammal. When threatened, it opens its mouth wide to show off these teeth, but this is mostly a bluff—if further hassled, it will pretend to be dead (hence the term playing possum). Lying down with its mouth open and dripping saliva, it exudes a fluid from its anal glands

Lucky Number Thirteen

Though marsupials famously have a pouch in which their young develop, they aren't born in that special pocket. They have to find their way there on their own, immediately after being born. Opossum babies are very small—at birth, they are about the size of a honey bee! These tiny, blind, pink babies (called joeys) must crawl two inches to the pouch, and no matter how many joeys were born (sometimes over twenty), mom only has thirteen nipples available. Later, as they develop, the mother opossum carries the babies on her back.

Where to See Them

This urban animal lives in, under, and near our homes. If you don't see one in your neighborhood, keep watch in the early evening on **Trips 8**, **10**, **11**, and **24**.

Although sometimes used as a common name for the opossum, *possums* are actually a distantly related group of marsupials that live in Australia, New Zealand, New Guinea, and the island of Sulawesi.

Reptiles and Amphibians

American Bullfrog

Rana catesbeiana

This is one big frog, with a booming voice to match. American bullfrogs are the largest frogs in the United States. The biggest can reach over eight inches, with hind legs up to ten inches long. In Los Angeles, they're often heard but not seen. Listen for the distinctive deep and droning call as you stroll near lakes and reservoirs.

Bullfrogs are native to the central and eastern United States. However, people have moved them around so much the exact borders of their native range are unknown. We've even introduced them to Canada, Mexico, western Europe, Asia, South America, Hawaii, Puerto Rico, and other Caribbean islands. They've caused significant problems in all these places and are listed as one of the world's worst invasive species by the International Union for Conservation of Nature.

The Other Other White Meat

In the mid and late 1800s, as California's population was exploding, so too was the demand for frog legs. The largest frog in California at that time was the native California red-legged frog, but in less than fifty years, its numbers were dramatically reduced by overhunting and habitat loss. Importing and releasing bullfrogs

Can be BIG, up to 8 inches long

Skin fold running from eye, over and around the tympanum (ear drum)

Green, tan, or light brown with darker speckling

in local waterways provided a new, reliable, and easy-to-find source of frog legs. Plus, bigger frogs meant bigger legs.

Unfortunately, people quickly discovered that bullfrog meat wasn't as tasty as red-legged frog meat so hunting pressure remained high on the native frogs. Later, as interest in eating frog legs dried up, bullfrogs were free from their limited hunting pressure. With an increasing number of cattle ponds and reservoirs to thrive in, their numbers skyrocketed. Red-legged frogs haven't been as lucky.

Big Appetites

More bullfrogs means bad news for just about any critter smaller than a bullfrog. Bullfrogs will eat almost anything they can fit inside their mouths, including all the usual frog foods like insects, spiders, and earthworms, but also small mammals, birds, snakes, and turtles. Studies have found that smaller frogs, including young bullfrogs, can make up more than 80 percent of an adult bullfrog's diet. It's no wonder this generalist predator is thriving.

In warm areas it takes six to eight months for bullfrog tadpoles to transform into froglets. In cooler areas, it may take over a year, and in some conditions, up to three years.

The good news is the bullfrog problem has a solution. If ponds are allowed to dry down in summer, bullfrog tadpoles don't have enough time to fully develop and populations can be eradicated.

The Water Problem

The problem isn't just that people brought bullfrogs to California, but that they also built perfect habitats for them. In the past, our long, dry summers were a big problem for bullfrogs because they need a permanent source of water for their large tadpoles to develop. But cattle ponds and reservoirs stocked with non-native fish and crayfish are perfect for them.

Where to See Them

Bullfrogs can be found in areas with permanent water, which in the LA area mostly means man-made ponds and reservoirs. Ballona Freshwater Marsh (**Trip 5**) and the ponds in Franklin Canyon (**Trip 8**) have bullfrogs, including some absolute giants. They can also be found on **Trips 3**, **14**, and **21**.

Blainville's Horned Lizard

Phrynosoma blainvillii

The flat, round, toad-like appearance of horned lizards gives them their common name, horny toad, and their genus name—*Phrynosoma* means toad-bodied. Their large, blunt heads, and crown of rearward facing spines makes them easy to recognize. They also have spiny scales on their back and tail. They can be yellowish, brown, or reddish brown, often matching the soil and rocks where they live. The patterns on their body, including a pair of dark blotches on the neck and dark wavy bars on the back, work with their jagged spines to break up the outline of their bodies and keep them camouflaged. If you see a rock scurry for cover, take a closer look; it's probably a horned lizard.

Blood in Your Eye

Camouflage is a great first line of defense for horned lizards, but it's not the last. If a predator grabs a horned lizard, the lizard will rock its

Crown of horns around blocky head

Flat, oval-shaped body

Two rows of fringe scales along edge of body

head from side to side, stabbing with its horns. Some snakes have been found dead with a horned lizard stuck part way down its throat, horns protruding through the snake's body!

If a predator is persistent and neither camouflage nor defensive horns work, horned lizards have yet another back-up plan. They can shoot blood from their eyes—or more precisely, from a sinus that sits just below their eyes. They try to shoot the attacker in the face and have surprisingly good aim. Coyotes, foxes, domestic dogs, and bobcats all find the blood distasteful enough to end their attack. Scientists haven't discovered what makes the blood so repulsive to dogs and cats, but many think it's toxins from the ants that make up a major part of a horned lizard's diet. In the few reported cases in which horned lizard blood was shot into the eye of an unsuspecting human, the person reported intense pain and short-term vision loss. Consider some chic protective eyewear if you want to get up close and personal with these southwest dwellers.

No Native Ants, No Horned Lizards

Blainville's horned lizards used to occur from the LA Basin and adjoining valleys up to about 7500 feet in the local mountains. They were common neighborhood lizards for many Angelenos up into the 1950s. Over time these lizards have become a rarer sight, and they're now almost entirely gone from lower elevations. The declines are caused by conversion of land for agriculture, increasing urban development,

Diet studies have found that large ants make up over 85 percent of the Blainville's horned lizard's diet.

and especially the spread of non-native Argentine ants. Horned lizards specialize in eating large-bodied native ants, especially harvester ants (*Pogonomyrmex* species). They don't eat the invasive newcomers, so as their preferred food has disappeared, so have they.

Where to See Them

Look for these lizards in areas where you see big-bodied ants such as harvester and carpenter ants. Horned lizards can be found in coastal sand dunes, grassland, scrub, chaparral, and forest areas and are most likely to be seen late February through June. They still occur at higher elevations in the Santa Monicas and Verdugos, as well as throughout much of the San Gabriel Mountains. **Trips 1** and **16** are your best bets.

California Newt

Taricha torosa

Somewhat stocky, medium-sized salamander

Rough, granular skin when on land

Reddish-brown above, orange below

California newts begin life in the water. As creeks dry up in the summer months, the larvae absorb their gills and fin-like tail and transform into small versions of the adults. Then they leave the water and spend the next few years on land, growing bigger in underground burrows, beneath logs, and in areas with moist soil and plenty of insects and small critters to eat.

Once they reach adulthood, newts return to the water to breed. During and shortly after winter rain storms, dozens, sometimes thousands, of adult newts make their annual migration to their local creek or pond. Pond breeders often arrive toward the start of the rainy season, but many creek breeders arrive later, after the threat of floods has mostly passed. If you hike creek trails at this time of year, you may witness this amazing migration.

Males stay in the water for a few months—females stop by for much shorter periods to lay eggs. Because males spend months swimming around in search of females, they undergo a really dramatic change. Their rough skin becomes smooth, and their tails get bigger, flatter, and more fin-like. Females also get smoother skin, but a much less dramatic tail change. In early summer, males leave the breeding site and once again take on their typical rough-skin and standard tail—until the next breeding season when the whole process starts again.

A Toxic Defense

During the annual migration events, newts wander across the landscape as if they have no fear of predators, trudging through open areas in the middle of the day. Their confidence comes from their incredible toxicity. Newts harbor an extremely potent neurotoxin called tetrodotoxin, which can affect the nervous system if ingested. If you touch one, be sure to wash your hands and avoid touching your eyes or mouth.

Other species that use tetrodotoxin as a defensive chemical include the blue-ringed octopus and pufferfish.

From above, newts' rough, brown skin provides great camouflage. If a sharp-eyed predator does try to grab it, the newt arches its back and raises its tail, exposing its bright orange underside, a warning of the newt's toxicity.

Some raccoons, otters, and ravens have learned to flip newts over, slit open the belly, and selectively eat the inner parts that don't have toxins. If you find a newt carcass—sometimes turned partially inside-out—it's a tell-tale sign that a clever predator won the battle.

Where to See Them

Thanks to introduced predators, finding newts in Southern California isn't as easy as it once was. A creek with crayfish or a pond with lots of bullfrogs and mosquitofish is unlikely to have newts. However, they still live in the larger coastal-flowing creeks of the Santa Monica and San Gabriel Mountains. Try **Trips 1**, **4**, **14**, and **15**. Remember: look but don't touch, and leave their aquatic and terrestrial habitat undisturbed.

Common Side-blotched Lizard

Uta stansburiana

In many parts of the desert southwest, these small, grayish-brown lizards are the most abundant lizard species. In the LA area, they can be difficult to tell apart from the larger western fence lizard. If you have a side view, the telltale blueish black side-blotch just behind the front limbs, for which the species is named, is an easy giveaway. Side-blotched lizards also have a double row of dark blotches or crescents down their backs, which are covered by small granular scales unlike the large, spiny scales of the fence lizards.

Side-blotched lizards like open areas with scattered rocks and boulders they can perch on and keep watch for predators. If they spot one, it's a quick dash into hiding spots beneath or between the rocks. These lizards are rock and ground dwellers—they don't use fences, branches, or logs nearly as much as the western fence lizard.

Small, brownish
lizard

Dark blotch usually
present on side

Small
pebble-like
scales on back

Rear of thigh tan or
light gray like much
of lizard's body

Blue vs. Orange vs. Yellow

Common side-blotched lizards have brightly colored throat regions. Males can have different colored patches on their throats, and their throat color usually matches up with their mating behaviors. Orange-throated males guard territories, mating with the females that reside there. Blue-throated males guard individual females. And yellow-throated males are sneaky. They mimic females to sneak past other males to find a mate. Blue-throated males can usually chase off the yellow-throated sneakers but are usually chased off by aggressive orange-throated males. Each color type can beat one type but loses to another—it's lizard rock-paper-scissors.

This dynamic results in a year-to-year population cycle (remember, these lizards typically live only about one year). When orange territory-guarders are most common, the yellow-throated sneaker males have higher reproductive success. The next year when the yellow males are most common, the blue-throated mate-guarders do best. When blue-throats are common, the territorial orange-throated males then do well, repeating the cycle.

If You Build It, They Will Leave

We may call this lizard the "common" side-blotched lizard, and it is the most abundant lizard in many parts of its range, but it's much less common in the LA Basin than it once was. They avoid grasslands and areas with thick vegetation, so irrigation is a problem for them. As the arid and semi-arid habitats they prefer, like sandy washes, broken chaparral, and open forest with little understory, have been invaded by non-native grasses and converted to neighborhoods, strip malls, and industrial areas, they've gotten scarce.

Where to See Them

Today, you're most likely to find side-blotched lizards in the foothills, but remnant populations can still be found in the LA Basin. For example, the Sepulveda Basin (**Trip 3**), the Bette Davis Picnic Area near Griffith Park, the Bowtie Parcel and other dry areas of the former Taylor Yard (near **Trip 10**), and little bits of open habitat along the lower LA and San Gabriel Rivers still have them. Similarly, they can be found in the isolated hills that rise out of the LA Basin including the Baldwin Hills (**Trip 6**), Palos Verdes Peninsula, and Chino-Puente Hills (**Trip 20**).

Look for side-blotched lizards in open, rocky areas with scattered vegetation anytime it's warm, and especially in spring and summer. **Trips 1**, **2**, **13**, **16**, and **25** also have them.

Side-blotched lizards are largely an annual species. The juveniles hatch in the summer months and breed the following spring. Very few adults survive to a second breeding season. However, recent studies have found individuals can occasionally live as many as seven years.

Garden Slender Salamander

Batrachoseps major

The garden slender salamander is brown, with a pale gray belly and short, stubby limbs. It's a little bulkier than other slender salamanders, which keeps it from drying out too fast, allowing it to survive in its favored habitat, coastal sage scrub and chaparral. Nevertheless, it spends drier months underground, using earthworm burrows, tunnels left by decomposing roots, and mammal burrows as passageways and hideouts. In wetter months, and in areas with sprinklers, you can find them above ground cruising for worms, earwigs, caterpillars, and other small insects to eat.

Cartwheeling to Safety

Slender salamanders are on the menu for alligator lizards and several species of birds and snakes in California. Luckily, they have a variety of incredible defense strategies. When harassed, they often curl into a tight coil. By rapidly uncoiling, they can propel themselves into the air, landing nearly a foot away where they remain motionless in hopes of avoiding detection. They can also rapidly flip or flex their long bodies to cartwheel away from danger.

If leaping to safety doesn't work, their skin excretes a glue-like substance so sticky it can glue a hungry snake's jaws together or glue parts of the snake to itself so it can't keep attacking. They'll also wrap their tails around the snake's neck to prevent it from swallowing. If none of those defenses work, slender salamanders, like many lizards, can drop their tails. The tail wiggles around distracting the predator while the rest of the salamander hides or crawls to safety.

The Salamanders among Us

Los Angeles is actually home to three species of slender salamanders, all of which are difficult to tell apart, even for experts. In fact, it wasn't until the 1960s that scientists realized the three species were distinct. By then, the city was heavily developed, with much of the remaining habitat in private property.

The Museum's community science projects like RASCals are helping scientists finally collect data on where the different species are found. They're also studying whether urban development is reducing and fragmenting the salamanders' habitats, or whether the increased use of water through irrigation is creating new opportunities in residential areas.

Where to See Them

Easiest to find in the winter months, especially right after rain. Look for them on the ground in the early evening, or search under flower pots, logs, and other objects any time of day. Just be careful to set those objects back in the exact same spot to preserve the hiding place and not squish any little critters. You can find them on **Trips 12**, **14**, and **25**, and in yards, vacant lots, or other urban open spaces.

Darker on top, pale underbelly

Short, stubby legs

Long, slender body, with tail up to twice as long as body

Slender salamanders are some of the nearly five hundred species in the family Plethodontidae, a group commonly called lungless salamanders. Lacking lungs, these salamanders absorb oxygen through their skin, which must be kept moist to function properly.

Gophersnake

Pituophis catenifer

Narrow head, though may be more triangular during defensive displays

Tan background color with dark brown blotches on back and sides

The gophersnake is the longest snake in our area and also one of the most commonly encountered. They have a tan or yellow background color with a series of brown or black blotches down the middle of their backs. This pattern is excellent camouflage. When predators like hawks, foxes, coyotes, bobcats or people do find a gophersnake, it puts on a big act that looks much like a rattlesnake's defensive display. It raises off the ground, inflates with air to look bigger, hisses loudly, and flattens its head to look more triangular like a rattler's. It also shakes its tail, which in dry grass or leaves creates a rattling sound.

The gophersnake hopes this bluff will cause any potential predators to think it is a venomous rattlesnake that should be left alone. Unfortunately, if the attacker is a human, they might be more likely to try and kill it.

Beyond Gophers

As you'd guess, gophersnakes do eat gophers, and you'll often find them cruising around grassland habitat in search of the subterra-

In general, snakes, especially larger species, don't do well around people. They lose their habitat to development and are persecuted by people with misplaced fears. Larger snakes also tend to have larger home ranges. That sounds nice, but in urban areas, it means crossing roads during the search for food, shelter, and mates. Many urban snakes get run over by cars.

nean mammals. But they're also dietary generalists who eat ground squirrels, mice, rabbits, other small mammals, lizards, and bird eggs and nestlings (they're excellent tree climbers).

Gophersnakes tend to be active hunters, seeking out burrows and nests. They usually kill with constriction, wrapping coils around their prey and squeezing it to death.

Where to See Them

From coastal dune habitat to high in the mountains and down into the deserts. They especially like grassland and scrub habitats, including coastal sage scrub and chaparral. **Trips 1**, **9**, **13**, **14**, **15**, and **19** are best for seeing these attractive serpents.

Pacific Treefrog

Pseudacris regilla

From green to brown, spotted or plain; individuals can change colors

Small but loud

Dark stripe across side of face and through eye

These frogs come in a variety of greens and browns and are able to change the darkness of their shading (light green frogs can quickly change to dark green, and tan frogs to dark brown) for excellent camouflage. Many have dark patterns on their backs and upper legs, and, regardless of color or pattern, they all have a dark mask or band running across their face and through the eye. The enlarged discs on their fingers and toes act like suction cups, helping the frogs climb.

The One and Only Frog that Says *Ribbit*

Frog calls are just like bird calls; both are produced mostly by males to attract females and announce territory ownership. As with birds, each frog species has a slightly different call.

Nevertheless, people all around the world seem to think that frogs say *ribbit*, just like cows say *moo*.

In fact, only one species of frog in the entire world says *ribbit*—the Pacific treefrog! Because it calls loudly and is relatively common in and around Los Angeles, this frog was easily recorded for background sounds in movies and TV shows. Although they're only found in western North America, you can hear Pacific treefrogs in movie and TV scenes set all over the world. The frogs calling in the background as Rambo runs through the jungles of Southeast Asia were likely recorded in LA foothills.

During the late winter and spring breeding season, you might hear a *ribbit* or two during the day—but return at night and you could experience a deafening chorus as dozens of males try to attract a female.

Pacific treefrogs make other calls too and each one serves a different function. In fall and early winter, especially after rains, they'll give infrequent, short, one-syllable calls, often from hiding spots in burrows or shrubs. Listen for these while hiking near seasonal creeks and ponds.

Where to See Them

Trips 1 and **14** are great places to hear and see them.

155

Red-eared Slider

Trachemys scripta elegans

Shell patterned above; underside yellow-orange with black blotches

Red stripe behind eye, can be faded in older males

Medium to large; shell up to 14.5 inches long

Historically, California was home to only one widespread freshwater turtle, the western pond turtle. Due to overharvesting for turtle meat, wetland loss, river channelization, and other types of habitat destruction, western pond turtles have become increasingly rare in the Central Valley and LA areas.

However, nearly every LA resident has turtles within walking distance of their home. Like bullfrogs, bass, and crayfish, the non-native red-eared slider can thrive in Southern California because we've built permanent water on a landscape that was historically dry in summer.

What's in a Name?

The first part of the red-eared slider's name comes from the distinctive red stripe on the side of their heads just behind the eye. The second part comes from the habit of wild turtles sliding off logs and rocks into the water when they sense danger.

Not all red-eared sliders have the red stripe. As adult males age, they lose their coloration, their skin and shells taking on a darker appearance. These old males can easily be mistaken

▲ A wild native western pond turtle is now a rare sight in the LA area.

for the native western pond turtle, which can also sometimes be a dull brownish-gray. An easy way to tell the two apart is that western pond turtles have especially long tails, and male red-eared sliders have especially long claws on the front feet.

How to Take Over the World

Typically found in urban ponds, reservoirs, and waterways—places close to cities, with an endless supply of no-longer-wanted pet turtles—red-ears are fast growers. They reach

> Female red-eared sliders can lay up to three clutches of eggs in a year with up to twenty-five eggs in each clutch.

over four inches long in a few years and, in a few more, can be twice that. Females, which get larger than males, can grow to over twelve inches. Turtles that start out small and cute are soon big, smelly, and sometimes prone to bite or scratch. Once big aquariums or backyard ponds with expensive filters become necessary, some irresponsible pet owners give up and release them.

THE GENERALISTS WIN

These turtles do so well in so many different places because they're not picky eaters. Young red-ears are mostly carnivorous, eating a variety of invertebrates including insects, snails, and worms or scavenging larger meals like dead fish or birds. As they age, they eat more plants and algae, but will still scavenge on carcasses or eat the occasional live animal. In a few cases, large red-ears have even been seen pulling unsuspecting birds into the water for a feathered feast. Regardless of where they find themselves, they seem able to find plenty of food.

Where to See Them

In huge numbers in the man-made ponds and reservoirs on **Trips 3**, **5**, **6**, **8**, **19**, **21**, and **24**.

Southern Alligator Lizard

Elgaria multicarinata

The southern alligator lizard is the most widespread lizard species in the LA area. They don't make it into local deserts, but they can be found just about everywhere else, including the most urbanized parts of our cities. Check your backyard or the landscaping around your apartment complex; you're very likely to find them. Although they're widespread, you won't often spot them without looking because they don't bask in the sun like many other lizards. They prefer cooler, hidden areas like gardens, shrubs, and woodpiles, and sometimes

> Alligator lizards' diverse diet includes insects, scorpions, spiders, and occasionally larger items like bird and lizard eggs and baby lizards, birds, and mammals. They're also big fans of slugs, caterpillars, grasshoppers, and brown and black widow spiders—making them a friend to local gardeners.

Large, bony scales with ridge or keel down middle

Fold of skin on lower sides of body

▲ Baby alligator lizards have a more muted appearance than the adults and are often mistaken for skinks or other lizards.

A Tale of Tails

An alligator lizard's tail can be up to twice as long as its body. Their tails are somewhat prehensile, allowing them to grasp branches. This helps with climbing shrubs and small trees—the best places to find tasty caterpillars, bird eggs, and nestlings. However, finding an adult alligator lizard with a complete, original tail is uncommon. When attacked, an alligator lizard can self-amputate its tail. The detached tail flips, flops, and flails about distracting the predator and giving the lizard a chance to escape. This ability is called tail autotomy (autotomy means self-cutting).

A new tail will grow, but it won't be a perfect replacement. It will look slightly different than the original, have a rod made of cartilage at the center instead of bones, and won't be as flexible or as prehensile. Tail loss can have huge consequences for the lizard. A female who has recently lost her tail may have to skip a breeding season because she has lost the energy reserves needed to develop her eggs.

Where to See Them

Alligator lizards can be found from sea level to about 6,500 feet in the LA area, and from behind your bookshelf to under the oak tree in your favorite mountain forest. They especially like areas with a bit of moisture, so streamside habitat in the foothills or a well-watered vegetable garden are good places to look. **Trips 1**, **4**, **8**, **14**, **15**, **18**, **19**, and **20** are good alligator lizard hangouts.

beneath your refrigerator or living room sofa. Their more natural habitats include grassland, chaparral, and forest, and they're especially fond of grassy areas along creeks.

Not a Snake, Not a Gator, Not a Skink

Adult alligator lizards have a slender, snake-like appearance with short limbs and a long tail. Their bodies are tan, brown, or reddish-brown with dark bars highlighted with lighter spots running across their bodies. They have relatively large heads and powerful jaws, which they sometimes hold open, exposing their teeth to warn off attackers (making them resemble their alligator namesakes). Adult males have bigger, more triangular heads than females. A narrow fold of skin on each side of the body—think of it like an elastic waistband on your favorite pair of pants—allows their bodies to expand after a large meal or as a female develops a clutch of eggs.

Starting in mid-summer, adorable baby alligator lizards start popping up. At first glance, these look like a whole different species. They lack the darker crossbars of the adults and often have a single broad stripe of red or brown down their backs. By late fall or early winter, they start to develop the more typical color pattern.

Western Fence Lizard

Sceloporus occidentalis

Have you ever seen a local lizard doing push-ups and head bobs? If so, it was probably the western fence lizard. Often called blue bellies by kids across California, they're the most commonly observed lizard in the LA area, occurring in a variety of habitats from urban backyards at sea level to pine forests high up in our mountains.

Small to medium-sized lizard

Larger ridged scales on back ending in a small point or spike

Yellow bar across rear of thigh

Lizard push-up displays, bird songs, and frog calls are all advertisement signals. Males use these to announce territory ownership and attract females. It's the animal equivalent of saying "Hey ladies, check me out!"

Western fence lizards are smallish, gray-brown lizards that bask atop walls, logs, boulders, and, of course, fences. From these overlooks, they dart out and grab prey. Adults have a vibrant blue patch on each side of their bellies, which are especially large and colorful on males. Their chin region also has a blue patch. During breeding season, some adult males will have blue specks on their backs as well, making them look bedazzled in turquoise sequins.

Young ticks, called nymphs, love to drink blood from western fence lizards. Fortunately for us, fence lizard blood has a protein that kills the bacterium that causes Lyme disease. If you're bitten by an adult tick that fed on a fence lizard when it was a nymph, you're protected from Lyme disease thanks to our blue-bellied friends.

Lizard Calisthenics

In addition to push-ups and head bobs, adult male fence lizards also announce territory ownership by flattening out their sides and neck region to display their bright blue patches. If a trespassing male ignores these warnings, the two are likely to fight. These battles determine the size of each male's territory. A larger territory means more potential mates.

Chameleons Aren't the Only Ones

In the lizard world, chameleons are famous for their ability to rapidly change skin color, but western fence lizards can do it too. Male fence lizards live by the mantra "the early lizard gets the rock." During the active season, males want to spend as much time guarding their territories as possible. In the mornings, and whenever the weather is cooler, they need to warm up quickly. Making their skin darker allows them to absorb more of the sun's energy more quickly. They also position themselves perpendicular to the sun to maximize the amount of skin exposed to its warming rays. As the lizard warms up, he lightens in color and turns parallel to the sun's rays to maintain a perfect operating temperature. Females can also change color, but to a lesser degree. If you see a big dark fence lizard in the morning, it's almost certainly a male trying to warm up fast.

Where to See Them

Western fence lizards are common residents of the LA area, though they are not as widespread in urban areas as southern alligator lizards. They're easiest to see basking on walls, boulders, logs, low branches, and fences in spring and summer months. **Trips 1**, **2**, **4**, **6**, **8**, **9**, **11**, **12**, **14**, **15**, **18**, and **20** are especially good.

Western Rattlesnake

Crotalus oreganus

The western rattlesnake is the most commonly observed snake in our area, with the gophersnake a close second. Spring and summer have the most rattlesnake activity. In winter, they hide below ground in abandoned mammal burrows or tucked into rocky crevices, but the occasional winter warm spell will bring out a few to enjoy the sunshine.

Their coloration varies from a light tan to nearly black. A series of dark blotches running down their backs eventually expands to bars near the tail. Usually, you can quickly identify them by their wide, triangular head and the rattle at the end of their tail.

The Best Defense

Rattlesnakes are mostly ambush hunters. While gophersnakes, kingsnakes, and other species actively search out prey, rattlesnakes set up along a common mammal pathway, like a ground squirrel trail or a mouse runway. Here, they wait, sometimes for days, for a meal to come along. They mostly eat small mammals, but will eat lizards, snakes, birds, and even frogs or the occasional insect.

In summer's heat, rattlesnakes are mostly active at night. Their sense of smell helps them find prey in the dark. Like other snakes, they flick their tongues out and pull scent molecules into their mouths to "taste" whatever's around them. Rattlesnakes can also sense infrared radiation, which allows them to detect things like warm mice and rats hiding nearby. This is especially useful at night when warm, little mammals are surrounded by cool evening air.

While waiting in ambush, or while out basking in the sunshine, the snake hopes its camouflage will allow it to go undetected by potential prey and by potential predators. While other snakes may flee at the approach of a person or other large, potentially deadly

What to do if you see a rattlesnake:

- Give it space.
- Back up and take a different path if it doesn't move off.
- Take a picture from a safe distance and submit it to the RASCals project (nhm.org.rascals).
- Celebrate that you got to see it.
- In the rare situation when someone is bitten, stay calm and get to medical help as quickly as possible (old advice about snake bite kits, sucking out the venom, or ice should all be ignored).

predator, the rattlesnake is likely to stay motionless, relying on camouflage and lack of movement.

THE RATTLESNAKE'S RATTLE

Rattlesnakes want to go unnoticed, but if a predator gets too close, a rattlesnake will use its rattle to warn off the larger animal. The rattle is made of keratin, the same material in your fingernails. When a rattlesnake is born, it has a tiny prebutton, which is basically a cap on the tip of its tail. During the snake's first shed, this prebutton is replaced by a button, the first segment of the rattle. With only one segment, these young rattlesnakes can't produce any sound. Each subsequent shed produces another segment, which can then slap against each other and produce sound. It takes a few sheds before a rattle will produce the loud characteristic warning.

Rattlesnake Moms

Rattlesnakes have maternal care, which means that moms look after the young. They also have live birth, which in our area usually takes place in the late summer. Females will find a safe spot, such as an abandoned mammal burrow, and give birth to around four to twelve young. She keeps watch over them for the first week or so and will actively defend them against potential predators. Once the babies

have their first shed (usually about seven to ten days), mom and babies head their separate ways.

Where to See Them

Rattlesnakes don't fare well in urban areas and have disappeared entirely from the Baldwin Hills. They are, however, a commonly seen snake on hikes in the Santa Monica and San Gabriel Mountains, and there's an isolated population on the Palos Verdes Peninsula. **Trips 1**, **9**, **13**, **14**, **15**, **16**, **18**, and **20** are your best bets.

Each year, around 7,000–8,000 people are bitten by venomous snakes in the United States, and only about 5 die as a result. More than half of the bites are to people who chose to interact with the snake or did nothing to move away—doctors call this an "illegitimate bite"—and include people handling snakes or trying to kill one, which is an especially common way people get bitten.

Rattle on end of tail

Triangular head

Dark blotches down back turning to bars towards tail

Heavy-bodied

161

Snails and Slugs

Common Garden Snail

Cornu aspersum

The common garden snail is large, brown, and easy to identify. It's the most commonly seen snail in Los Angeles and can be found on sprinkler-wet sidewalks in nearly every neighborhood, chowing down on prize vegetables in backyard gardens—even on your plate in upscale French restaurants.

Thin, spherical shell

Brown to yellow-tan bands, blotches, or streaks

Body is tan, gray, or brown with a bumpy appearance

You Eat Them, They Eat Your Garden

The common garden snail was first introduced to California in the 1850s with escargot farms. Whether the snails escaped from the farms, or were dumped by fed up farmers, we'll probably never know. They were likely introduced multiple times and are still (along with other species of snails and slugs) being introduced today—potted plants make perfect homes for stowaways.

This snail can lay between 30 and 120 eggs at a time. The eggs are covered in layers of protective film and a thin, calcium-rich shell. The baby snails hatch out of their eggs with tiny, delicate shells of their own.

Many gardeners don't like this snail. It eats a large variety of fruits and vegetables—everything from carrots and cabbages to apples and

Like other snails, the common garden snail is a hermaphrodite, which means it has both male and female sex organs. When a pair comes together, each harpoons the other with a love dart, which introduces hormones to induce mating. To reproduce, they intertwine their bodies and extend their penises from behind their heads to exchange sperm. Mating can take anywhere between four and twelve hours!

apricots. Flowers are also a favorite food. In some instances, entire beds of freshly planted zinnias have been devoured in a single night.

Snails are pros at what scientists call aestivation, a prolonged dormancy to escape the frequent hot dry spells of Southern California. To retain as much moisture as possible, common garden snails retreat into their shells and hunker down. They seal off the entrance to their shell with slime, which, when it dries, looks like delicate parchment paper.

Where to See Them

This snail is most easily seen on trips in the wetter, winter or spring months or in heavily irrigated areas like lawns. Look for them in planter beds and yards near you or keep an eye out on **Trip 12**.

Trask's Shoulderband Snail

Helminthoglypta traskii

In small pockets across Los Angeles and in our local canyons—from Tujunga Wash to the Palos Verdes Peninsula—this snail is holding on. According to the International Union for Conservation of Nature, it's a critically endangered snail with dwindling numbers in the region. However, it could be living in LA backyards or parks near you!

There are at least seven species of shoulderband snail that live in California, three of which call Los Angeles home (the other two are the Southern California and transverse range shoulderbands). They're hard to tell

Despite being critically imperiled, California shoulderband snails are understudied, which means there could be more species here that scientists haven't yet discovered or described.

Shell somewhat flattened

Dark amber or brown band running down the middle of the shell

Body brown in color and bumpy in appearance.

163

apart, but all three species found in the LA region have an easy-to-spot shoulderband that swirls around the shell. The Trask's shoulderband snail (sometimes called peninsular shoulderband) has a cinnamon-brown shell with a dark chestnut-brown band. When fully grown, it's about half the size of a common garden snail.

Where Has My Little Snail Gone?

Nestled in paper boxes and glass vials in the Museum's malacology collection (malacology is the study of snails, slugs, octopuses, squids, and other mollusks) are dozens of Trask's shoulderband snail shells. There are shells from Elysian Park, Palos Verdes, Griffith Park, Arroyo Seco Canyon, Hermosa Beach, Baldwin Hills, Ballona Creek, and many locations in the San Gabriel Mountains. Almost all are from before the 1950s, allowing scientists a look back in time to see when and where Trask's shoulderband lived in the LA area. Unfortunately, there aren't quite enough specimens in the collection to get a complete map of the past. Jann Vendetti started the SLIME community science project (Snails and slugs Living in Metropolitan Environments) to better understand the health and distribution of our local snail and slug populations. Today we map current locations for shoulderband snails and other species so we can understand how these species have responded to urbanization, and track future changes.

Where to See Them

These snails are hard to find. Look for them after rains in undisturbed areas, particularly in the coastal sage scrub and chaparral habitats. Remember this is a critically endangered species—carefully flip logs and rocks to spot them (be sure to put them back as they were). Follow slime trails and look at old shells. You're most likely to find them on **Trips 13** and **25**.

Striped Greenhouse Slug

Ambigolimax valentianus

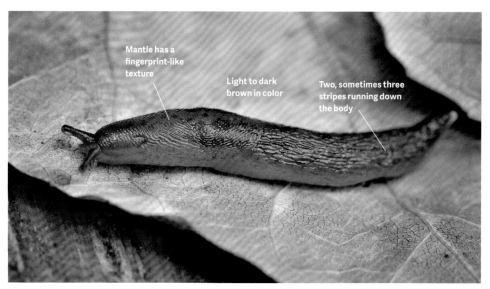

Mantle has a fingerprint-like texture

Light to dark brown in color

Two, sometimes three stripes running down the body

Once confined to Spain and Portugal, the striped greenhouse slug can be found throughout Los Angeles, particularly if you're out and about at night in irrigated areas.

In the early 1900s there were two publications that looked at the slugs of Los Angeles—the striped greenhouse slug was not mentioned in either, which means it likely had not yet been introduced. Somewhere between 1912 and 1940 the slug showed up, and now there are millions of them here.

Lungs, Crystal Pee, and Secret Shells

Like all other land-dwelling slugs and snails, the striped greenhouse slug has a lung-like sac under its mantle. (The mantle is the fleshy lobe behind the head.) To breathe, it just has to tighten the mantle to move air inside its body. Look closely and you can usually see the breathing pore, known as a pneumostome, slowly opening and closing.

Living on dry land is hard for snails and slugs; they have to make sure they don't dry out. One way they conserve water is with an alternative to liquid urine, excreting instead hard crystals made of uric acid. Many birds and reptiles that live in hot, dry climates use this strategy too.

Some people refer to slugs as "snails that have lost their shells." While it's impossible for an individual snail to lose its shell, since body and shell are attached, you could say that slugs have lost their shells over time through evolution. The striped greenhouse slug still has a small, plate-like, internal shell.

Where to See Them

These slugs are easy to find. They're gregarious, so look for groups of them in damp, irrigated yards, parks, and greenhouses. Follow slime trails and you could find a compost bin full of them. You're most likely to find them hiding during the day, or out and about at night, on **Trips 7** and **12**.

Most land snails and slugs have two sets of tentacles—sensory tentacles on the bottom for smell, and longer ocular tentacles with eyes on top.

Mushrooms, Slime Mold, and Lichen

Turkey Tail Fungus

Trametes versicolor

Alternating bands of light and dark growth

Velvety to the touch

Tiny pores on the underside

Shaped and striped like a turkey's tail

On rotting logs in our local mountains or sprouting out of old tree stumps on university campuses, the beautiful, leathery turkey tail fungus can be found year round. Its alternating bands of color (from yellow, red, brown, gray, or black) and texture (velvety or smooth) and its turkey-tail shape make it easy to spot. However, there are many lookalike fungi, including the aptly named false turkey tail, and often it takes experts to tell them apart.

Mycelia: the Hidden Life of Mushrooms

Turkey tail fungus is a type of saprobe fungi, which means it eats wood—usually decomposing deciduous trees, but sometimes conifers too. When food is abundant, the fungus is mostly hidden, living inside and feeding on the decaying wood. If you were to open up a stump or log, you'd see a network of white strands, or mycelia, which are fungal cells that grow into long threads. When the fungus is ready to find a new place to live, or if food runs out, the mycelia grow a spore-bearing, fruiting body—a mushroom. In this species, the mushroom is the fan-shaped shelf sticking out from the log or stump. Sometimes there can be dozens in highly photogenic arrangements.

Most mushrooms disappear after a few hours or days, but turkey tail mushrooms are made of sturdier stuff and can be found in the same spot year after year. Find one in your neighborhood or along your favorite trail and watch it grow and change colors over seasons and years.

When the turkey tail fungus is ready to reproduce, it develops whitish-yellow spores, which it releases by the billions through tiny pores. If the spores land in a favorable spot, they will germinate, find food, and grow.

Fungi like the turkey tail can break down lignin—a complex tissue in wood and bark that gives trees rigidity and doesn't rot easily. Some fungi can also break down complex compounds harmful to the environment. Scientists are beginning to study using fungi as a method of environmental restoration. This is called *mycoremediation.*

▲ An aggregation of turkey tails.

Where to See Them

Look for turkey tail fungus shelves growing out of dead and decaying tree stumps, downed wood, and rotting fence posts or decking. Most likely to be found on **Trips 1**, **4**, **8**, **14**, and **15**.

Yellow-staining Mushroom

Agaricus xanthodermus

Popping up on dew-wet lawns across the city, or on irrigated golf courses in Griffith Park, this white mushroom looks an awful lot like *Agaricus bisporus*, a mushroom you'd add to your breakfast omelet. However, the yellow-staining mushroom can cause severe stomach cramps, vomiting, and diarrhea. Don't eat mushrooms you find growing in your lawn!

Turns yellow when bruised

White cap and stipe (stem)

Gills turn from pale to chocolate brown as spores mature

167

Los Angeles lawns host a handful of white mushroom species. Though some are edible, you should never eat a wild mushroom unless you're a skilled mushroom hunter. The easiest way to identify this little white mushroom is to bruise it then smell it. It will turn yellow and smell like ink or iodine.

Did Fairies Dance Here?

Yellow-staining mushrooms can often be found growing in arcs, or perfect circles on lawns. These phenomena are called fairy rings in the belief that fairies danced on the spot overnight. However, there's nothing supernatural about a fairy ring's origin. The center of the ring is where a germinating spore has landed, producing strands of fungal cells that grow outward in all directions. As the fungus spreads, it feeds on organic matter in the soil, eventually, sending up a cluster of mushrooms in a tell-tale circle.

Spore Prints

Avid mycologists, the professional term for mushroom experts, have a good trick to help them identify mushrooms—they make spore prints. These help determine the color of a mushroom's spores and are a fun activity for nature-lovers of all ages. (As always don't disturb mushrooms or any other species in protected areas.)

First, take the cap off a mushroom, then place it on a piece of black or white paper for a few hours—the spores will land on the paper and be easy to see. Spores come in many col-

▲ This mushroom has pinkish-brown spores. Other mushrooms have white or green spores.

ors, from black, brown, white, and even green! If you're not sure what color spores your mushroom will have, try putting one on black paper and one on white. The yellow-staining mushroom has a dark, chocolate-brown spore print.

Where to See Them

Look for yellow-staining mushrooms on irrigated lawns of parks, golf courses, and cemeteries. Most likely on **Trips 18**, **21**, and **24**.

Dog Vomit Slime Mold

Fuligo septica

Frequently seen growing on wood chips or lawns

Bubbly textures that vaguely look like scrambled eggs

Varies in color from yellow to pinkish brown when fresh

That odd yellow or pink fluffy mass sitting in mulch-filled planters and garden beds is dog vomit slime mold. Sometimes mistaken for a fungus, this organism is actually a plasmodial slime mold. Most of the time it lives as a single cell amongst dead wood and mulch. It feeds by engulfing its food—living bacteria and mushroom spores. When it runs out of things to eat, or conditions are otherwise not great for survival, the individual cells come together and fuse into one large mass called a plasmodium. This is the life stage we see and mistake for a dog's regurgitated dinner. Eventually the mass takes on a sponge-like structure as it forms spores that spread into the environment.

Dog vomit slime mold can tolerate very high levels of zinc and other toxic metals, sometimes even converting them from toxic to inactive forms. Scientists are researching how slime molds can be used to eradicate environmental pollutants.

Voyaging Vomit

Spores are like plant seeds—filled with enough genetic material to grow a whole new slime mold. Dog vomit slime mold spores are purplish-brown to black—when they're released, the whole plasmodium turns dark. The tiny spores float through the air, landing on new territory and starting the cycle again.

Scientists have studied the movements of slime mold masses and even had them solve puzzles in experiments. They put the slime mold in a maze with a food source and over time it solves the puzzle to find the food. A dog vomit slime mass can move up to three feet overnight!

Where to See Them

Look for dog vomit slime mold in gardens or planters that use woody mulch, particularly after rains or excessive watering. Most likely to be found on **Trips 7** and **12** after repeated rain events.

Lace Lichen

Ramalina menziesii

Hanging from branches of oaks growing on bluffs and canyons above the Pacific Ocean, a light green, netted plant-like structure wafts in the breeze. As finely constructed as hand-made lace, this organism isn't a plant, it's a lace lichen. Lichens are composite organisms, made up of two or three distinct life forms.

Lichen = Fungus + Fungus + Algae

Lichens are complicated! Some mistakenly think of them as plants, even giving a few species names from the plant kingdom, like reindeer moss or Spanish moss. But they have no roots as most plants do and reproduce by spores instead of seeds. Lichens are unique because they are a combination of three living organisms—two species of fungi plus an algae or cyanobacteria (a group of bacteria that get their nutrients through photosynthesis like plants do). The fungi are the dominant partners, giving the lichen most of its characteristics and an ability to absorb inorganic nutrients. The algae or cyanobacteria allow the lichen to do what no fungus can—make food out of the sun.

Hangs in clumps

Net-like structure

Pale yellowish-green to gray in color

It was thought that both parties mutually benefit from this association, but recent research found this isn't always so. In some instances, the algae is "captured" by a fungus and doesn't benefit, which makes the fungi a parasite.

Who Likes Lichens?

In certain areas along our California coast, trees hang heavy with curtains of this Spanish moss look-alike. Animals, including deer and rabbits, like to eat it, and birds use it to line their nests.

California is the first state in the nation to designate a state lichen—it took seven years for the lace lichen to gain this status, and on January 1, 2016, the California Lichen Society celebrated its long-fought effort. Though California has 1,500 species of lichen, members chose lace lichen for a number of reasons: it's easy to recognize, it's common throughout much of coastal California, and it's one of the most unique and beautiful lichens in the world.

Old and Hardy

Lichens are able to withstand some pretty extreme conditions. When it gets too hot, too cold, or too dry, they can shut down their metabolism and enter a state of inactivity, sort

Remind yourself what makes a lichen with this dad joke: when Freddie fungus met Alice algae they immediately took a lichen to each other. Since then, their relationship has been on the rocks.

of like a bear hibernating through the winter. As soon as favorable conditions return they wake back up again. This lets them survive a long time—some lichens in the Arctic are thought to be 8,600 years old. While they're able to stand environmental extremes, they don't usually do well with pollution. That's one reason lichen diversity is pretty low in urban settings. Because lace lichens have so much surface area, they are particularly prone to airborne pollutants. Scientists have begun using them to monitor air quality.

Where to See Them?

Lace lichens can be found along the coast and up to 130 miles inland. Look in areas where oaks grow on the Channel Islands or in the canyons of the western Santa Monica Mountains.

Plants

Arundo
Arundo donax

Tall, potentially over 20 feet

Leafy stalks look like bamboo

Grows along rivers and in other wet areas in thick clusters or clumps

Tall and green and vaguely tropical looking, arundo grows along the LA River in Frogtown. Some people think it looks like sugarcane, others like bamboo. Goats can eat arundo, but because the leaves contain concentrated salt, silica, and other noxious chemicals, not much else can. Once arundo enters a stream, it rapidly takes over and changes the streamside ecosystem.

Arundo is one of the fastest growing plants in the world, capable of growing nearly four inches per day.

No Seeds? No Problem

Arundo flowers are large, silver to brown or purple, feathery plumes up to two feet long, which produce lots of small and sterile seeds. The seeds don't spread it—instead it relies on underground rhizomes to reproduce. They break off during floods, and after washing up against a bridge or sandbank, they establish a new colony downstream. These sections can sprout even after months of drying in the sun—just add water and some soil that's been torn up by a storm or bulldozer.

Worst of the Worst

Arundo is apparently native to eastern Asia, although it has been moved around by people for so long its exact native range isn't precisely known. In California, arundo dates back to the early days of the Los Angeles Pueblo. Back then, it was used to thatch roofs and woven into mats and screens. Later, it was intentionally planted to help control erosion in drainage ditches. Now it sprouts up along the LA River and other local riparian zones, wild and difficult to manage.

Arundo grows in dense mats, crowding out native streamside plants, and starving animals of food and shelter. Its seeds are too small for birds to eat, and most native wildlife shuns arundo as nest material. The situation gets worse when water is low and stalks are dry. Arundo is a fire-adapted species that burns easily, and its roots are anchored in wet soil so can re-sprout once conditions improve. Native willows, cattails, and adjacent stream species aren't adapted to fire and don't fare so well. For all these reasons, arundo makes the International Union for Conservation of Nature's list of "100 of the World's Worst Invasive Species."

> Musically inclined? Arundo is the major source of reed mouthpieces for woodwind instruments. You can also use dried arundo stalks to make wind chimes and panpipes.

Biologists and land managers responsible for restoring stream habitats would like to get rid of arundo completely—they spend a lot of time and money dealing with it. But homeowners still plant it as a windbreak, and, because it grows so quickly, some people want to use it as a biofuel. Arundo will likely be with us for a long time to come.

Where to See It

Moist areas and streambeds with soil; water must be nearby, even if from an underground spring or yard runoff. **Trips 10** and **19**.

Blue Gum Eucalyptus

Eucalyptus globulus

Tall, white-trunked trees

Often can be the tallest trees in the neighborhood

Gray and brown bark, peeling off in long strips

Loose, narrow-angled leaves hang downward

Blue gum eucalyptus trees are tall, graceful, and as popular with wintering warblers, who gobble insects off infested leaves, as they are with herons, who nest in them at the Sepulveda Basin Wildlife Reserve and Silver Lake Reservoir. They're the most common big tree you'll see along the freeway from San Diego to San Francisco.

Blue gum eucalyptus leaves shimmer in summer sunlight and their subtle pastel bark brings on the urge to paint watercolor. Or—and this view is held by many foresters and botanists—they're weedy pests that make bad wildfires worse and outcompete California native plants for water, nutrients, and sunlight—a devil plant whose arrival ruined Southern California landscapes. In the blended ecology of modern California, we need to navigate between both views.

Eucalyptus Booms and Busts

Blue gum trees were imported to Los Angeles in the 1870s as timber trees. But it turns out their wood cracks and twists as it dries and isn't a good timber crop. They next became popular as windbreaks at citrus farms—though they're not always effective there either.

Memories are short, so eventually people started planting these trees again. Abbot Kinney, best known as the architect who developed Venice, was chair of the California Board of Forestry and interested in finding ways to prevent floods and erosion caused by ranching. In the 1890s, he promoted the blue gum heavily, pitching it as a miracle plant that could help everybody get rich. The fad lasted into the early 1900s when the bottom fell out of the eucalyptus market yet again, but by then the tree was firmly established in the area.

Forest Fire Fiends?

There are many species of eucalyptus and not every species is as invasive in California as the blue gum. Eucalyptus leaves contain a lot of oils. You're likely familiar with them—they're

Some eucalyptus trees grow truly huge. A blue gum in Northern California is 135 feet tall with a trunk circumference of 56 feet.

▲ Tan, pink, and gray bark peels off in long, papery strips.

often used in cough drops and syrups. These oils are highly flammable, creating a fire hazard as leaves and shreds of bark accumulate under the trees. In Australia, native fungi break down this debris, but since the fungi aren't found in California, the oil-rich leaves stay on the ground until a cigarette butt or lightning strike turns the eucalyptus grove into a firestorm.

Burning eucalyptus trees can be explosive, sending sparks or flaming debris far ahead of the main fire, helping it spread. Eucalyptus have a life cycle that depends on fire for survival. The trunks can regenerate even if some branches have burned off, and the hard, triangular seedpods (called pips) open up *after* a fire, releasing seeds from their protective casing to take advantage of the freshly cleared landscape.

Where to See It

Most people in Los Angeles live within walking distance of a eucalyptus tree, but among the places where you can see large blue gums, **Trips 2**, **8**, **12**, and **24** all have eucalyptus trees of particularly robust size. You can see the groves first planted by Abbot Kinney at his Santa Monica Mountains forestry station on **Trip 4**.

Bush Sunflower

Encelia californica

Abundant daisy-like flowers

Sprawling bush 2–4 feet tall and wide

A big patch of this native sunflower can look like an exploded daisy factory. It brightens even the most drizzly June gloom, and when the sun comes out it's even better, with saturated yellow flowers that burst exuberantly from vibrant green leaves. You may want to pick a bouquet for someone special—but don't! Leave the blossoms, full of nectar and pollen, for the many insects that rely on them for food.

This member of the daisy family is a Southern California local. It can only be found along the coast and mountains from about Santa Barbara County to Baja California. One of the more common species in coastal sage communities, it is, for much of the year, one of the showiest plants on local hillsides.

Nature's Supermarket, Condo, and Rec Room

After winter rains, the bush sunflower's first flowers attract insect pollinators ranging from honey bees to flies, butterflies, and beetles. Small insects attract larger ones, including ladybugs that feast on aphids. Lesser

The name *sunflower* is used for a wide variety of plants with large, golden yellow blooms. Many have young flowers that turn to follow the path of the sun over the course of the day; this is called *heliotropism*. One indigenous word for the bush sunflower translates to *it watches the sun.*

Bush sunflowers use ants to help distribute their seeds, which are covered in a fleshy structure called an elaiosome. Ants love elaiosomes because they're oil-rich and nutritious. They use the coating as a carrying handle to bring the seeds back to their nest. After eating the elaiosome, they discard the seed in a midden, or waste disposal area. When next season's rains come, these seeds are pre-planted and ready to grow.

goldfinches land in summer and fall to eat the seeds, and some butterflies eat the leaves. The dense, shady leaves also provide important cover for lizards, snakes, chipmunks, and ground-feeding birds like towhees. Certain beetle species spend their entire adult lives in this bush. It's a miniature nature city in one compact, attractive plant.

Naturally Pretty

The bush sunflower is one of the most popular plants for Southern California native plant gardens. With modest mid-summer watering, it can produce blooms deep into summer, and if it starts to get too bushy, it's easy to trim back. Be sure to leave a few flowers long enough for seeds to ripen and ensure you a new crop of seedlings next year. Your neighbors will thank you for brightening up the neighborhood, and your local bee population will thank you for all the pollen.

Where to See It

A number of hikes and coastal areas feature this plant (including **Trips 1**, **2**, **4**, **6**, **9**, **11**, **13**, and **20**), but the most reliable is **Trip 15**, Eaton Canyon, where it can be prolific around the visitor center and trailhead.

California Buckwheat

Eriogonum fasciculatum

This small, low shrub is butterfly heaven when in flower, can bloom for half the year, and is also drought- and frost-resistant. Its leaves are small and needle-like, which helps it conserve water. In midwinter, with most of the flowers gone, this plant looks like a rosemary or a super-scaled-down bonsai pine. By early spring, the whole plant becomes lollipopped with clusters of small yet perfect flowers. These flower clusters can serve as an informal calendar. They start out pale pink in spring, slowly change to creamy white by mid-summer, and in the fall, dry into a deep rust-red.

One to three feet tall with needle-like leaves

When the plant is dry, it shows a range of rusty brown hues

California buckwheat leaves look and feel a bit woolly. They're covered with small hairs called trichomes, which protect the leaves from heat and wind by trapping a layer of air that acts as a barrier. In coastal populations, the hairs are typically only on the bottom side of the leaf. Inland, they're on both sides.

▲ Each California buckwheat flower by itself is truly dinky (smaller around than a pencil eraser), and the entire cluster is about the size of a walnut. Yet clusters cover the plant so thickly it seems to burst with a thousand cotton balls.

Something for Everyone

For a small plant with small leaves, the California buckwheat provides a huge benefit to the entire food chain. Although hummingbirds are too big to visit, most nectar-feeding insects queue up for a sugar rush. Besides the expected honey bees (buckwheat honey has a rich, musky taste—the merlot of the honey world), many butterflies use this plant, including metalmarks, hairstreaks, and several blues. Other members of the buckwheat fan club include wasps, bees, flower flies, and tachinid flies. Stand and watch a blooming buckwheat—it's hard not to be amazed by the incredible insect diversity.

Hardy Survivor

California buckwheat has evolved to endure our boom and bust rain cycles. It can thrive in years of more-than-usual rains (and in over-watered gardens as long as the soil drains well), but also knows how to tough it out in the dry years that inevitably follow. It has a two-tier root system—a deep central taproot keeps it anchored on steep hillsides and goes down deep for the best chance of finding long-term water, while a skirt of shallower, more surface-connected roots captures rain as soon as it falls.

Another reason California buckwheat does so well here, is it can grow in a number of plant communities. It loves our mosaic of habitats, including coastal sage scrub, sand dunes, grasslands, and hillside chaparral. It can be found from sea level up into the pine belt of Angeles Crest and out into the Mojave Desert.

Where to See It

Trips **1**, **2**, **4**, **5**, **6**, **7**, **8**, **9**, **11**, **13**, **14**, **15**, **20**, and **25** all feature California buckwheat and other native plants. You can find additional species of buckwheat in the Museum's Nature Gardens (Trip 7), including several that, outside of cultivation, are known only from the Channel Islands.

Because buckwheat harbors beneficial insects, some organic vineyard managers grow strips of buckwheat in the middle of their grape rows.

California Poppy

Eschscholzia californica

Often found in extended colonies

Low to ground

California is the "Golden State" not just because of the Gold Rush of 1849, but also because of our iconic state flower. In the days of sailing ships, Spanish sailors could see golden, poppy-covered hillsides from far out at sea. These days, a late spring drive over Tehachapi Pass can reveal spectacular displays high above Interstate 5.

In some years California poppies bloom as early as March, but usually they come later and linger all the way through June. Once a plant is done blooming, the fallen petals cover the ground like small orange handkerchiefs.

One blossom per stem

Open, cup-shaped flower is a deep, saturated orange

Orange Above, Orange Below

The blooms of the California poppy are so intensely orange, on a sunny day it can feel like somebody has cranked nature up to its most vivid setting. The orange runs in both directions, with bright blooms above and a carrot-colored taproot below. This long, thin root allows the plant to find water deep in the soil so it can survive dry periods.

Poppy flowers are cup shaped, like a Dutch tulip or a small teacup. They're pollinated mostly by beetles, and also by bees. Flower size varies by time of year; on average, later blossoms are smaller than earlier ones. California poppies don't have nectar, so hummingbirds, butterflies, and other nectar seekers don't come around. Instead, bees and other insects gather pollen.

Where to See It

In wet years, you can see California poppies at many of the sites featured in this book, especially at the Antelope Valley Poppy Reserve only a short drive away in Lancaster. Thanks to an increase in native landscape planting,

The California poppy is not the poppy we pin to our shirts on Memorial Day. And it's not the poppy that gives us opium and poppy seeds. But it is a California ambassador, spreading sunshine throughout the world. Today, you can find it growing wild in many places with a Mediterranean climate including Chile, Australia, New Zealand, and South Africa.

you also might see California poppies along freeway margins. When not in bloom, they're easy to overlook. Two places to start learning them—and places likely to have blooms even in lean years—are Arlington Garden (**Trip 12**) and the Museum's Nature Gardens (**Trip 7**).

California Sagebrush

Artemisia californica

Leaves are small, dense

3–6 feet tall

Color varies from green to light gray

This plant has a lot to give. It's a treat for the nose—even if you just brush past them while hiking, its leaves release that classic sage scent, cowboy cologne. Oils in the stems and leaves create the aroma, which also discourages animal and insect pests from having a nibble.

It's also a visual treat—the soft, fine-textured leaves create a delicate, almost feathery look that changes halfway through the year. In the rainy season, California sagebrush produces larger, greener leaves, and in the summer, smaller, grayer ones. The second batch uses less water, helping sagebrush get through the dry season. When it gets too dry for even these leaves, the plant is drought-deciduous: its leaves die (they may or may not fall off) and a new set emerges in the next rainy season.

Native Americans use smoke from sage leaves during pre-hunt cleansing ceremonies, and hunters sometimes rub the plant on their body to mask their human scent.

Its Name Is on the Ecosystem

California sagebrush has an entire ecosystem named for it: the coastal sage scrub plant community. The most common community members are California sagebrush (of course), California buckwheat, ceanothus, manzanita, other types of sage, and sometimes cactus.

Bees and other insects visit sagebrush flowers for nectar and pollen, and, because California sagebrush often blooms late in the summer, it's an important source of food. Birds use it for nesting; chipmunks and lizards use it for shade.

One bird in particular has its destiny tied to California sagebrush. The California gnatcatcher only nests in areas with dense sagebrush. This bird doesn't migrate, living its entire life here in California and adjacent Baja California. There may be as few as 2,500 pairs of California gnatcatchers left, which is why preserves in places like the Palos Verdes Peninsula matter so very much.

Where to See It

California sagebrush is mostly a lowland species—you won't find it in the high mountains. It occurs in the native plant garden at the La Brea Tar Pits, at the Museum's Nature Gardens (**Trip 7**), and Point Vicente Park (**Trip 25**), as well as excursions **1**, **3**, **4**, **5**, **6**, **8**, and **9**. It is widespread in natural areas.

Ceanothus (California Lilacs)

Bigpod Ceanothus

Ceanothus megacarpus

Up to nine feet tall

Leaves are small and dark green

Hoary-leaved (or Thick-leaved) Ceanothus

Ceanothus crassifolius

Large bush common in Southern California chaparral

Evergreen

Lavender-blue or white flowers in spring

Can form dense thickets

What feeds deer, makes bees happy, turns entire hillsides white or blue, is seen by millions of people every day, and yet is invisible? The answer is a key genus that's well represented in California wildlands: *Ceanothus*. There are more than forty ceanothus species in California, and all are generally called California lilacs. They grow near some of the busiest freeways in the world, yet most folks don't know they're there.

As with so many of our native plants, ceanothus may seem at first glance sort of dull and forgettable—just another drab, olive-colored

For some plants, their common name is also their genus name. When used as a common name, it should be lowercase (such as ceanothus). When referring to genus, the name should be capitalized and italicized as is standard for scientific names (*Ceanothus*). Some examples include plants of the genera *Ceanothus*, *Eucalyptus*, *Ficus*, and *Acacia*.

bush. A closer look lets us enjoy its variety of forms, the subtle fragrance of its blossoms, and even the beauty of its braided stems. Our local ceanothus plants—the two most common of which are featured here—are found nowhere else in the world. Bigpod ceanothus is especially common at lower elevations of the Santa Monica and San Gabriel Mountains; it is replaced at higher elevations by hoary-leaved ceanothus.

Both are amazing organisms. They can survive droughts, grow back after fire, provide nectar to an impressive array of insects, and, without being asked, year after year put on a springtime flower display that rivals the best lilacs in a flower show.

A Perfect Partnership

Like all plants, ceanothus use the most basic ingredients—energy from the sun, carbon dioxide, and water—to make food. Through photosynthesis (the Latin roots mean *putting together by using light*) the plants create sugar and at the same time give off oxygen—thanks, plants!

But ceanothus also performs the remarkable chemical feat called nitrogen fixation. All plants need nitrogen, but it's often hard to get. Ceanothus has a mutualistic partnership with bacteria that grow on its roots—it gives the bacteria food and shelter, and the bacteria help supply the plant with nitrogen by pulling it from the air and changing it into a form the plant can use. When ceanothus dies and decomposes, the nitrogen returns to the soil for other plants to enjoy.

Seasonal Color

Just as New England has fall foliage, California has spring days when entire hillsides glow blue and white with ceanothus blooms.

Most ceanothus plants bloom from early winter to early summer. Bigpod ceanothus starts its parade as early as December, but sometimes not until March, depending on when we get rain. You can see it all through the Santa Monica Mountains and up the coastal slope of the San Gabriels. Just as one plant finishes its display, another kicks into action, blooming in succession as you go toward the Angeles Crest. The show typically lasts well into June if the rains have been decent.

In drought years ceanothus may hunker down, shedding some leaves, maybe dropping a branch or two, but a particularly rainy winter will send them into an explosion of flowers. As the small fruits of the ceanothus dry out in summer, tension builds until the capsule explodes with a clear *pop*, flinging thousands of seeds in all directions.

Where to See It

A classic chaparral plant, ceanothus can be found on **Trips 1**, **8**, **9**, **15**, and **16**.

Chaparral Yucca

Hesperoyucca whipplei

You've probably seen this plant, or at least its flowers. This California native lives most of its life low to the ground, often hidden from view by other plants. But in spring, seemingly overnight, all the yuccas along the 210 Freeway bloom at once, sending up flagpole stalks topped by thousands of creamy white flowers. Each stalk points down to the circle of spikey, fibrous leaves at the base, as if to say, "Hey everybody, I'm here!"

If you're trying to take a picture, be careful lining up the perfect shot. These plants often grow together, one every few feet, and the tips of their leaves are sharp and rigid—they've earned the name "Spanish bayonet," with concentric rows of their sharp tips pointed outward, like an aloe vera plant crossed with a porcupine. Back into one, and you'll be sorry.

Yet from a safe distance, a hillside of chaparral yucca in bloom is a tremendous sight. Another common name for this plant, "our Lord's candle," is a good description of the flower stalk, which looks like a torch or flame being carried in a holy procession.

A Lock-and-Key Relationship

Chaparral yucca offers a classic example of mutualism. Every chaparral yucca is pollinated by just one species, the California yucca moth. The moth lays her eggs inside a flower so the young can feed on the seeds. The pollen inside yucca flowers is stickier and stringier than in most plants, so most insects avoid it the same way you avoid gum on the sidewalk. But the yucca moth can handle this stringy material, so it goes from plant to plant, gathering pollen and laying eggs. It only lays eggs on chaparral

Clusters of creamy, fragrant flowers

When flowering, central stalk rises to 10 feet tall

Stiff, bayonet-like leaves

Pincushion shape sits low to the ground

The name *yucca* ("YUCK-uh") is related linguistically but not botanically to the brown, South American root that is used to make manioc, cassava, and tapioca. That edible root is spelled *yuca* ("YOU-kah") and comes from *Manihot esculenta*, a woody shrub.

yucca—nothing else will do—and the yucca relies solely on this moth to pollinate its flowers. Each depends entirely on the other.

When they finish eating some of the seeds, the caterpillars drop to the ground, pupate (change from larva into adult moths), and fly off to find more blooming yucca plants and continue the cycle.

THE MYSTERY OF SYNCHRONIZED BLOOMING

This is a classic case of "you never see just one." In a bloom year, it seems like all the chaparral yuccas know to bloom at once, each exploding its single stalk into the sky. Each plants will do this just once in its lifetime, and since they want to be sure they have a good chance for pollination, practically all the yuccas bloom around the same time, offering up a huge feast for the moths. Scientists aren't entirely sure how they do this. It could have to do with the timing of rains, or of fires, but the exact trigger that gets so many plants blooming at once remains a mystery.

The Swiss Army Knife Plant

Few native plants are as utilitarian as chaparral yucca. Native people use the fiber for baskets, ropes, brooms and brushes, and fishing nets; they use its charcoal for tattoos and dead stalks as tinder. It's edible as well—you can roast the stalks, use it to make flour and seedcakes, or boil and eat the flowers. Animals share our interest. Carpenter bees make nest chambers in the stalks, while yucca longhorn beetles and black yucca weevils tunnel into (and help to decompose) dying plants.

Where to Find Them

Trips 2, **13**, **14**, **15**, and **16** are the best.

Cheatgrass and other Brome Grasses

Bromus species

Fringing every freeway onramp and carpeting every hillside, a silent killer hides in plain sight. Deceptively emerald after a good rain and brittle tan the rest of the year, cheatgrass is one of the worst pests in the American West. Los Angeles has cheatgrass plus several look-alikes, including a species with slightly longer heads (called the awns) with the horror

6–18 inches tall

Bright green after winter rains

Much of year, plants are a dry light brown or tan

Seed heads detach easily and stick to socks or pet fur

film name of "ripgut brome." Another, which turns pinkish when it dries out, is called red brome.

▲ Most of the year, bromes and cheatgrass are dry and yellow.

You've encountered these plants. If you've ever taken a shortcut through a vacant lot, the golden seed heads stuck in your socks or in the fur and ears of your dog are theirs. The smoke from a new brushfire on the local news probably isn't coming from smoldering native plants but from these grasses—the first to die in summer and also the first to burn.

Cheatgrass is so good at burning, and so good at coming back first after a fire, it's changing the fire ecology of entire ecosystems. Plant communities that used to have big fires every twenty, thirty, even fifty years, now have fires every five. That's too quick for native plants to recover, and it creates an endless cycle of grow and burn, grow and burn. With a few exceptions, almost every brushfire in Southern California starts with tinder-dry, invasive grasses catching fire and spreading across a hillside or freeway edge.

Where the Deer and the Antelope Play

Here's how grass in Los Angeles is supposed to work: native perennial bunchgrasses grow in clumps with bare ground in between that reduces the risk of fire spreading. Their deep root systems hold moisture into mid- and late summer, making them fire resistant and good food for deer and antelope. Plus they're tall, providing shade and shelter for little critters.

When plants like cheatgrass or red brome move in, everything changes. First, cheatgrass hogs water and nutrients in the soil, making it hard for native bunchgrasses and other plants to get started. Then it sends out so many seeds it overruns native plants to form a continuous flammable mass. When animals need food or shelter in summer, very little is left because the cheatgrass has already died. Studies have shown it even raises temperatures in its immediate area, making baked soil harder and hotter.

The Black Fingers of Death

Land managers have experimented with using sheep and goats to graze cheatgrass to the ground early in spring, reducing the potential summer fuel load and catching it before it flowers and produces seeds.

More promising is a type of fungus jokingly called the black fingers of death. It doesn't damage native plants but attacks cheatgrass seeds in the soil before they can sprout. Testing is going on now, and perhaps someday it could be applied across much of the western United States.

Where to See It

Start with the nearest vacant lot, but if that doesn't work, Baldwin Hills (**Trip 6**), Debs Park (**Trip 11**), the trailhead of Icehouse Canyon (**Trip 17**), Powder Canyon in the Puente Hills (**Trip 20**), and the roadsides of Point Vicente (**Trip 25**) all have an abundance of bromes and cheatgrass.

Coast Live Oak

Quercus agrifolia

1–2-inch long, leathery leaves lined with spiny teeth

Usually dense, leafy trees

Coast live oaks are abuzz with life. Thousands of species of insects, birds, mammals, reptiles, amphibians, and fungi make a living in and around these trees. Some are attracted by the shelter of the tree canopy, others by the rich, organic leaf litter beneath, and still more by the tasty acorns that grow through summer and drop in fall. All the Native American tribes of the LA area used (and many still use today) acorns as food. Deer and black bears graze on acorns in fall to get ready for winter, and acorn woodpeckers stash many thousands of nuts for the year ahead.

Spanish settlers associated coast live oaks with fertile soil and found them useful as a source of building material and shade. As a result, most missions are found near this tree.

Specialized Leaves

A classic, mature coast live oak has a dense, dark green crown covering the tree almost all the way to the ground. Up close, its leaves are surprisingly small and tough, usually not even as long as your thumb. The topmost leaves are thick and small, with more layers of cells devoted to photosynthesis. These leaves are packed so tight they create a solid umbrella, soaking up maximum sunlight but also cooling the tree's interior. Leaves on shady interior branches are thinner, wider, and flatter, with just one layer of photosynthetic cells. They capture stray light that filters through the crown and don't need to be as armored as their upstairs neighbors.

185

▲ Even after acorns fall off or are eaten, the cups remain for many months.

▲ An oak gall. The wasps inside drill tiny exit holes when they're ready to fly away.

You've Got a Lot of Gall

Over two hundred species of wasps make galls in the twenty different oak species of California. Mama wasp needs a place to leave her eggs, one protected from harm but with a good, close-at-hand food source. Solution? Oak twigs and leaves. She lays her egg inside the wood or leaf along with chemicals that cause the tree to grow new tissue over and around the wound. Inside this swollen shelter, the larva develop with plenty of plant tissue for food.

Though appearances and locations vary, a typical oak gall looks like a wooden ping pong ball or small apple placed mid-twig (they're often called oak apples). You can spot them near the thin ends of branches or scattered on the ground. For leaf galls, look for round or star-like growths on the underside of oak leaves. The gall's shape can help identify the wasp species.

Some predators and parasites have figured out the galls' secret. Competing wasp species and small birds like titmice search out active galls, so not all gall dwellers make it to adulthood. But it works out often enough that galls appear frequently on oaks—you can find them yourself with minimal searching.

Some wasps enlist oak trees in a clever gall defense. In a chemical interaction that's not fully understood, the wasp larva inside the galls trick the tree into creating a sugary honeydew just outside. Ants love this and will defend their sugar factory against all attackers, keeping the wasps inside safe.

Where to See It

Hahamongna has great examples of coast live oak right in the parking lot (**Trip 14**); these trees are also found on **Trips 1**, **2**, **4**, **8**, **9**, and in many other foothill parks and preserves.

Oak apple galls are full of bitter tasting compounds called tannic acids. The tannins can be soaked or squeezed out and have been used to tan leather, make ink and dyes, and clean wounds.

Coyote Brush

Baccharis pilularis

2–8 feet tall

Dense bush

Branch tips often covered with creamy white, cottony seed heads

This large, bright green shrub is one of the most common native plants of the California landscape. Built for surviving drought, this waxy-leaved bush has a central root that drills straight down for ten feet or more, searching for water and anchoring the plant against intense winter rains. Usually it is a tall shrub, but on coastal bluffs, strong, cool winds create dense bonsai forms—still the same plant, just hunkered down against the elements.

The Smells of Summer Chaparral

Plants use a variety of strategies to keep animals from eating them. Coyote brush produces oil on its leaves that makes them taste bad to deer and other grazers. On hot days, the oil evaporates with a rich, incense-like smell. This evaporation helps the plant stay cool the same way sweat cools you off after a workout.

> Coyote brush is a real insect magnet, particularly when it is in flower. One study identified 221 species of insects associated with this plant.

▲ The white and tan flower "fuzz" indicates this plant is female.

Male or Female?

Coyote brush has separate male and female plants, as you can see in the fall when the flowers bloom. Flowers are very small (about the size of a pea) and cover the bush all over, looking something like dirty snow. Male flowers are yellow and cream colored. Female flowers are white. In the fall, female flowers will have long hairs that help their tiny, black seeds float on the wind like small soap bubbles. When not in bloom, males and females look the same.

Where to See It

Coyote brush is widespread in our coastal scrub and chaparral plant communities and can be found on **Trips 1**, **3**, **8**, and **25**. Once you learn what it looks and smells like, you'll notice it on many hikes.

Floss Silk Tree

Ceiba speciosa

Pink, hibiscus-like flowers

Trees can grow 40–60 feet tall

Massive, green gray trunk often covered with large spikes

Despite stereotypes that declare Los Angeles a concrete jungle, trees like this, with their showy, orchid-pink blossoms and green, spine-covered bark prove the city has surprising nature. Many plants can grow in our mild Mediterranean climate, and this tree is an example of past Angelenos trying to bring something unusual into their backyards.

In their native range, floss silk trees are found in northern Argentina, Bolivia, Paraguay, Uruguay, and southern Brazil. Much of this range overlaps with that of the yellow-chevroned parakeet, which loves to tear into the seedpods in search of large black seeds. Now that both species have been introduced to the area, you can observe this South American dynamic along the sidewalks of Los Angeles. But here, eastern fox squirrels compete with parakeets for those tasty seeds.

The immense seedpods—twice the size of our supermarket avocados (watch out below when they fall!)—burst open to reveal silky white "floss" that bushtits and hummingbirds use to line their nests. The soft filaments help the large seeds float on the wind, carrying them far away so the tree doesn't compete with (and shade out) its offspring.

Bees like floss silk blooms, as do humming-birds and sometimes other nectar-attracted birds like tanagers and orioles. In the fall, after the flowers have been pollinated, the tree drops its pink crown creating a carpet of blooms. They look beautiful, but walkers beware—they're incredibly slippery on sidewalks!

Hardworking Bark that Bites

The floss silk trunk is covered with triangular prickles or spikes—watch where you lean—and it often swells towards the bottom of the trunk, like a bowling pin. Under the thorns the trunk is smooth and light green, especially when the tree is young (later the bark becomes grayer and more wrinkled). The color comes from chlorophyll, the pigment that makes plants green and aids in photosynthesis. That means even when the tree has dropped its leaves for the year (as it often does before blooming), the trunk can help turn sunlight into food.

Where to See It

Listen for the yellow-chevroned parakeets screeching as they zoom past overhead—they will take you to the nearest floss silk trees. You can find some near the Museum's Nature Gardens (**Trip 7**) and as a street tree all around Los Angeles.

▲ Parakeets love floss silk seedpods here in Los Angeles just as much as in their native South America.

189

Manzanita

Arctostaphylos species

Manzanita is Spanish for *little apple*, but this evergreen chaparral shrub is usually identified by its smooth maroon-red bark. The branches often rise up out of a central trunk like modern sculpture; the tallest ones are themselves the size of a small tree. Most manzanitas have leathery, smooth, medium-to-pale green or gray leaves that vary in size and shape depending on species. In all types, the leaves are very flat, and usually held vertically to minimize the amount of surface area exposed to the sun.

Little Apples for All

Manzanitas are great friends of wildlife. When in bloom, fragrant, bell-shaped, white to pale pink flowers attract crowds of hummingbirds and insects.

Even more noticeable than its bee-filled bouquet is the manzanita berry crop. Once the small reddish-brown fruits are ripe, lots of animals want in—bears, foxes, coyotes, squirrels, and quail. Even if you don't see the critters themselves, the seeds filling their scat will tell you who's been feasting on berries. In the past, California's grizzly bears gorged on manzanita berries for hours, hence the name bearberry. Native Americans dry the berries to store for winter, making a kind of fruit punch from them, using them in jelly, or eating them fresh. The leaves and bark can be used to make teas as a treatment for upset stomach.

Grow in Winter, Sleep in Summer

Manzanitas are long-lived shrubs. Our local species are large bushes or smallish trees. In other parts of California, you can find mountain or coastal species that grow very low to the ground. Regardless of size and form, all manzanitas share gorgeous bark, with swirls of red and gray wrapping around like an exotic

Large shrub or small tree

Red-brown bark

Oval, leathery leaves

barber pole. Sometimes the red bark peels off in long curls. This allows for expanding growth and signals the end of the winter growing season and onset of summer dormancy.

In Case of Fire

Manzanita plants use two strategies for making sure they persist after a fire. Some species can resprout from their base—the fire burns the above-ground parts of the plant and triggers the burl at or below ground level to sprout. Others rely on spreading their seeds widely. Even if the original plant dies, the heat of the fire causes seeds buried in the soil to sprout while there's little competition for space. A few burl sprouters are believed to be over one thousand years old, but on average, most manzanitas live less than fifty years.

Where to See It

California is the world headquarters for this group, with five species occurring in LA County and over fifty statewide. This is an easy plant to locate in Angeles Crest. Try **Trip 16**.

Mexican Fan Palm

Washingtonia robusta

Convertible sports cars, a perfect sky, and rows of tall, stately, oh-so-thin palm trees: what could be more Hollywood than that? Except Hollywood's palms aren't native. The Mexican fan palm came to Southern California with the Spanish missions as a source of fronds for Holy Week celebrations. It also may have been planted to provide thatching for house roofs. Beautification projects in the 1930s planted huge numbers of palms along barren city streets, ensuring its status as an iconic symbol for Hollywood, Malibu, and living *la vida buena*. In some areas they can form dense monocultures. Because of their tendency to crowd out other species in areas near water, Mexican fan palms are sometimes listed as an invasive species.

Los Angeles's other common palm is the only one native to our state—the California fan palm. It only occurs naturally in desert oases but was brought to the city where its massive trunks line streets in older neighborhoods and cemeteries. Like so many of us humans, the city's palms originally came from somewhere else.

Be a Palm Reader

It may seem like there are several kinds of fan palm, since some have beards or petticoats of dead fronds hanging down and some

are smooth and clean, right to the top. But the difference is only due to machetes and chainsaws.

In their untended state, fan palms have lots of dead fronds. However, these are highly flammable, provide habitat for unwanted rats to nest in, and are a falling hazard (particularly

Crown of fan-shaped leaves

On some trees, a beard of dry fronds

Single tall trunk

▲ A row of trimmed Mexican fan palms in Santa Monica.

during windstorms), so most planted fan palms are trimmed by work crews. The picture postcard silhouette is a Tinseltown fabrication.

Another iconic LA palm tree is the Canary Island date palm. It's easy to distinguish from the other two. On average, fan palms are taller and thinner, while date palm trunks tend to be chunky, like a temple column. Fan palm fronds are broad and shaped like an old-fashioned lady's fan. Canary Island date palms belong to a group called the feather palms, and their fronds look like long, shaggy feathers—think Shakespeare's quill pen. There are more kinds of palms than just these three, of course. Nobody's quite sure how many of the world's two thousand palm species have been planted in Los Angeles.

Where to See Them

It's hard *not* to see fan palms in the city. They're planted along many streets, including Sunset and Hollywood boulevards and Rodeo Drive in Beverly Hills. You can also see them along the LA River (**Trip 10**).

The oldest palm tree in Los Angeles is in Exposition Park, a California fan palm that survived multiple replantings before ending up near the Figueroa Street entrance. It may be over 150 years old.

Peruvian Pepper

Schinus molle

This is probably Los Angeles's first non-native tree, having come to California around 1825. The Peruvian pepper produces small, pink peppercorns, which Spanish padres dried and ground to zest up their meals. They planted pepper trees at the missions and the earliest haciendas and pueblos, partly for the peppercorns, partly for the shade provided by their

aromatic leaves, and partly for the timber—their wood was favored for making saddles.

Birds like the peppercorns too, and they help the tree spread. They eat the fruit then poop out the seeds away from the parent tree—inadvertently planting them with a dab of starter fertilizer. Between the birds, missionaries, and early settlers, this tree has become

10–30 feet tall

Leaves are delicate, long, and hang loosely downward

Small, pink or red berry-like fruits

Bright green foliage appears feathery from a distance

so common across coastal regions of Central and Southern California that it's often called the California pepper despite its ancestry.

Its soft, weeping-willow profile and common role as a street tree make it an iconic part of the LA botanical experience, joining the ranks of the Mexican fan palm and eucalyptus as being both widely planted and widely recognized. Even if you don't know its name, you've almost certainly seen it.

Tolerant of drought, not fussy about soil types, and able to endure full sun or partial shade, this tree is well-suited to our climate. You can see it along freeway edges, in the courtyards of historic churches, or dotted across foothill canyons. But because it can take over hillsides and crowd out native plants, the California Invasive Plant Council lists it as an invasive species.

Spice Mix

The peppercorns you grind onto your dinner usually come from the black pepper, which is native to India and grows as a large tropical vine. The Peruvian pepper is more closely related to dandelions, roses, and oak trees. However, if you have a colorful mix of peppercorns in your pepper grinder, the red and pink ones are from either a Brazilian or Peruvian pepper. These species are both in the cashew family—someone allergic to tree nuts might also have an allergy to pink peppercorns.

Where to See It

The largest tree at Arlington Garden (**Trip 12**) is an especially venerable pepper. **Trips 2**, **6**, **8**, **11**, **13**, **14**, **18**, **19**, and **20** also give you a chance to study, and smell, this aromatic species.

Pines

Ponderosa Pine

Pinus ponderosa

6–8-inch needles mostly in bundles of three, sometimes two

Straight, tall trunk can grow to 200 feet

Canary Island Pine

Pinus canariensis

Usually grows to 50 feet but can reach 100 feet

Upswept or drooping side branches

Found in parks and along streets, (not in mountains)

In the blended magic of LA botany, two pine trees from opposite sides of the world help fill out the local landscape. The most common pine in our neighborhood parks, college campuses, and median strips is the Canary Island pine, named for islands off the coast of Morocco. Native ponderosa is even bigger, taller, and more majestic, best appreciated in the Angeles Crest high country.

Both trees have reddish bark, classic pine cones, long, evergreen needles, and lots and lots of squirrels.

Built to Survive

A mature pine tree is the ultimate survivor. Thick, fire resistant bark? Check. Leaves reduced to über-minimalist needles that are windproof, snow-proof, freeze-proof, and super drought-resistant? Check. Energy conservation, so that the same needles last for three or four years? Check. A pollination plan that doesn't need any animal helpers—just the wind? Check and check.

Pine needles are so tough few things can eat them. And when they die and fall off, the needles release chemicals into the soil that help the parent tree by keeping other plants from growing around the base.

Even the roaring Santa Ana winds that send eucalyptus trees crashing down on cars and porches don't usually harm pine trees. Their trunks are immensely strong, and their

California has eighteen native pines, more than any other state. The list includes bristlecone pine, the world's oldest—some nearly 5,000 years old—and Torrey pine, North America's rarest.

▲ The large puzzle-piece appearance of ponderosa pine bark makes the trees easy to identify.

needles so thin and tough the wind slides right through without stopping. Pine trees aren't indestructible however; they're vulnerable to bark beetles, which can devastate pine groves.

Where to See Them

Charlton Flats (**Trip 16**) is ponderosa central. Canary Island pines, very common on our streets, are also found in the parklands adjacent to Sepulveda Basin (**Trip 2**), around Exposition Park (**Trip 7**), Franklin Canyon (**Trip 8**), and in Bonelli Park (**Trip 18**).

Ponderosa pines have deep fissures in their bark. Place your nose in this valley and take a deep whiff (make sure there are no small cobwebs to inhale, first). These trees often smell of vanilla or butterscotch cookies. Another local pine, the Jeffrey pine, shares this trait.

Poison Oak

Toxicodendron diversilobum

The genus name means poison tree, and that's fairly accurate. Like its close relatives poison ivy and poison sumac, our poison oak contains an oil that gives most people an itchy, blistery rash. Some folks suffer more than others and reactions may change during a person's lifetime. Firefighters who breathe in smoke from burning poison oak can have a painful reaction in their throat and lungs.

Nevertheless, this beautiful native plant is part of our natural environment, and luckily,

once you learn how to spot it, it's not hard to avoid. This rhyme helps: leaves of three, let it be!

Hollywood's Fall Colors

Poison oak leaves are slightly lobed with rounded edges, often shiny, and come in groups of three. They also change with the seasons. In spring, leaves are greenest and shiniest. In summer, many are tinged with red, and in fall, it's an explosion of red, yellow, and orange. If you're hiking and see a plant starting

Lobed leaves in clusters of three

Sprawling shrub or low vine

Color varies from glossy green in spring to orange or red in fall

to turn a mix of red and green, treat it with respect—it's probably poison oak. Though some plants keep a few leaves year-round, most drop their leaves in late autumn. Watch out for this "naked" poison oak—you can still get a rash from the leafless stems.

Poison oak produces white flowers followed by white berries in summer and fall. Birds love these berries: one study identified over fifty species that feed on them and inadvertently help spread the seeds.

Where to See It

From the M*A*S*H site at Malibu Creek State Park (**Trip 1**) to the weedier parts of Whittier Narrows (**Trip 19**), poison oak is found in oak woodlands and coastal sage scrub. A good place to learn how to identify it is Eaton Canyon (**Trip 15**), where it is well-labeled on the trails around the Visitor Center.

Poison oak rashes are caused by an allergic reaction to urushiol, an oil found throughout all parts of the plant. If you think you've come into contact with urushiol, wash the area as soon as possible using soap (dishwashing soap is best) to cut the oils and a washcloth to rub them off your skin.

Horses don't seem to react to the oils in poison oak and, like deer, enjoy eating the plant. Dogs can get poison oak rashes but usually have a higher tolerance than people, and their fur provides some protection. But beware! Humans can get a poison oak rash by petting a dog that has been romping in poison oak.

Southern California Black Walnut

Juglans californica

Small to medium tree

Fern-like compound leaves that face each other down the stem

One or several trunks

Fruit starts green and ripens to brown

In the wild, black walnuts won't look like the nuts we buy at Thanksgiving. The familiar shell is hidden inside another layer—one that's thick, green, and furrowed. It looks more like a small, wrinkled lime than a walnut. Getting the nut out from the husk takes a bit of work. And once you reach the nut you may feel a bit cheated, because it's much smaller than the hybrid varieties most of us are used to. Still, you *can* eat it, and what you don't want, the jays and squirrels will be happy to consume. In the shade of walnut trees, you'll find old shells split in half, evidence that some critter recently enjoyed a meal.

A Southern California Specialty

The Southern California black walnut lives here in our biodiversity hotspot and no place else on Earth. But it's only found in the coastal mountains of the Ventura and LA areas.

Around Los Angeles, the best remaining walnut woodlands are on the north slopes of the Santa Monica Mountains and in the San Jose (between West Covina and Pomona), Chino, and Puente Hills. Farther south, it becomes increasingly uncommon with only a small number of walnut stands at the southern limit of its range in San Diego County. And that's it! This is a true Southern California specialist.

Although the Southern California walnut is often thought of as a stream species, because it prefers riparian habitat, it also does fine on steep, partially-shaded hillsides. It's usually found in oak woodlands but occasionally creeps into chaparral and coastal sage scrub. Once upon a time, Benedict, Laurel, Coldwater, Topanga, Bronson, and all the LA canyons would have had walnuts. Some still do, and many more could in the future. If you're thinking of changing your yard to include more native species, this is a good one to consider.

Black walnut husks are full of tannins and have been used for thousands of years for making ink and a brown dye for fabrics and leather. The dye is extremely strong, so if you start picking at a black walnut husk, be sure to wear gloves or you might end up with stained hands for several weeks.

THE WALNUT BUSINESS

Southern California black walnuts acted as rootstock to help start the English walnut industry. Inserting the twig of an English walnut into a slit carved onto the stump of a California walnut produced a hybrid tree with superior fruit. This system is still used today.

Walnuts were (and are) a big business. The first commercial hybrid California-English walnut orchard was planted in San Diego in 1845 and today the industry has an annual production of just under a billion dollars. If you've mixed walnuts into your brownies, they probably grew in California, descended from trees cultivated in the Southland.

Where to See Them

Oak woodlands, hillsides, and stream edges, including **Trips 1** and **4**. Some grow in Griffith Park (**Trip 9**), including in the Old LA Zoo, facing the small cages farthest from the parking lots. Powder Canyon in the Puente Hills (**Trip 20**), takes you into one of the largest remaining Southern California black walnut woodlands.

Toyon

Heteromeles arbutifolia

Toyon, also called California holly or Christmas berry, has been the official native plant of the City of Los Angeles since 2012. It's a tall bush or small tree with white flowers in summer, vivid red berries in winter, and perky, slightly serrated, two- to four-inch long evergreen leaves all year around. In early summer the showy flowers are magnets for insect pollinators, which help grow those bright red fruits. If you cut open a berry—technically known as a pome—the inside looks a lot like the core of an apple.

Urban legend says this plant is the "holly" for which Hollywood was named. Even though that's not the case, it's still a cheerful part of the landscape and a good food source for robins, cedar waxwings, coyotes, and other chaparral inhabitants.

Find a Single Tree to Study

When learning plants, it's often easier to study them in isolation. With one all by itself, you can focus on the new plant's shape, color, and distinctive features. A good place to learn toyon is in the Museum's Nature Gardens. The Huntington Library and Gardens in San Marino also has a good selection of toyon in the entry plaza.

More often, nature is a crazy parade, with few things occurring in isolation. You'll almost always find toyon mixing it up with other plants featured here (manzanita, ceanothus, chaparral yucca) and a number of other common sage scrub and chaparral species, like lemonade berry and laurel sumac.

Where to See It

Rustic Canyon (**Trip 4**), the Museum's Nature Gardens (**Trip 7**), Mt. Hollywood (**Trip 9**), and Eaton Canyon (**Trip 15**) are some of the many hikes on which you will come across Christmas berry.

Red berries
in winter

Bright green
leaves have
toothed edges

This is one of the few California native plants that holds onto its original name. Toyon is a Spanish transcription of the plant's Ohlone name, a tribal group resident from San Francisco to Salinas.

Western Sycamore

Platanus racemosa

Before eucalyptus were introduced, western sycamores were almost always the tallest trees in LA lowlands. They became what's known as witness trees and were used as significant boundary markers. One called the Eagle Tree still stands in Compton today; it once marked the northern edge of Rancho San Pedro.

The Tree with Curves

These leafy trees often bend and twist into curious shapes, and they like to be near water but not in it. With Los Angeles's floodplain forests all but gone, we mostly encounter western sycamores as park trees, such as along Arroyo

Tree with white
to gray mottled
bark

Found near
streams
and wetter
canyons

Irregular
branching
pattern
creates
see-through
effect

▲ Hand-shaped leaves are green in spring and summer, turning yellow or tan before dropping in fall and winter.

▲ Dangling seed heads.

Seco in Highland Park or downslope from the Old Griffith Park Zoo. Their trunks are pastel blends of white, gray, even pale green or pink. The bark flakes off in thin, curled sections. Sycamore leaves are broad and hand-shaped, similar to maple leaves.

Their distinctive seedpods form chains of round pods, which dangle from the ends of branches, each tied to the pod above like linked plastic monkeys. These fruits, green in spring and brown in fall, are hard and walnut-sized and protect tiny, fuzzy seeds.

Western sycamores provide valuable habitats for a variety of local wildlife. Western tiger swallowtail butterflies feed on its leaves and pupate on its branches. Anna's hummingbirds make their nests with the hairs from the underside of the leaves.

Western sycamores don't make good timber—the wood corkscrews, breaks, and splits into odd chunks. The sycamores themselves even have a hard time with it. Their branches can crack off, leaving hollows and divots, some quite deep. These turn out to be perfect for wildlife. Owls, wood ducks, raccoons, and parrots all find them just right for making a den or nest.

Where to See Them

Especially when young, these trees need water, so if you see a western sycamore, there's either a lot of underground water now, or there was once. **Trips 1**, **3**, **4**, **7**, **15**, and **19** all have sure bet western sycamores. If visiting the LA River at Frogtown (**Trip 10**), just upstream, the Bette Davis Picnic Area on Riverside Drive has many mature sycamores, most with leaning, curving trunks that beg to be climbed. (Careful though: some people are allergic to the hairs on the leaves.)

White Sage

Salvia apiana

White sage has something for everyone. Gardeners appreciate the handsome shrub for its striking silver foliage, dramatic floral display, and bold scent. Bees like it (its scientific name, *apiana,* refers to the Latin word for bees, *apium*) and produce a delicate and flavorful honey from its flowers. Native Americans consider it sacred and essential for ceremonies. Other everyday uses include boiling the leaves for tea as a cold remedy, using it as a deodorant (a University of Arizona study demonstrated its antibacterial properties), or gathering seeds to eat whole or ground into *pinole* (a grain-rich) flour.

Flower stalks 2–6 feet high with white, sometimes pale pink blossoms

Leaves waxy, sometimes sticky, and very aromatic

Bush up to three feet tall

The Scent of Ceremony

White sage has a strong aroma (some people love it, others compare it to dirty socks) and grows on steep hillsides, accepting drought and blistering sun. The silvery-white leaves reflect sunlight, which helps the plant conserve water.

Bundles of white sage leaves are sold as smudge sticks for burning—many believe the smoke will cleanse a space or heal a person. As this practice grows more popular, overharvesting wild plants is a serious concern, particularly for Native Peoples who hold it as sacred. Grow white sage in your garden instead of picking it (or buying it harvested) from the wild.

Sage Pollinators

Today the most common visitors to white sage flowers in urban Los Angeles are European honey bees. But before they were introduced, native insects like bumblebees, moths, and flower flies did the job. These insects still visit today.

Carpenter bees, a species of very large native bee, seem too big to fit inside white sage flowers, but a recent study showed they can still get in by pushing the flower's lower lip down, the way you use your foot to open the lid on a kitchen trashcan.

Where to See It

Look for white sage in coastal sage scrub and chaparral plant communities. This includes **Trips 1**, **9**, **11**, **14**, **15**, and **20**, along with the various preserves of the Palos Verdes Peninsula, including Point Vicente (**Trip 25**). You can also find white sage in the Museum's Nature Gardens (**Trip 7**) and outside the La Brea Tar Pits and Museum.

Wild Cucumber

Marah macrocarpus

Sprawling vine that can be big as a car, spreading up to 20 feet

Large, hand-shaped leaves

Seedpod is spiky and kiwi fruit-shaped

Seedpod is green when fresh, brown when dry

A green, sprawling vine with white, star-shaped flowers and a spikey, grenade-sized seedpod, the wild cucumber lives a Jekyll-and-Hyde life. Right after winter rains begin, it sends out long shoots that green up with four-inch leaves and tendrils, reminding some people of wild grapes. It flowers as early as January, and by the time the heat of mid-summer comes, the seedpods are dying dry husks.

Giant Roots and Spiky Seeds

The majority of the wild cucumber plant lives underground as a massive tuber that looks like a huge, ugly potato. The record-setter was 467 pounds, but even in less exceptional cases, these tubers can weigh 100 pounds. The stored energy in this modified root allows the plant to sprout vigorously after a fire. The green shoots sprawling over blackened earth or climbing burned tree trunks can be very striking.

Wild cucumber seedpods are remarkably fierce looking. When mature, they split open with a pop, scattering seeds for yards. The pod stays on the vine and dries out through fall and winter—tan, almost white, and bristling with dozens of thin, pale spines. It's is filled with a loofah-like structure made up of tiny knitted threads. Over time, the spiked husk disintegrates, and cucumber loofahs litter the ground.

Where to See It

In spring, **Trips 1** and **15** almost always have plenty of wild cucumber. Look for it as you hike along trails anywhere there's a good mix of native vegetation, both along creeks and in drier, shrubby areas.

If crushed wild cucumber tuber is scattered into a pond or small stream, it releases a substance that stuns fish. This was a common way for some Native Americans to catch fish. Crushing up these tubers also produces a liquid extract that can be used as a natural soap.

▲ A dry wild cucumber seedpod.

FIELD TRIPS

VENTURA
COUNTY

SANTA
CLARITA

*Santa Susana
Mountains*

*Simi
Valley*

CHATSWORTH

SAN
FERNANDO

UPPER
LOS ANGELES
RIVER

Simi Hills

CANOGA
PARK

RESEDA

③

Verdu

BURBA

THOUSAND
OAKS

AGOURA
HILLS

Santa

Monica

Mountains

S a n

Santa

①

⑧

NORTH
SANTA MONICA
BAY
MALIBU

④

BEVERLY
HILLS

SANTA
MONICA

⑥

*Point
Dume*

⑤

*Santa
Monica
Bay*

SOUTH
BAY

REDONDO
BEACH

TORRAN

RANCHO
PALOS
VERDES

㉕

*Point
Vicente*

0 ————— 10
miles

:: WATERSHED BOUNDARIES ::

CalWater 2.2.1 | California Department of Forestry and Fire Protection
frap.cdf.ca.gov

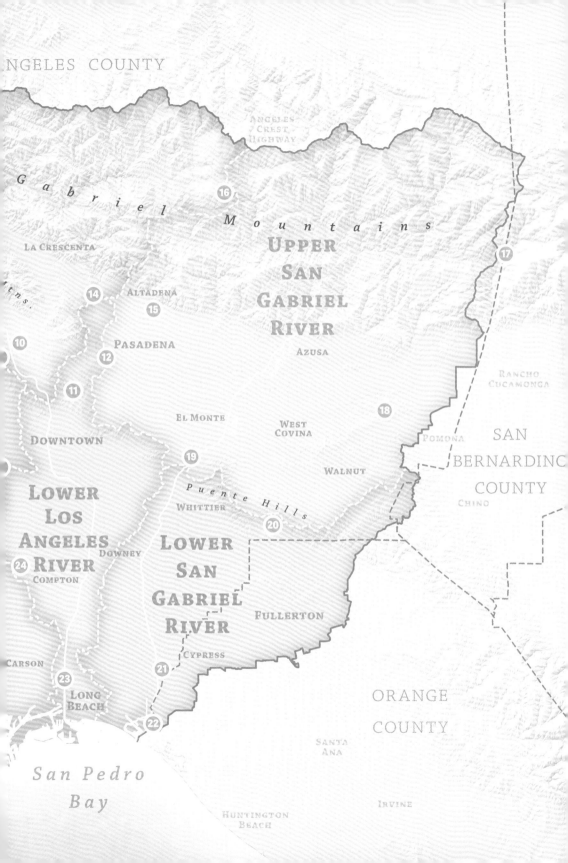

Although nature is all around us at all times — sidewalk snails, lawn mushrooms, and light pole–perching birds included — there's something fun about making a special trip to new or familiar places. Whether you're looking for charismatic megafauna (like bighorn sheep or green sea turtles) or just want to check out a new-to-you nature spot, the following twenty-five trips will help you get to know Los Angeles's nature firsthand.

Here are some tips to help you get the most out of your LA nature adventures:

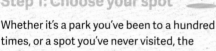

Step 1: Choose your spot

Whether it's a park you've been to a hundred times, or a spot you've never visited, the beauty of nature is that it's always changing.

Step 2: Choose the time

The time of the year and the time of the day will impact what you see. Bird watching is usually best in early morning. Lizards and snakes are most active in late morning during spring and early summer. If you hope to see deer, early mornings and evenings are best. Coyotes, skunks, opossums, raccoons, and bats are some of the nighttime specialists you can observe shortly after sunset. Winter rains will bring a new crop of green plants peeking out from the brown grass, and a few months later in spring, wildflowers will brighten your trip. In our mild, Mediterranean climate, adventures can be had year round, although the mid-day summer heat, especially in chaparral, should be avoided—the critters are all wisely staying in the shade at this time, and you should too. Try heading up in elevation or towards the coast during the summer to find cooler temperatures.

Step 3: Prep your pack

Packing for a nature adventure is part of the fun. What animals and plants do you expect to find, what tools will help you experience them better? How will you stay comfortable while out and about? Here are some essentials for your pack:

FOR YOUR COMFORT:

- **Sunscreen, hat, water, snacks, additional clothing** as needed for the weather (rain jacket, warm sweater, water shoes, etc.).

FOR NATURE SPOTTING

- **Binoculars** (great for birds, butterflies, and dragonflies). Pro tip: using only one eye, look through the wrong end of the binoculars and they become a makeshift magnifying lens.

- **Hand lens or magnifier.** Great for seeing insects and other tiny plants and critters up close. Pro tip: hold your magnifier in front of your smartphone's camera lens and it will help you get the perfect picture of tiny things.

- **Camera.** Whether with your smartphone or other camera, pictures of what you find will not only help you keep memories, they can also become data points for community science projects. Share your finds with us by tagging **#wildLA** in your social media posts.

- **Field guides like this one**. Although they can be heavy, field guides help novice nature explorers identify what they find. Get familiar with your guide before you go—there's nothing quite as frustrating as trying to flip to the right page as that really cool bird flies off into the distance.

- **Maps** are helpful for getting to your spot and navigating once you're there. Pro tip: if you don't have a paper map, snap a picture of maps displayed at the trailhead.

- **Field journal/notebook**. Some people like taking notes or drawing pictures of what they find. It could be a place to list all the different species you see that day, or somewhere to jot any strokes of genius you may have on the trail.

Step 4: Make our trails and your adventure beautiful

Wonderful weather and millions of Southern Californians means our trails get a lot of use. Try to pick up at least one piece of litter on every excursion (you may never look at helium balloons the same happy way again). You can be proud of yourself, and the next person down the path will appreciate your effort.

Keep music turned off. It could detract from someone else's nature experience and might cause you to miss hearing a lizard scurry through the leaves or a bird celebrating spring or a rattlesnake politely telling you that you're getting too close.

Step 5: Put your nature eyes on

Every time you go outside (and even sometimes when you're inside) put your nature eyes on. It's as easy as declaring your intention to notice nature. Look closely where you step. Look up as you walk down the street. Listen to the birds as they fly overhead. Sit quietly on a park bench and see who comes by. Take a moment to stop and smell the roses, but think about turning over that leaf to see what's living on the underside. Keep your eyes and ears open, and your adventure can begin.

Malibu Creek State Park

Famous as the *M*A*S*H* film site, this 8,000-acre park has fifty miles of trails that explore streams and valleys, oak forests, rocky cliffs, and a beautiful lake.

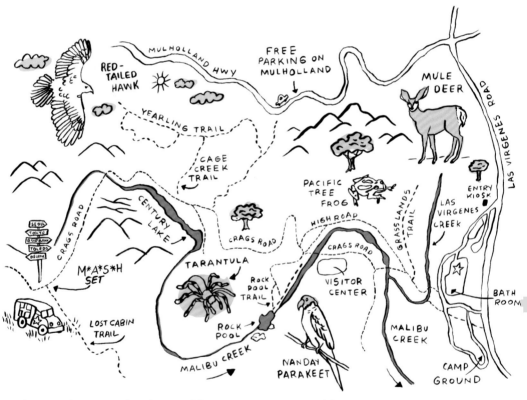

Few parks so perfectly combine great scenery with abundant wildlife. You can hike for an hour, a day, or a full week and not run out of paths to explore or streambeds to investigate. With oak forests, grassy hillsides, and a year-round lake, it's no wonder this site is considered the crown jewel of the Santa Monica Mountains.

KEY
☆ PARKING
---- TRAILS / DIRT ROADS
═══ PAVED ROADS
═══ BIKE PATHS

▲ If nanday parakeets are around, it's not hard to find them—they're even yakkier than acorn woodpeckers.

◀ Calm days in fall and winter create perfect reflections in Malibu Creek's pools.

Familiar Territory

Even if you've never been here before, you've probably seen these rugged hills and open, sycamore-filled valleys in a movie or television show. The most popular hike goes two miles each way to visit the *M*A*S*H* set, used for filming both the 1970 movie and the subsequent television series. Starting from the main trailhead near the campground, you'll be following the well-named Crags Road. Along the way you'll pass the camera-ready sandstone bluffs of Goat Buttes and experience wild California at its best. Coast live oak, valley oak, scrub oak, sycamore, and Mexican elderberry trees create a plant community that provides shade for us and shelter and food for many animals.

Before Europeans arrived, this was all Chumash territory. The word "Malibu" comes from a Chumash word, *humaliwo*, which means "the surf sounds loudly." Along the Malibu coast they hunted marine mammals, fished, and foraged for shellfish; inland they harvested acorns and a variety of wild berries and hunted rabbit and deer.

If you notice a large hawk turning in close circles on broad wings, it's probably the red-tailed hawk. Acorn woodpeckers, *yak-yak-yakking* and swooping tree to tree, are also long-time residents.

Nanday parakeets are more recent arrivals. Also called the nanday conure or black-headed parakeet, they are native to Brazil and Argentina, but escaped captivity to naturalize here. These foot-long birds are green with a black head and chin, red feathers on each leg, and blue-tipped wings. Look for them in sycamore trees with broken branches and hollow spots in the trunk, which they carve out with their sharp beaks to create nesting holes.

WHERE: 1925 Las Virgenes Road (at Mulholland Highway), Cornell, CA 91301; between 101 Freeway and Pacific Coast Highway.
PARKING: Parking lot fee required; limited street parking.
DIFFICULTY, DISTANCE, ACCESS: Easy to moderate. 3–4 miles is average; longer options possible.
FACILITIES: Bathrooms, picnic areas, and a campground.
BEST TIME: Year-round. Wildlife spotting is best early in the day.
SPECIAL NOTES: No dogs allowed beyond the parking and camping areas. Bring your bathing suit for the Rock Pool swimming hole.

Century Lake and the M*A*S*H Site

About halfway to the M*A*S*H site, a side trail leads to Century Lake. This human-made lake was created over one hundred years ago and on still days it reflects the surrounding cliffs like a mirror. Redwood trees, planted when the dam was built, still thrive here, offering a tiny glimpse into the ancient world, when saber-toothed cats roamed native redwood forests across Southern California. The top of the dam is off limits, but the lake is just a short detour from the main trail.

Staying on the main Crags Road trail takes you to the signpost and abandoned trucks that mark the M*A*S*H site. Just before you arrive at the site itself, the trail goes through a narrow, rocky section with a lot of dense, short trees. These arroyo willows help us know water is present just underground. Willows always mean there's water nearby, even if you can't see it or splash in it. Many of the streams in the park dry up by mid- to late-summer—to see the park at its wettest and lushest, visit in late winter or early spring. Most years, a few deeper sections of Malibu Creek and Las Virgenes Creek will keep water throughout the year. Look for non-native turtles and bullfrogs in these pools. This is also a good place to spot Pacific treefrogs.

▲ Listen for the Pacific treefrog's distinctive *ribbit*.

🚩 The famous M*A*S*H signpost framed by the ruins of an old ambulance.

▼ Century Lake has been a backdrop of many movies, including *Planet of the Apes* (1968).

TRIP 2

Chatsworth Oaks Park

Let kids be the leaders as you explore fun sandstone rock formations, oak trees, and historic trails at this ideal afternoon getaway.

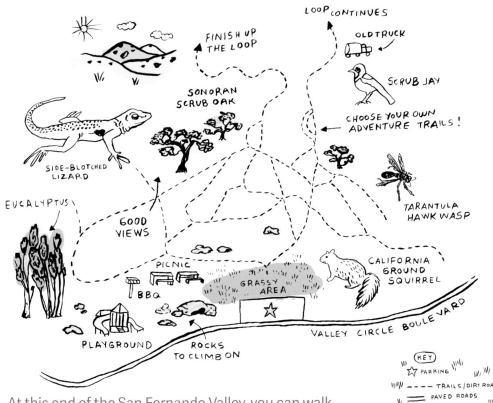

At this end of the San Fernando Valley, you can walk through the history of Los Angeles. Rocks tell the first part of the story: the tan sandstone was laid down under the ocean over sixty million years ago, far to the south. Layers of silt accumulated thousands of feet underwater and, with heat, pressure, and time, became solid rock. Plate tectonics brought the rock north and to the surface through a combination of uplift and erosion.

WHERE: 9301 Valley Circle Boulevard, Chatsworth, CA 91311

PARKING: Free off-street parking. Handicap parking available (but see access).

DIFFICULTY, DISTANCE, ACCESS: Easy. A network of trails provides a choose-your-own adventure day with short to medium length excursions. Trails mostly too rough for strollers and wheelchairs.

FACILITIES: Picnic tables, barbecue pits, and a playground.

BEST TIME: Can be done any time of day, any season. Hot in summer.

SPECIAL NOTES: This site is open dawn to dusk, all year, and there's no entrance fee. Chatsworth Nature Preserve (the large park across the street) is open only select days of the year. Keep your dog on a leash to keep it out of poison oak and away from bridle paths.

Stone quarried near here helped build Los Angeles. Chatsworth sandstone shows up everywhere, from churches in Pasadena to the breakwater at San Pedro.

Originally, these rocks were gray. A chemical change called oxidation (essentially, iron in the stone "rusting") gave them their warm, orange color. A darker sheen shows up too. Called "desert varnish," this layer of orange-yellow to black rock is formed from windborne particles—clay and other substances—that chemically bind to each other when it is particularly hot outside.

The stagecoach route to San Francisco from downtown Los Angeles passed near here and climbed up over Santa Susana Pass. Views enjoyed by stagecoach travelers also attracted movie and TV producers—many Westerns were filmed nearby in the 1940s and 50s.

During the Cold War, Nike missiles on the hills around Chatsworth protected Los Angeles from the threat of Russian bombers, and engineers from the nearby Rocketdyne Test Center developed rocket engines. At one time, low-power nuclear reactors were in operation here, contributing to an urban legend about local glow-in-the dark cats.

▲ This park is named for oaks, but the tallest trees in it are these blue gum eucalyptus near the parking lot.

Nature and More Nature

▲ Watch for desert varnish while rock scrambling—it often makes a great handhold.

◀ Plate tectonics brought these layers of sandstone, formed below an ancient sea, to the surface here, providing a perfect spot for people and wildlife to scramble about.

◀ If a huge insect helicopters past you, it's likely a tarantula hawk wasp.

Your nature study can begin in the parking lot. The huge central tree is an oak, almost certainly several hundred years old, and the tall eucalyptus trees on the edge of the grassy play area are blue gums.

Listen for the *yak-yak-yak* of an acorn woodpecker and keep an eye out for flocks of blue scrub-jays making their rounds through the park. The smaller flitting songbirds might be lesser goldfinches—watch for a yellow tummy and black cap—or they may be yellow-rumped warblers, whose jaunty daub of yellow earns them the folk name "butter butts." Both species sometimes drink at the dog bowls put out near the water fountains. The dinky, all-gray birds in chittering, fast-moving flocks are usually bushtits.

Tarantula hawks, those large, blue-black wasps with orange wings, sometimes show up near the parking lot too. They won't bother you unless you bother them. Watching calmly presents little risk.

You may see red-tailed hawks working up the ridges or circling on rising columns of warm air (called thermals). They patrol the hills in search of food and nesting materials. Also riding the thermals are large, black, slightly less graceful birds that fly with a rocking motion on stiff, V-shaped wings—these are turkey vultures. They only eat dead food, called carrion, which they can find by sight but especially by smell—the "smell-o-vision" parts of their brains are particularly large. Sometimes they skim right over the trees with inches to spare, and if they're low enough to the ground, you can make out their red, naked heads.

The casual hiker who begins scrambling over the rock formations at Chatsworth Oaks may later end up climbing at Stoney Point—the tall, sandstone summit 2.5 miles to the northeast. For decades, Stoney Point has been a training ground for Southern Californians who have gone on to become some of America's greatest rock climbers.

◄ Keep an eye out for native sugar bush. Its berries attract lots of birds.

◄ California ground squirrels thrive in open, grassy areas throughout the park.

◄◄ A turkey vulture waits for the morning air to warm, so it can ride the thermals and look for roadkill or other carrion.

Best Hikes to Try

As you gain a bit of altitude over the parking lot, look south, and you can see a large, fenced-off nature reserve, ending in a distant hill. That hill is the 1919 dam for Chatsworth Reservoir, once part of the water supply system of the LA Aqueduct but no longer in service because the dam doesn't meet current earthquake standards.

At this park, it's up to you to create your own route. The further you get from the road (and the earlier you're out), the better your chance for spotting a shyer animal like a ground squirrel or a flock of quail. There are many short, kid-friendly options radiating out from the parking lot. Appoint a leader and let fate be your guide—most trails loop back to the main park sooner or later, and open views make it pretty hard to get turned around. When in doubt, just go back downhill, listening for the occasional passing car and taking the wider, more heavily used path at each junction.

TRIP 3

Sepulveda Basin Wildlife Reserve

Visit this hidden oasis to look for some of the reserve's 267 species of birds and celebrate the "start" of the LA River.

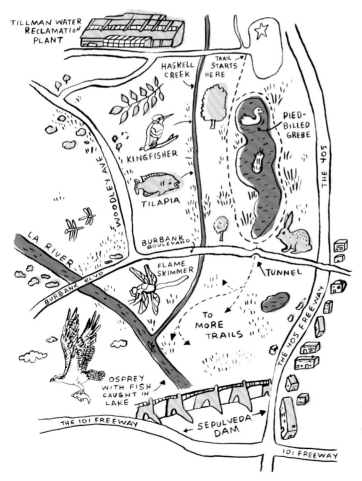

WHERE: 5600 Woodley Avenue, Van Nuys, CA 91411

PARKING: Free parking in paved lot close to the 405 and 101 freeways. Handicap parking available.

DIFFICULTY, DISTANCE, ACCESS: Easy. Less than a mile (or connect segments to hike further). Mostly level, wide paths accessible to strollers and wheelchairs.

FACILITIES: Restrooms and picnic tables at the parking lot.

BEST TIME: Bird diversity is highest from October to April.

SPECIAL NOTE: No dogs allowed.

217

Ospreys snatching carp, egrets nesting in trees, California towhees, and desert cottontails scurrying off early-morning paths—something always is going on here, especially in winter and especially before the glaring hot sun of a midsummer day.

To find the reserve, turn off Woodley Avenue and drive past the cricket fields to the last parking area you can find. Restrooms (and sometimes volunteers with loaner binoculars) are here, next to handsome, white-barked sycamores and lawns full of gopher mounds.

The trail around the main lake can't be seen from the parking lot, but just head downhill away from the lawns. Once you reach the tall coyote brush (often frosted with pale flowers), the main loop trail will come into view.

◄ A baby cottontail sniffs the air for danger.

This site is listed as a "birding hotspot" on eBird.org. You can review species checklists the night before your visit and find out which bird species you're most likely to see.

Birdwatching Made Easy

Many of the birds in the species identification section of this book can be spotted by the lake. You may also discover a white pelican, a serene flotilla of Canada geese, or the submarining dive-and-surface of a pied-billed grebe. Hawks and turkey vultures circle overhead, and male red-winged blackbirds perch on lakeside bushes and cattails, loudly claiming their territory.

► Red-winged blackbirds can be found near marshes and lakes throughout Southern California.

▼ A young black-crowned night heron stalks non-native mosquitofish.

The male red-winged blackbird is glossy black with red-and-yellow wing patches, like decorative shoulder pads. Its liquid, oddly gurgling call is easy to identify. It usually gets typed out as *konkk-luh-reeee*—but it's easier to hear than to transcribe. Any spring visit will teach it to you quickly. You can find blackbirds here year-round, even when they're not yodeling.

The big, dark birds with long tails that look glued on sideways are great-tailed grackles. Itty-bitty bushtits chitter in nervous, always-on-the-go flocks, investigating bushes and the lower branches of trees. Mid-sized birds include towhees, sparrows, thrashers, and robins. As at most birdwatching sites, walking quietly and being out early usually brings best results. On weekends, you'll see photographers out with their fanciest cameras and longest lenses, all waiting for that perfect shot.

Turtles and Trees

Side trails west of the main lake will take you to Haskell Creek. Watch for belted kingfishers, non-native red-eared slider turtles, nesting mallards and wood ducks, and schools of non-native fish, mostly tilapia and mosquitofish.

Shamel ash trees, native to Mexico and now found all over Southern California, line the creek, mixing with native plants like mulefat, California walnut, elderberry, western ragwort, and mugwort. Of course, the usual non-native and invasive species can be found here too—castor bean, fennel, thistle, and mustard. Restoration efforts attempting to suppress introduced plants and replace them with native species make this area a perpetual work-in-progress, with lots of volunteer opportunities for anybody who wants to help.

The tall, more open canopy trees with solid, corrugated gray trunks and green, heart-shaped leaves are Fremont cottonwoods. Summer cottonwood leaves often flutter in the slightest wind, creating a mosaic of shimmering shade. In the fall, leaves turn yellow, red, and brown, while in winter the cottonwoods are bare, budding out again in February and March.

You'll also find willow and eucalyptus trees here—botanically, this site is a good example of blended nature, with native and non-native species hashing it out, side by side.

Haskell Creek and the Birth of the LA River

The Sepulveda Basin is close to the start of the LA River (it technically begins where Calabasas and Bell Creeks join a bit farther upstream). Here at the Sepulveda Dam, more water is added from the Donald Tillman Reclamation Plant as it releases water into Haskell Creek.

What's a reclamation plant? Wash your hands, run the dishwasher, or go to the bathroom, and that dirty water has to go somewhere. In a city like Los Angeles, this is a substantial amount of wastewater—hundreds of millions of gallons per day. In the San Fernando Valley, wastewater flows through an elaborate network of sewer pipes to Tillman—which trivia buffs will

◄ Morning mists and beautiful scenes can be found just a few hundred yards from the 405 Freeway.

> The LA River right above the Sepulveda dam is a prime spot for local kayaking. The area opens as a recreation zone on Memorial Day and usually runs through Labor Day—check the Mountains Recreation & Conservation Authority's website (mrca.ca.gov) for details and links to kayak tour providers.

recognize as Starfleet Academy in *Star Trek*—where it is cleaned and released. Although the LA River's water volume also includes natural spring water, rainfall, street runoff, and side tributaries, most of the flow in the dry season starts here at the Tillman plant.

FLOOD CONTROL AND FREEWAYS

One interesting man-made feature found on the lake's loop trail is a stone monument as tall as a person. An inscription on the base explains, "At a two-year flood level, the water would be at your feet. At a twenty-year flood level, the water would be three times higher than this stone. At a fifty-year flood level, the water would be four times higher than this stone."

In other words, if we want to keep having a city where we have a city now, we need dams like this one. It and Hansen Dam (further north by the 210 Freeway) are here not because there *could* be flooding, but because there *was* flooding. At the time of construction, the area was mostly ranches and orchards—since then the city has flowed up and around the dam all the way to Santa Clarita—a reverse flood of houses, roadways, businesses, and restaurants. Without controlling, delivering, and managing water, there could be no city here. You can get a good view of the dam from the 101 Freeway just west of the 405.

Go West

If you want longer walks than the bird stroll inside the main reserve, bridges cross Haskell Creek and trails zigzag west and north back out to Woodley Avenue (where you can park). At the bottom end of the lake there's a path that parallels the 405, then enters a tunnel under Burbank Boulevard to access scrubby fields and a network of trails between the lake and the 101 Freeway. You'll rejoin Haskell Creek on this side of the roadway and can follow it all the way to the LA River itself.

TRIP 4

Rustic Canyon

Hiking along an oak-shaded stream offers cool temperatures on hot days. Explore the remains of a creepy ranch from the 1930s, and spot interesting birds and plants year-round.

WHERE: 1501 Will Rogers State Park Road, Pacific Palisades, CA 90272

PARKING: Free street parking on Amalfi Drive (near intersection with Capri Drive); walk a short way up Capri Drive and Casale Road to Murphy Ranch trailhead.

DIFFICULTY, DISTANCE, ACCESS: Moderate. Three miles round trip is average; longer options possible. Not suitable for strollers or wheelchairs.

FACILITIES: No bathrooms or picnic areas unless you go to Will Rogers State Historic Park.

BEST TIME: Good year-round with the most wildlife likely early in the day.

SPECIAL NOTE: No dogs. There's an entrance fee for Will Rogers State Historic Park.

SULLIVAN FIRE ROAD TO "DIRT" MULHOLLAND DRIVE

TO CAMP JOSEPHO BOY SCOUT CAMP (PRIVATE PROPERTY)

REDWOODS

MURPHY RANCH

JOSEPHO SPUR TRAIL

STEEP

SULLIVAN FIRE ROAD

STAIRS

RIDGETOP TRAIL

TO THE "HUB"

TOPANGA STATE PARK

RUFOUS-SIDED TOWHEE

POWER BUILDING

BACKBONE TRAIL

RUSTIC CREEK

GATE

INSPIRATION POINT

RUSTIC CANYON TRAIL (UNMAINTAINED)

CASALE

SOUTHERN ALLIGATOR LIZARD

AMALFI

SORRENTO

WILL ROGERS STATE HISTORIC PARK

POLO FIELD

CAPRI

AMALFI DRIVE

SUNSET BOULEVARD

KEY
☆ PARKING
---- TRAILS / DIRT ROADS
═══ PAVED ROADS
═══ BIKE PATHS

POISON OAK

WESTERN SYCAMORE

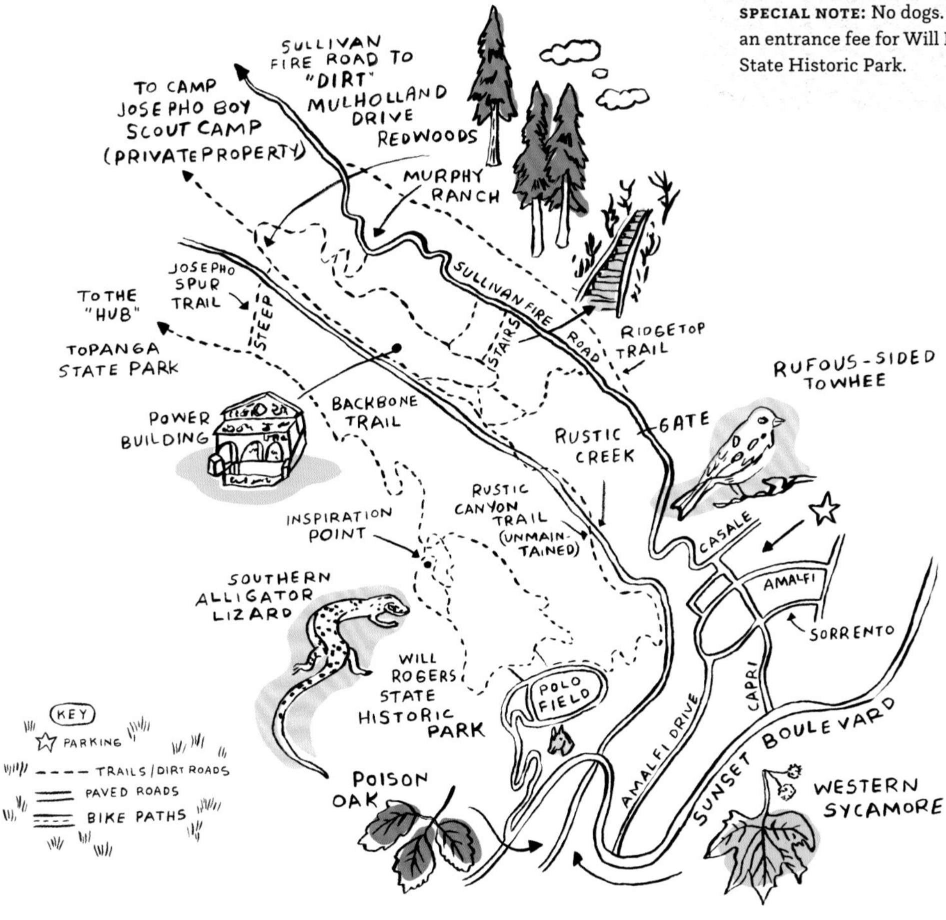

Rustic Canyon is home to the fabled ruins of Murphy Ranch, but even without these surreal and heavily-tagged structures, this hike to a cool, shady stream would still be a favorite among LA nature lovers. You start up high, on a fire road that offers views from the Pacific Ocean to the mountains, then traverse bands of native brush to drop down into the surprisingly cool and welcoming inner canyon. Water runs here even in summer, flowing out of springs higher up the canyon.

The stream-fed vegetation here is an example of riparian habitat—a fiesta of willow trees, sycamores, frogs, native flowers, and running water creates a plant community once found throughout the canyon bottoms of the LA foothills. Take a deep breath: the air smells wet, not quite a river and not quite a marsh, but a blend of both. Many riparian zones in the Southland have been turned into houses and streets—Rustic Canyon lets us experience California's not-that-distant past.

▲ Poison oak is common in the cooler, shaded canyons of the Santa Monica Mountains. Stay on the trails to avoid it.

▼ This shady tree-filled canyon provides a welcome respite from summer heat.

Nature's Air Conditioning

To reach the canyon, park on the wide, well-tended streets of the Riviera neighborhood north of Sunset Boulevard. Walk west to pick up Sullivan Fire Road and follow that north along the top of the canyon. Trails drop into the canyon from this main fire road, with hundreds of concrete steps, seemingly going straight up and down.

Experienced hikers can come in from the bottom of the canyon, starting in Will Rogers State Historic Park and following the creek upstream from there. Expect wet feet and poison oak as the price of adventure.

Whatever your approach, you'll end up at Murphy Ranch, about a third of the way between the beach and Mulholland Drive. In the shade of willows, oaks, and sycamores, the temperature will be twenty degrees cooler than on the sunny hillside. Think of it as nature's air conditioning, making this excursion an especially good one for summer (still bring water, sunscreen, and a hat for the hot chaparral sections into and out of the canyon).

Not-Quite-Native Redwoods

In the canyon bottom, at the top end of Murphy Ranch are redwood trees, considered non-native to this area. However, not that long ago, probably as recently as 15,000 years ago, during the time when the La Brea Tar Pits were trapping mammoths, saber-toothed cats, and dire wolves, redwoods were found farther south than they are today, including here in the coastal canyons of the Santa Monica Mountains. While 15,000 years may sound like a lot, this is only about eight redwood tree lifespans. In that relatively short time, the range of redwoods has retracted northward.

These Murphy Ranch trees, however, show us that conditions aren't all that off for redwoods to survive in coastal Southern California. If the region received a bit more moisture, redwoods could make a comeback. Although Murphy Ranch has been unoccupied for decades, these trees are still able to get enough moisture to survive in this steep, shaded canyon. A handful of the trees died in the prolonged 2011–2016 drought, but some are still holding on, forcing us to ponder the definition of native. If they were here eight redwood generations ago, and are still found two hundred miles to the north, then what makes them non-native?

▼ Murphy Ranch graffiti makes for a surreal urban nature experience.

A Lost Nazi Hideout?

Some people call this trip the Nazi Ranch hike. That oversimplifies things a bit. Although rumors are as thick as June gloom fog, what seems to be true is that an eccentric couple, Norman and Winona Stevens, hired a series of top-shelf architects in the 1930s and 40s to draw up plans for a four-story mansion and related infrastructure. On paper it was a sort of "Hearst Castle South," and may or may not have been affiliated with plans for a pro-Nazi utopian colony—some names have been removed from surviving documents and pseudonyms abound.

In the end, nothing large was ever built, though fuel tanks, workshops, and outbuildings survive. After World War II they were abandoned, and in time became colorfully painted

and systematically vandalized. After the Fire Department had to rescue one person too many from unstable structures, the City of Los Angeles began boarding up some buildings and tearing down others. Don't worry—if you like to photograph graffiti, plenty of painted walls remain.

Nature doesn't need spray paint to be colorful, though. On this hike you might see a robin-sized bird sporting a chestnut vest under a jet-black topcoat, the spotted towhee. Males sing from exposed perches, but usually you'll see one or two birds shuffling around in shaded leaf litter, hoping to uncover beetles and spiders. They also like poison oak berries. If a snake is in the area, towhees join the other understory birds to fuss and scold—what ornithologists call "mobbing." They surround the predator and hiss their displeasure at the enemy in their midst.

Walking back to the car, look for the matilija poppy—large, floppy petals and a yellow center make it easy to spot. This is the largest flower of any California native plant; it was suggested for the state flower in 1890 but lost the vote to the orange poppy we know so well. Why limit ourselves to only one? Maybe California could have two or three or even ten state flowers—as this hike can show, we have many to choose from.

▲ Matilija poppies are also called fried egg plants.

🐁 Arriving early (or staying late) makes it easier to discover nighttime residents like this curious brush mouse.

▼ Look for the spotted towhee on the ground, scratching among the bushes.

Ballona Wetlands

Follow Ballona Creek to the Pacific Ocean
and explore fresh and saltwater wetlands.
An observation platform in the saltwater
marsh offers great birdwatching.

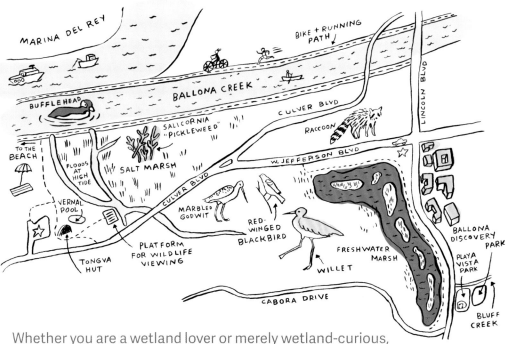

MARINA DEL REY

BIKE + RUNNING PATH

BALLONA CREEK

BUFFLEHEAD

CULVER BLVD

TO THE BEACH

SALICORNIA "PICKLEWEED"

RACCOON

LINCOLN BLVD

FLOODS AT HIGH TIDE

SALT MARSH

W. JEFFERSON BLVD

VERNAL POOL

CULVER BLVD

MARBLED GODWIT

RED-WINGED BLACKBIRD

BALLONA DISCOVERY PARK

PLATFORM FOR WILDLIFE VIEWING

FRESHWATER MARSH

PLAYA VISTA PARK

TONGVA HUT

WILLET

CABORA DRIVE

BLUFF CREEK

Whether you are a wetland lover or merely wetland-curious,
Ballona will help you get your fill of this unique habitat. The wetlands in the
Ballona area used to be extensive, covering almost two thousand acres—
approximately half the area of Griffith Park. Most of that land is now developed,
but thanks to the work of some dedicated individuals, including the Friends
of Ballona Wetlands, six hundred acres of precious habitat (about 450 football
fields' worth) have been preserved as a state ecological reserve. There are saltwater and freshwater marshes, vernal pools, and even remnant coastal sand
dunes. Much of the six hundred acres is off limits to visitors. It is one of the
few remaining places in coastal Los Angeles where marsh birds (and hundreds

KEY

☆ PARKING

‑ ‑ ‑ ‑ TRAILS / DIRT ROADS

═══ PAVED ROADS

▭▭▭ BIKE PATHS

Marshes are low-lying areas where the ground is generally waterlogged at all times and regularly inundated with water (at high tide or in the wet season).

▲ These pilings mark where a railroad bridge once crossed the wetlands.

of other species) can flock without being disrupted by humans. To get an idea of what much of Los Angeles used to look like, or to spy on the hidden lives of marsh-dwelling animals and plants, head down to this sliver of land between Marina del Rey and Playa Vista.

There are three areas to visit at Ballona—Discovery Park, the freshwater marsh, and the saltwater marsh. Both Discovery Park and the freshwater marsh are open daily for walking, bird watching, or just soaking in the view. The saltwater marsh is only open a few days each month when LA Audubon hosts their "Open Wetlands" days (info at losangelesaudubon.org) and the Friends of Ballona Wetlands lead marsh tours (info at ballonafriends.org).

History of Ballona

Two hundred years ago, not long after the city was first settled, it was really hard to reach Ballona and the adjacent coastline. But as Los Angeles's population grew and the Pacific Electric cable-rail lines were built, many more Angelenos were able get to the beach. The increase in beachgoers drove development. Restaurants, hotels, and other amenities were built

over the wetlands. Thanks to the automobile boom, this trend continued. Today, the wetlands still feel the pressure of human expansion, but efforts by concerned community members, the staff and volunteers of local non-profit groups, and local government agencies help protect this precious habitat.

BALLONA BACK IN TIME

Imagine time-traveling to three hundred years ago and standing at what is now the intersection of Jefferson and Lincoln boulevards. You find yourself in the middle of a giant wetland that extends in all directions. There are marshes fed by saltwater from the ocean, and freshwater marshes filled by rain and by the countless creeks and streams that crisscross the landscape. The roar of traffic becomes the calls of thousands of birds, and car exhaust is replaced by a salty tang in the air.

The Ballona lagoon, a salt-water lake separated from the ocean by sand dunes, is close by. The place is alive with plants and animals, and there are humans too. The Gabrieleño/Tongva search for shellfish and other marine delicacies. In the distance you see smoke from a fire and the outline of many domed structures called *kiiy*. They're built from the same reeds that line the water's edge.

No Gabrieleño/Tongva villages remain today, but you can see a model kiiy at Discovery Park. To learn more about the Gabrieleño/Tongva people, visit the Kuruvungna Springs Cultural Center and Museum in the Sawtelle neighborhood.

> The LA River used to turn sharply westward near present-day downtown, flow to Santa Monica Bay, and empty into the Pacific Ocean via today's Ballona Creek. An 1825 flood carved a new channel that headed south, meeting the ocean in Long Beach instead.

WHY ARE WETLANDS IMPORTANT?

The remaining wetlands are still home to many animals. Ballona is an important stop on the Pacific Flyway, so it's no surprise that dedicated bird watchers have counted 320 species of birds in the area around Ballona (including both the salt- and freshwater wetlands, the bluffs, parks, and the adjacent residential neighborhoods). On any given day during spring or fall

► A male bufflehead duck shows off its distinctive white and dark color pattern. These are most commonly observed in the lower reaches of Ballona Creek and at the freshwater marsh.

◀ Rare in urban Los Angeles, the burrowing owl nests on the ground and even hunts in the middle of the day. Burrowing owls are reported from the Ballona Wetlands more than any other place in the LA area, usually from October through March.

migrations, hundreds of birds can be seen by eye and through binoculars, including the phalarope, a slim-billed sandpiper that flies all the way to and from the Arctic.

Without these wetlands, migrating birds would have a near impossible time making their long journeys. They need wetlands like we need freeway rest stops, a place to relax and grab a bite to eat to fuel up for the journey ahead. But these marshes are for more than just the birds. They're also fish nurseries, water and air filtration systems, places for groundwater to refill aquifers and buffer zones that help protect human homes and other property from floods.

Saltwater Marshes

Just down Jefferson towards the beach is the saltwater marsh. Although this part of the wetlands is only open to the public a few days each month, it's well worth a visit. You can join a guided tour or explore the trails at your own pace.

A number of crisscross trails explore the marsh, but your best bet is to make a bee-line for the observation deck that sits almost in the middle of the salty habitat and is a great spot to look for marsh wildlife. Over 220 species of birds have been recorded in this location. There are common species like brown pelicans, mallard ducks, and California gulls, and many other shorebirds of the long-legged and long-billed variety.

Shorebirds, as their name implies, hang out along the edges of water. Their long legs and splayed feet allow them to walk through the mud without sinking or getting stuck. Tiny clams and crustaceans burrow and hide in the sticky-dark ooze, but shorebirds' long bills allow them to dig deep and find their favorite snacks. Many shorebirds have bills equipped with extra sensitive tissue at the end, which allows them to know when they've found something worth eating.

▶ The whimbrel's curved beak helps it find food on the water's edge.

A SALTY PLANT: PICKLEWEED

Done with shorebird identification? The observation platform is also a great spot to look for an edible salt-loving plant—pickleweed, also known as *Salicornia*. Pickleweed is a *halophyte,* a plant adapted to high salt environments. It grows all along the banks of Ballona's saltwater marsh and can be seen on menus or sold in grocery stores labeled as sea beans, sea asparagus, or glasswort. The small shoots are crunchy with a salty aftertaste. They're best harvested in summer when they're bright green. As autumn approaches the plants turn red and develop a tough inner core, which is much less appetizing. Harvesting pickleweed isn't allowed in these protected wetlands, but you can try growing it in pots in your garden at home. Bon appétit!

Seasonal Vernal Pools

Visiting in spring means you might miss some overwintering birds, but after heavy rains the wetlands have many other things to offer. Wildflowers sprout along the trails, snails come out from their hiding spots, and the vernal pool fills up. Vernal pools are seasonal wetlands that fill with spring rains and go dry during the summer. In Southern California, our vernal pools are dry more than they are wet. Still, after significant rains, they fill up and explode with life for a few weeks. As raindrops fall, the tiny fairy-shrimp slumbering in the earth sense it's time for action. Hundreds of tiny eggs, pupa, seeds, and other

When full, the vernal pool at Ballona Wetlands is home to thousands of fairy shrimp. These tiny, translucent crustaceans swim upside down using eleven pairs of leaf-like legs which also facilitate breathing and feeding. After heavy rain, look for them feeding on algae and plankton at the pool's surface.

Prior to urban development, the El Segundo Sand Dunes wrapped around the coastline of the Santa Monica Bay. Some reached 150 feet in elevation! Remnants of this once massive dune complex can be found here at Ballona Wetlands and at the coastal end of LAX's runways. The hilly streets of western El Segundo, Manhattan Beach, Hermosa Beach, and Redondo Beach remind us that sand dunes once stretched across this area. In Manhattan Beach, Sand Dune Park and Polliwog Park—named for the spadefoot toad tadpoles that once thrived in vernal pools—are also reminders of the sandy past.

suspended life-forms transform from their dormant state into their fast-paced pond lifestyle. Fish can't usually access these pools, which allows these tiny creatures a chance to thrive without predators.

Sand Dunes

Any place with lots of sand and wind strong enough to move it will have coastal sand dunes. Once formed, dunes protect the area behind them from wind and waves and provide a place for plants to grow. Here at Ballona, expensive homes and beachfront property stand where most of the dunes used to be. The eight acres of remaining dunes are blanketed with ice plant, a fast-growing succulent that was initially introduced to keep the dunes from moving. Unfortunately, ice plant forms dense mats that outcompete native plants—now volunteers spend time removing it from the dunes and re-planting native species.

Extend Your Trip

After walking all the trails around the saltwater marsh, you can extend your trip by heading down Ballona Creek to the beach. As you walk along the paved bike path, you might spot California sea lions in the creek. With each step toward the ocean, think about what this space looked like before all the houses, hotels, and shops were built and why it's so vitally important to protect the few fragments of habitat that remain.

TRIP 6

Kenneth Hahn State Recreation Area

Enjoy some of the city's most stunning views of the San Gabriel Mountains and downtown Los Angeles. Grassy banks for kids to roll down and hilly trails to climb.

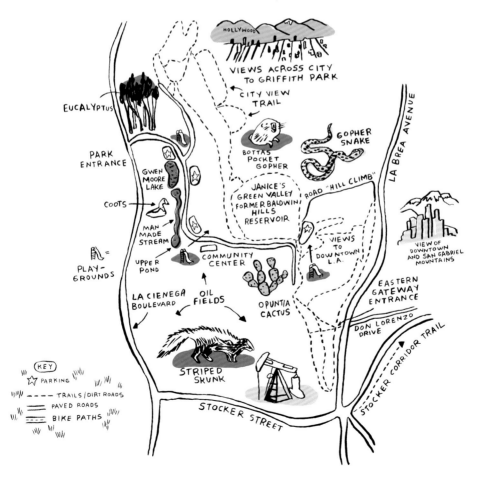

On the border between Culver City and Los Angeles, Kenneth Hahn State Recreation Area rises above the city and offers a bird's-eye-view of Los Angeles. The park sits at the eastern end of the Baldwin Hills, a low mountain range which rises above the city between the communities of Baldwin Hills, Leimert Park, Inglewood, and Culver City. Thanks to oil, water, and steep slopes, these hills were saved from the creep of tract-home developments. Today, the park welcomes people from all over Los Angeles to hike the seven miles of trails, fish in the lake, or simply sit in the grassy bowl of a long-disused reservoir.

▲ A clear wintertime view of downtown Los Angeles with the San Gabriel Mountains in the distance.

WHERE: 4100 South La Cienega Boulevard, Los Angeles, CA 90056

PARKING: Free parking weekdays. Fees apply weekends and holidays.

DIFFICULTY, DISTANCE, ACCESS: Variable, but mostly easy. Some of the trails and paths are wheelchair and stroller accessible.

FACILITIES: Bathrooms, playgrounds, and picnic amenities.

BEST TIME: Immediately after winter storms clear, smog-free air and snow-capped mountains behind downtown Los Angeles provide a spectacular view.

Oil and Water

The Inglewood Oil Field was discovered near here in 1924. Today, from some of the park's hilltops, you can still see hundreds of giant, bird-like machines bobbing up and down. They're called pumpjacks, and every day they pump 7,500 barrels of oil out of the country's largest urban oil field.

In 1947, the LA Department of Water and Power began construction on a large dam and reservoir. However, a great place for drilling oil turns out to be not such a great place to build a dam. It sat on an active fault line, and over the years the land beneath the reservoir shifted. On December 14, 1963, the

▲ Water pouring from the Baldwin Hills reservoir after the dam's collapse.

◄ The dam's failure flooded the community below with 292 million gallons of water.

dam collapsed. KTLA news helicopters televised the whole catastrophe—five deaths and the loss of five hundred homes—in one of the first broadcasts of live aerial footage.

Today these 401 acres are protected for the people and wildlife of Los Angeles. The site of the former reservoir is now the grassy bowl of Janice's Green Valley. That industrialized oil drilling and dam building are responsible for such a tranquil scene is yet another example of Los Angeles's ever-changing relationship with nature.

Paths for Wildlife and Humans

These hills are habitat for some species that have been displaced by urban sprawl in the LA Basin. When the park is open you can see animals and plants of all sorts. But what about at night? Scientists from the Natural History Museum put motion activated cameras in the hills to see what animals use the park after dark. As expected they saw coyotes and raccoons, but they were happily surprised when gray foxes turned up. It turns out the park and surrounding Baldwin Hills are full of wildlife, some here because of humans (abandoned cats, dogs, and rabbits), some because they tend to do well near urban areas (raccoons, opossums, mice, and rats), and some because this space is far enough from urbanization that they can make do (the gray fox).

Humans are taking the hint, building a new thirteen-mile trail to increase connectivity between wildlife habitats. Once it's completed, people and animals will be able to safely walk all the way from Kenneth Hahn State Recreation Area to Venice Beach. The trail is scheduled to open in 2019, and scientists will be interested in seeing which animals use the new path.

Coastal Sage Scrub Wonders

Parts of this park are covered with coastal sage scrub habitat. Among the usual scrub habitat suspects, you'll spot coastal prickly pear cactus. In places it adorns hillsides like a giant prickly blanket. Starting in

late spring prickly pears set forth their bright reddish-purple-colored fruits—called *tuna* in Spanish and prickly pear in English—the La Tuna Canyon offramp on the 210 Freeway, and the wildfire that burned here in the autumn of 2017, are named for them.

The fruits are edible and can be turned into jams and candies or used as a novelty ingredient in cocktails. The spiny pads of the cactus are also delicious. The spines are a defense mechanism for protection from hungry animals, but people have been removing spines and eating cactus pads in salads, salsas, and stews for centuries.

Birdwatchers have identified 174 species of birds in the park. It would be a surprise for visitors not to see black phoebes flitting around the grassy areas looking for insects. Down by the fishing pond, water birds are in residence year-round. Mallards and American coots are easy to spot any time, but keep a close eye out for smaller creatures. Aquatic snails cling to rocks along the pond's edge. If you take a moment to watch, you'll see them busy at work, scraping algae off the rocks with their tiny, rasping mouthparts—this is why aquarium owners love to keep snails in their tanks: free cleaning!

Although it's unlikely you'll see one of the Baldwin Hills' gophersnakes on your visit, you could easily spot their favorite food, the gopher. A giant clan of Botta's pocket gophers call the park home and you'll often see them peeking out of their well-engineered holes, weighing the need to find food with the desire to avoid predators. A not-so-wary gopher can become an unlucky bulge in a four-foot-long gopher snake's middle if it isn't careful.

Visiting the park throughout the year will reveal a surprise each season. Nesting birds in spring, lizards sunbathing in summer and fall, and mushrooms, snails, and slugs after winter rains.

▲ Look for the fan-shaped dirt mounds that mark the burrow entrances of Botta's pocket gophers.

▼ Prickly pear cactus tunas could end up on your toast.

Nature Gardens at the Natural History Museum in Exposition Park

Just four miles from downtown Los Angeles, visit a bee hotel, dip your toes in a fountain, and get elbow deep in a compost bin.

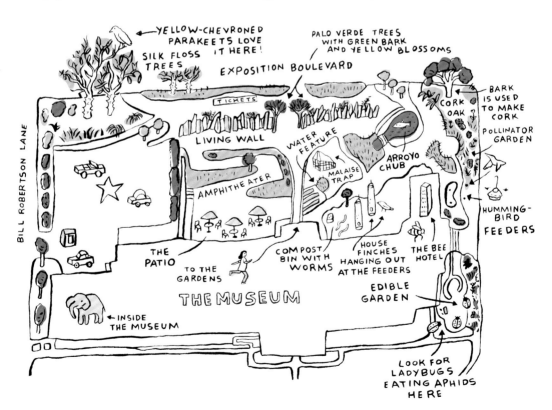

YELLOW-CHEVRONED PARAKEETS LOVE IT HERE!

SILK FLOSS TREES

PALO VERDE TREES WITH GREEN BARK AND YELLOW BLOSSOMS

EXPOSITION BOULEVARD

TICKETS

LIVING WALL

WATER FEATURE

MALAISE TRAP

ARROYO CHUB

CORK OAK

BARK IS USED TO MAKE CORK

POLLINATOR GARDEN

AMPHITHEATER

BILL ROBERTSON LANE

HUMMING-BIRD FEEDERS

THE PATIO

TO THE GARDENS

COMPOST BIN WITH WORMS

HOUSE FINCHES HANGING OUT AT THE FEEDERS

THE BEE HOTEL

THE MUSEUM

EDIBLE GARDEN

INSIDE THE MUSEUM

LOOK FOR LADYBUGS EATING APHIDS HERE

All the bottles, plates, and other objects unearthed during construction of the Nature Gardens now live in the Museum's history collection, which houses approximately 650,000 objects documenting Los Angeles and Southern California history.

Imagine tearing up asphalt parking lots and thirsty lawns and planting an urban wilderness in their place. A few years ago, that is exactly what the Natural History Museum did.

Museum scientists wanted to create a space that looked and felt like Los Angeles's altered nature—a space where visitors could see native and introduced species of trees, shrubs, and wildlife from throughout the city. Every plant, every rock, every dead tree trunk was placed for maximum habitat value. If an animal couldn't eat it, drink it, live or hide in it, then it didn't make the cut. As a result, visitors are guaranteed to see a diversity of the area's wild neighbors any day they come.

▲ Pollen comes in a huge variety of colors. Look closely at this honey bee's pollen sacs. They're purple because it has been collecting purple pollen from this *Phacelia* plant.

◄ The Living Wall was designed to have lots of nooks and crannies where plants can grow and animals can hide.

Digging through History

As they dug the pond and removed the lawns, construction workers found interesting objects. An old medicine bottle here, a broken plate there, even parts of old agricultural machinery. Museum historians collected over one thousand objects and linked almost all of them to the late 1880s. There was once a racetrack right next to where the Museum sits now—with a grandstand to sit in and a saloon to drink at. The first automobile race in Los Angeles was held here, and some say a number of camel races, too! (Staff haven't found any camel bones yet.)

► Flame skimmer dragonflies are often seen resting on plants around the pond. They sit still and wait, not moving until something tasty flies by or a photographer gets too close.

◄ This pond is home to hundreds of tiny fish, called arroyo chub, and a variety of immature insects, from dragonfly and damselfly nymphs, to backswimmers and midges.

Natives and Newcomers Welcome

To explore the gardens, pick up a Museum map and take a walk—any path will do. Every day there's something different to discover. Look out for five fifty-foot floss silk trees. These green-barked trees were planted over fifty years ago, and Museum staff worked hard to protect them during construction. As one Museum scientist put it, "I can almost imagine elves swinging down from the branches as I walk beneath them." No elves live in these trees, but exotic parrots often visit. Yellow-chevroned parakeets are also frequent visitors, especially in springtime when they feed on the large seedpods.

LIFE IN THE CRACKS
Explore the Living Wall and take time to look in all the nooks and crannies for crickets, spiders, and snails. Draping rosemary scents the air with volatile oils. Gently rub the waxy coated leaves (the wax helps the plant stay hydrated) and take a whiff—delicious to us, but a huge deterrent for insects.

WATER WORLD

There are good views of the waterfall from the pond bridge or the dock, which is also a good spot to catch a glimpse of the creatures living in this underwater habitat. The only fish living in the pond are arroyo chub, introduced as a natural form of mosquito control. Once abundant in the LA River, today chub can only be found in its upper reaches. Camera traps have caught hundreds of birds and mammals stopping by the pond for a drink or a bath. You can see the images inside the Nature Lab.

BIRDS

Over 170 bird species have been documented in the Nature Gardens. The three best spots to see them are:

- At the pond, bathing and drinking in the area above the waterfall. American crows have been seen dunking bread rolls in the water to soften them up before eating.

- By the Wildlife Viewing Platform, where feeders offer niger seeds. Below the feeders, you can see dusky-colored mourning doves picking at the fallen seeds. The most common bird seen clinging to the feeders has a reddish colored head and brown body—the common house finch.

- By the sugar-water feeders, visited in all but the rainiest weather by hummingbirds. There are usually two species—Anna's and Allen's hummingbirds—but occasionally rufous hummingbirds pass through in late winter on their way to southern Alaska.

VACANCY AT THE BEE HOTEL

The Nature Gardens were planted to attract the many bees (almost five hundred species!) that live in Los Angeles County. A number of homes for bees have been set up around the garden. These are not your standard bee hives—they're for solitary native bees. Unlike honey bees, which live in a communal hive with one queen bee, solitary bees do all their own work—collecting their own food, building their own nests, laying their own eggs, and

▲ Don't throw away those old wooden fence posts, they can be reclaimed and turned into a hotel for native solitary bees. Over 200 quarter-inch holes, 3–4 inches deep, were drilled into the wood to make the Museum's bee hotels.

▼ The most common species seen at the Museum's bird feeders are house finches and lesser goldfinches.

◀ The Erika J. Glazer Family Edible Garden shows that food for humans and habitat for wildlife can coexist in the same space.

caring for their young. Don't worry about getting stung. Because they have no queen and hive to protect, solitary bees are quite docile and slow to use their stingers in defense. Museum scientists have discovered fifteen species of bees using the Nature Gardens as habitat.

FOOD FOR BUGS AND HUMANS

The raised beds of the Erika J. Glazer Family Edible Garden might remind you of the produce section at your local grocery store. Depending on the season, a variety of familiar and exotic fruits, herbs, and vegetables grow here—everything from tomatoes, basil, and eggplants (a pizza garden!), to less well-known garden offerings like peanuts (you won't be able to see them because they grow underground), okra, lemongrass, and papaya. This garden is also home to an array of beneficial bugs.

There are over ten species of ladybugs—from the locally abundant convergent ladybug to the less common twice-struck ladybug. Twice-struck ladybugs break the classic ladybug mold of a red beetle with black spots. Instead, they're black with two prominent red spots—hence the evocative name. More ladybugs mean fewer aphids and other undesirable insects—great news for the Museum gardeners.

Science in the Gardens

The gardens were designed to function as a field site for studying nature in Los Angeles. They're a place for Museum scientists and the public to work together. An insect trap is set up to study the small flying insects that call this patch of urban wilderness home. A bat detector sits atop a pole by the pond, listening for bat echolocation signals every night. And camera traps, like the one near the pond, are moved around the Gardens to monitor what happens after staff and visitors go home.

You can help study the Nature Gardens. Bring your smartphone and take pictures of the plants and animals you find, then email them to nature@nhm.org, tag them #NatureinLA on social media, or upload them directly to iNaturalist.org.

TRIP 8

Franklin Canyon Park

Hidden in a hard-to-find canyon above Beverly Hills is a small reservoir surrounded by cattails and trees. It's perfect for spotting wood ducks and basking turtles or staging a romantic picnic.

WHERE: 2600 Franklin Canyon Drive, Beverly Hills, CA 90210

PARKING: Free parking in multiple lots around the reservoir.

DIFFICULTY, DISTANCE, ACCESS: Easy loop around the reservoir is mostly level and paved, but watch out for cars when you're walking on the road. Extend your trip with five miles of trails.

FACILITIES: Bathrooms and nature exhibits at the Sooky Goldman Nature Center. Picnic tables around the reservoir and Heavenly Pond.

BEST TIME: Good year round, particularly to escape the heat of summer in the shaded areas around the water.

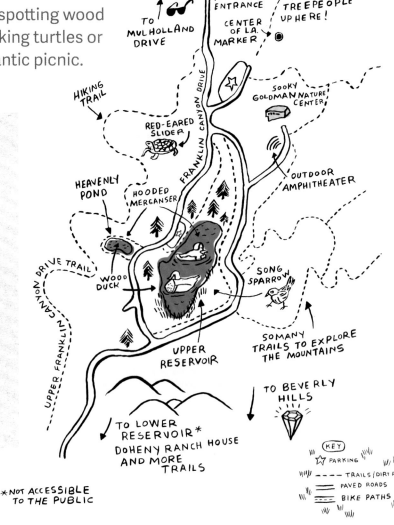

TO MULHOLLAND DRIVE

NORTH ENTRANCE

CENTER OF L.A. MARKER

TREE PEOPLE UP HERE!

HIKING TRAIL

SOOKY GOLDMAN NATURE CENTER

FRANKLIN CANYON DRIVE

RED-EARED SLIDER

OUTDOOR AMPHITHEATER

HEAVENLY POND

HOODED MERGANSER

WOOD DUCK

SONG SPARROW

UPPER FRANKLIN CANYON DRIVE TRAIL

UPPER RESERVOIR

SO MANY TRAILS TO EXPLORE THE MOUNTAINS

TO BEVERLY HILLS

TO LOWER RESERVOIR* DOHENY RANCH HOUSE AND MORE TRAILS

*NOT ACCESSIBLE TO THE PUBLIC

KEY
☆ PARKING
- - - - TRAILS / DIRT R
═══ PAVED ROADS
▬▬▬ BIKE PATHS

▲ The scenic upper reservoir is a popular filming location.

Franklin Canyon may seem familiar. Thanks to its proximity to Hollywood, the park has appeared in hundreds of TV shows and films. Most infamously, the reservoir appears in the 1954 classic *Creature from the Black Lagoon*. Maybe this is one reason there is no swimming or fishing allowed in the reservoir! It was also the spooky setting for scenes from *A Nightmare on Elm Street*, *Silence of the Lambs*, and *Twin Peaks*.

The Mountains Recreation and Conservation Authority operates traffic cameras in the park—be sure to come to a complete stop at the stop signs!

This park owes a lot to two very powerful early Angelenos, William Mulholland and Edward Doheny. In 1914 Mulholland and the LA Department of Water and Power constructed two reservoirs in Franklin Canyon—one in the upper canyon, and a larger one in the lower canyon. Then in 1935, oil baron Edward L. Doheny built his family a summer retreat and cattle ranch, part of which is still standing today. This protected the area for a time, but in the 1970s, activists had to step in to block planned residential developments.

In 1981, the National Park Service purchased 605 acres in the canyon—including the three-acre, upper reservoir. Today, you can visit the nature center named after Sooky Goldman, a prominent activist in the fight to protect this green space. The center is operated by the Santa Monica Mountains Conservancy and has variable open hours. Stop in to chat with a ranger or a volunteer Wednesday through Sunday to find out about programs and check out exhibits on local plants, animals, and cultural history.

◄ Franklin Canyon's ponds are good places to look for frogs and turtles, although the most common species, like this bullfrog or the ubiquitous red-eared sliders, are both introduced to California.

"Real" Nature

During World War II, the cottony fluff from cattail seed heads was used to stuff mattresses, life vests, and baseballs.

Along much of the banks of the reservoir thick growths of cattails—a common wetland plant—obscure your view. They are great for wildlife to hide in and are easiest to identify when the seed heads are present. Look for a brown, cigar-like growth that is velvety to the touch. Eventually, these disintegrate into a mass of cottony fluff and the individual seeds are carried away by the wind.

Take a walk under the low hanging branches of the deodar cedar near the reservoir—brush your hands over the short, spiky, green needles and take a whiff. The needles are scented with oils—including cedrol, used by the ancient Egyptians to embalm bodies—which help the tree protect itself from attacks by insects and fungi. This elegant evergreen tree is originally from the Himalayas. The reservoir isn't natural either. No matter how good it feels to us, here's something to contemplate—what makes nature authentic?

Introduced species aren't "supposed" to be here. They can wreak havoc on native species and ecosystems. But then again, today's migrating birds rely on this "unnatural" body of water. Nature in Los Angeles offers no easy answers to tough questions.

Birds Birds Everywhere (Also Turtles)

To see the maximum number of birds at this site, your best approach is silence. However, there are many species to see even if your group has trouble staying quiet. Community scientists and bird enthusiasts have documented 150 bird species in the upper canyon, and 90 in the lower

▲ Sapsucker holes create a mini version of the La Brea Tar Pits for insects, and a bonanza of sweet sap and insect protein for the bird to eat.

◀ Franklin Canyon is one of the best sites in the area to see wood ducks like this handsome male.

▶ Hooded mergansers dive beneath the surface to chase small fish.

canyon. The reservoir is home to year-round residents like the mallard ducks, while spring and fall migrants stop by for a break from their travels along the Pacific Flyway.

While wandering the trails, keep your eyes open for lines of small holes around tree branches and trunks. These are made by red-breasted sapsuckers. Every year, some of these striking woodpeckers fly down from Western Canada and the Pacific Northwest to spend the winter in our mild climate. Their name tells you something about how they feed—think of them as avian syrup farmers. They drill regular lines of holes, each about the size of BB gun shot, to tap the trees for their sweet sap. Throughout the day they revisit the holes to sip on the sap that's leaked out and feast on any insects caught in the sticky mess.

Many people admire the iridescent-green heads of male mallard ducks, but the wood ducks that live year-round at Heavenly Pond give them a run for their money in the costume department. As with most other birds, the male wood duck is showier (egg-laying females can hide better from predators if they blend in with their surroundings), with a multicolored bill and bright red eyes. Wood ducks nest in trees—they are one of the few ducks that have strong claws that can grip branches. Hooded mergansers are also cavity nesters, building in abandoned woodpecker holes, old snags, and tree cavities. Like many people, both of these duck species like quiet waters surrounded by large, old trees.

Some species of hummingbirds have learned to follow sapsuckers around to find their tapped trees. They can feed on the sap just like nectar.

It's almost impossible to miss the turtles. On warm sunny days, they'll be basking at the edge of the pond or on exposed tree roots and floating logs. The most common turtle species here are red-eared sliders and various soft-shelled turtles, which can have shells almost two feet long. None of these turtles is native to the area.

The Geographic Center of Los Angeles?

In the late 1980s, Allan E. Edwards wanted to pinpoint the center of Los Angeles. Edwards was a retired US Geological Survey staffer turned amateur historian and long-time Franklin Canyon Park docent. To pinpoint the geographic center, he took a map of the city, cut along the city's border and mounted it to cardboard. He then took the map and balanced it on a pin. Was it coincidence that the pin happened to stick in Edwards' beloved park? To commemorate the spot, Edwards erected a plaque under a tree. Follow the trail north of the main parking area and stand for yourself in the point that could very well be the center of Los Angeles.

Mount Hollywood and Griffith Park

Brilliant views of the iconic Hollywood sign, the LA Basin and San Fernando Valley, and, on a clear day, the Pacific Ocean. Coyotes serenade early-evening hikers.

WHERE: 2800 East Observatory Road, Los Angeles, CA 90027

PARKING: Park in the observatory lot, or skip the horrendous traffic and bike or take the Observatory Dash bus (multiple stops near street parking on Los Feliz Boulevard and North Hillhurst Avenue).

DIFFICULTY, DISTANCE, ACCESS: Moderate hike with inclines; loop is approximately two miles long. All-terrain strollers with buff parents only—trails can be steep!

FACILITIES: Bathrooms and drinking fountains in the observatory parking lot.

BEST TIME: Winter and early spring after rains, or early morning/late evening in summer to avoid blazing hot trails.

SPECIAL NOTE: Keep toddlers close at hand near steep trail edges.

245

Griffith Park is huge! It's the second largest city park in California, measuring just over 4,310 acres and bisecting Los Angeles's urban sprawl. It sits at the eastern end of the Santa Monica Mountains, giving views of the San Fernando Valley to the north and west, Glendale and the Verdugo Mountains to the east, and the LA Basin to the south. An important space for nature in the city, it's a corridor for some to move through, a year-round home for others, and a place for humans to connect with wildlife.

Griffith Park is about four times the size of San Francisco's Golden Gate Park and five times larger than New York's Central Park.

▲ The view looking north: all of Burbank and the Verdugo Mountains stand in crisp relief on a winter's day.

▼ Between 1885 and 1889 Griffith Park was an ostrich farm.

Ostrich Farm to Public Park

Around the year 1800, the Spanish government gave 6,647 acres of land to José Vicente Feliz as a reward for his work overseeing the civil administration of early Los Angeles. Rancho Los Feliz was born and included much of what is now Griffith Park and also some of the surrounding lowlands. In 1882, mining magnate Griffith J. Griffith purchased the land with plans for a series of public attractions that would help put Los Angeles on the map.

First, he opened an ostrich farm. A narrow-gauge railway took visitors from downtown to the attraction, where they could see herds of these giant African birds. After four years, Griffith closed the farm, but his passion was undeterred. In December of 1896, Griffith gave the land to the city as a Christmas gift. His only stipulation: "It must be made a place of recreation and rest for the masses."

Today, millions of people visit Griffith Park every year. Of the many spots to visit—from the LA Zoo and Botanical Gardens to the old zoo site where Shakespeare in the Park

◀ View of Griffith Park and the Hollywood sign looking northwest from Griffith Observatory.

plays are regularly staged—the Griffith Observatory and adjacent Mount Hollywood are among the most popular, particularly if a view of the iconic Hollywood sign is on the agenda.

HOLLYWOOD SIGN

The famous sign is visible from the observatory parking lot, but follow the Mount Hollywood trail a bit further up into the hills for a better view. Many believe that Hollywood was named for the California holly bush, also called toyon, that still grows on the hillsides, but this is just an urban legend. When originally constructed in 1923, the forty-five-foot-tall letters spelled out Hollywoodland, a name created by real estate developer Harvey Wilcox. In 1949, the last four letters were taken down, and today the sign acts as a symbol for Los Angeles's movie industry—rather than its native plants or the urban development that replaced them.

Toyon, which shares a common name with the famous sign, bears bright red berries in winter. In the 1920s, the state outlawed collecting these holly berries on public land because they'd become so popular as a winter decoration. Look for it along the chaparral-covered hillsides.

Some of the most common plants in Griffith Park are the small and often twisted scrub oaks, which line the trail from Ferndell to the Observatory.

Welsh immigrant, mining expert, and philanthropist, Griffith J. Griffith donated the land that makes up the park named in his honor. However, later in life he was notorious for ventures much less philanthropic. In 1903 he shot his wife (non-fatally) and was sentenced to two years in San Quentin State Prison.

After his release, he offered to pay for an observatory and theater, but public opinion of him was so low that city officials were reluctant to accept. Only after his death would his fortune be used to build what is now the Griffith Observatory and Greek Theatre.

◀ The berry of many names: toyon, California holly, California Christmas berry.

Halfway between a shrub and tree—you wouldn't want to climb or build a treehouse in them—they support a huge array of life and are easy to identify by their shiny dark green leaves cupped with spiky edges. Examine the oaks closely to discover birds, ants, and the round, tan galls—also called oak apples—that protect baby wasps.

SECRET GARDENS

As you hike towards Mount Hollywood, a line of non-native palm trees becomes visible. They grow in a section of the park called the Captain's Roost, a folk garden planted in the 1940s by a man known only as the Captain. He cared for it until his death. Two other folk gardens grow elsewhere in the park, Dante's and Amir's gardens.

Dante's View is closer to the top of Mount Hollywood (around the other side of the peak). It has picnic tables, drinking fountains, and a dog bowl for thirsty pups. Explore the terraced garden—there are lots of secret nooks with benches for quiet contemplation or friendly conversation.

The cultivated folk gardens sit in stark contrast to the park's naturally occurring vegetation. The garden plants are greener and more lush and are landscaped with exotic plants that require irrigation. Some conservationists believe the gardens should be torn out and re-planted with native species, while folk garden supporters advocate their value for hikers, picnickers, dog walkers, and as part of the park's history.

▲ A fiery skipper butterfly nectars at a Griffith Park flower.

TEN MISSING BUTTERFLIES

Between 1920 and 1960 John Comstock, one of the early entomology curators at the Natural History Museum, discovered fifty species of butterflies in Griffith Park. He gathered specimens and took field notes—all of which are still in the Museum's collection today. In 2011, two local scientists teamed up to repeat the study. Dan Cooper and Tim Bonebrake followed in Comstock's footsteps around Mount Hollywood and into the wilder, less explored parts of the park. They found forty of the fifty species, but ten were missing. These butterflies probably disappeared when the host plants that feed their caterpillars stopped growing in the park.

Why should we care about ten missing butterflies? Their disappearance points to the long-term impacts of urbanization and fire prevention on habitat. Griffith Park is a habitat island surrounded by an urban sea. Improving connectivity to nearby wildlands and increasing wildlife habitat in surrounding urban areas could help prevent future species declines and disappearances.

One butterfly still present in large numbers is the fiery skipper. On certain summer days, hundreds of them can be seen hilltopping. In this butterfly mate-location strategy, males fly to the top of a hill and wait for females to show up. It's not just humans who think Mt. Hollywood is a great date spot!

Griffith Park's Mysterious Mega-Fauna Stars

Griffith Park's most famous resident these days is the mountain lion P-22. The only lion known to have survived the hazardous crossing of the 101 and 405 freeways, he was first recorded on a camera trap in Griffith Park in 2012. His name, P-22, is an abbreviation for Puma-22, because he was the twenty-second puma collared and studied as part of the National Park Service's urban carnivore research program. You can read more about P-22 and the other mountain lions of the Santa Monica Mountains on the National Park Service website (**nps.gov/samo/learn/nature/pumapage).**

▲ A motion-triggered camera catches a glimpse of P-22 on his nighttime rounds.

You probably won't get to see P-22 on your visit—he avoids humans and only comes out at night—but if you're out early, you may see his tracks. They're as big as salad plates, showing just the outline of the fleshy pads, because like domestic cats, a mountain lion's claws are retractable. This is different than dog prints, where you can easily see claw marks. Also, cat heel pads have three lobes at the bottom versus the two lobes on dog heel pads. If you see dog prints on the trail, they could be from somebody's pet or they could be from a coyote.

Puma, cougar, mountain lion, catamount, ghost cat—all of these names refer to the same species, *Puma concolor.*

Nobody knows exactly how many coyotes live in Griffith Park, because no one has done a comprehensive study. Driving through the park at night, you can sometimes see them ambling along the roads, sidling through the golf course, or sauntering around the edges of the observatory. Picnic areas near the base of the hills are the best coyote-watching spots; at dusk, they often come out of the nearby chaparral to search for tasty picnic leftovers. At dawn you can sometimes see them returning home to bed down for the day. If you encounter them, look but don't approach. Remember these are wild animals, and while they're rarely aggressive, staying away helps them stay wild. It's safer for all involved.

Los Angeles's Big Park

Having a park like this in the city's backyard is a big deal. While parts of Los Angeles may be park poor—particularly the lowest income neighborhoods—Griffith Park is a huge resource for Angelenos to celebrate, enjoy, and protect. It is incredible that one of the world's largest urban areas has maintained a park this size, and as pressure for development continues and tourism increases, it's important for us to conserve this fragment of habitat.

LA River at Frogtown

A green and magical paradise just minutes from downtown that offers willow forests, herons, biking, kayaking, and fishing. Easy walks, pocket parks, sitting areas, and playgrounds make this a spot for all ages.

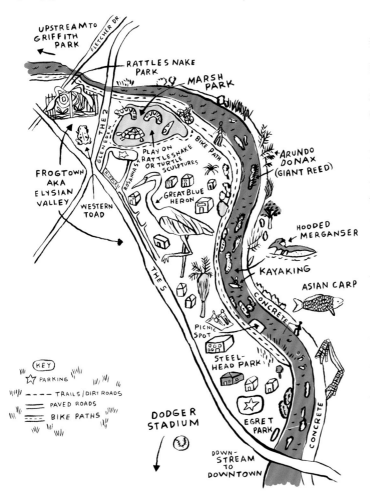

WHERE: Between the 110 and 2 freeways, near the 5 in Frogtown (a.k.a. Elysian Valley).

PARKING: Free parking on surface streets. Handicap parking and access is best at Marsh Park.

DIFFICULTY, DISTANCE, ACCESS: Easy. Can connect with longer bike rides if you wish. Good for strollers and wheelchairs—use caution walking on and crossing bike lanes.

FACILITIES: Bathrooms and picnic tables are available at Marsh Park.

BEST TIME: Any time of day, any season.

SPECIAL NOTES: Summer boating season start and stop dates vary. Stay out of the river channel during storms when water level can rise rapidly.

Many people don't know Los Angeles has a river.
Others consider the city's concrete riverbed a glorified storm drain that shouldn't count as a real river. The Frogtown section of the river helps to prove them all wrong. Go on an adventure and meet the damselflies, carp, and herons that call the river home. It's your portal into our watery past.

No Concrete on the Bottom = Life

This part of the river, called the Glendale Narrows, is extra special. It's one of only three sections that still has a soft, concrete-free, bottom. The other two soft-bottomed sections are the Sepulveda Basin and the area downstream of Willow Street (see Trips 3 and 23 for more details). A soft bottom allows trees and shrubs to take root. And where plants can grow, a whole community of birds, mammals, insects, fungi, and other organisms can thrive.

The Glendale Narrows weren't paved over because the bedrock that raises the Santa Monica Mountains is just barely below ground here. Water from underground aquifers is forced to the surface, so this part of the river has above-ground water for much of the year. Springs, pools, and backwaters dot the Narrows, and wildlife take full advantage. This soft-bottomed section starts on the north side of Griffith Park near the Bette Davis Picnic Area and continues with only a few concrete interruptions as the river turns south between Griffith Park and Glendale, all the way until it passes under the 110 Freeway.

PLANTS: THE BACKBONE OF THE RIVER COMMUNITY

Driving over the bridges that border Frogtown (Fletcher Avenue to the north, and Riverside Drive/Figueroa Street to the south) you get glimpses of a more natural space than the stark concrete channel that shoots through downtown. The predominant plants on the islands are native willow trees and stands of invasive arundo. Both provide cover for birds, insects, and the coyotes and bobcats that use the river as a wildlife corridor.

Another easily-spotted weed along the river has uses both medicinal and deadly. Castor bean plants have spiky seedpods and large, eight-fingered

▲ The three and a half million barrels of cement that paved the LA River met their match in the Glendale Narrows. Here, water rising up from underground aquifers meant the cement would never harden, so the river was left with a soft bottom of sand and cobbles.

▼ Kayaking the Glendale Narrows was piloted in 2013 and has grown increasingly popular. Although there are calm pools like this one, much of the route is made of easy to moderate rapids (Class I and II).

leaves that are typically green, though sometimes purple. The pods grow seeds the size of a coffee bean, which contain the castor oil used in medicine, in soap manufacturing, and as a perfume base. However, they also contain a toxic chemical called ricin, which is poisonous if ingested. Ricin has been used in many Hollywood plotlines (notably, the television series *Breaking Bad*).

FISHERMEN AND FISHING BIRDS

As you stroll or bike along the river, you may see people fishing. If you want to have a go, be sure to get the appropriate California Department of Fish and Wildlife license.

Friends of the LA River conducted a study in 2008, which looked at fish in this section of the river. Scientists sampled the river with seine nets and spoke with local anglers. They documented 1,214 individual fish representing eight species, none of which were native to the area. Mosquitofish, which local vector control officers put in urban ponds to keep mosquito levels down, were the most common. Coming in second was non-native tilapia, an African fish commonly seen on restaurant menus.

Not all fishing in the LA River is done by humans. Osprey, also known as fish eagles, are frequently seen in this part of the river. If you're lucky, you might see one dive and catch a fish in its sharp talons. They often eat the stunned fish atop the light poles that dot the riverbanks.

LIFE UNDERWATER

Other natural dramas unfold in the murky depths of the river. Hiding amongst the reedy edges of the river are fearsome predators: baby damselflies (the dragonfly's more petite and slender cousin). When they hatch, out of eggs the size of a rice grain, these babies are hungry. Immature damselflies are sit-and-wait predators, patiently waiting for lunch from a sheltered spot. When another insect, tiny fish, or even another damselfly swims by, its huge eyes sense the movement, and within a microsecond it thrusts forward jaws of death to grab its prey. Though voracious, they only grow to about an inch in length, and their fierce jaws are no match for larger predators, including fish and birds. Even large dragonfly nymphs will eat damselflies. It's a dangerous underwater world: eat or be eaten.

◄ Light poles make good osprey perches along the river.

▼ Green herons are quiet, patient hunters as they search for small fish in the shallows.

Toadtown?

Although this neighborhood is listed on the map as Elysian Valley, it is also called Frogtown. Walking along the asphalt bike lanes, there are murals and sculptures of frogs, but living, breathing frogs are now uncommon.

The name dates back to the 1930s. In summer, thousands of baby frogs—at their smallest about the size of a corn kernel—would emerge from the river, walking up the concrete banks onto sidewalks and into residents' yards. This continued through the 1950s and 1960s. One resident recalls walking along the street and finding it hard not to step on dozens of them at a time. Neighborhood kids started calling the area Frogtown and the name stuck.

The frogs in question were probably western toads. Following winter rains, these toads go into a breeding frenzy, with each female capable of laying over ten thousand eggs. Several months later, the tadpoles develop legs and metamorphose into tiny toadlets, which then go marching across the landscape in search of insects to eat and new places to call home. Toads are frogs, so the name Frogtown is still technically correct, but Toadtown would be more appropriate.

In recent years, western toads have become rare in Frogtown. Perhaps once a year, a lone toad is spotted along the bike path or in a backyard garden. The springs, pools, and backchannels that once made this region ideal for toads have been destroyed, and the upland habitat is now paved over and crisscrossed by streets. The channelized river provides few microhabitats safe from floods, so eggs, tadpoles, and adults can be easily washed away. Plus, non-native predators abound: mosquito fish eat toad eggs and tadpoles, sunfish and bass eat toadlets, and the American bullfrog eats all stages from tadpoles to adult toads.

▲ Museum entomologist Lisa Gonzalez samples the river for aquatic insects, which can say a lot about the river's water quality and ecosystem. Swarms of mayflies, for example, feed bats, swallows, and swifts.

Pocket Parks and Habitat Restoration in Action

Habitat restoration is the act of restoring or renewing habitat that's been degraded by human activities. Few places illustrate its importance in urban areas as well as the pocket parks along the LA River. The concrete embankments of the river are almost void of wildlife and plants, but a few steps away in the pocket parks, it's another story. Community activists and agencies like the Mountains Recreation and Conservation Authority have worked together to build spaces that celebrate nature and provide habitat for a mix of wildlife. See for yourself in Marsh, Rattlesnake, or Egret park.

Try to find a western fence lizard on the concrete-lined riverbanks. You almost certainly can't—but a few feet away, you'll find many. Walk through Marsh Park and the lizards will tell you what they view as good habitat. You

▲ Standing on top of the Sunnynook Bridge, the view north hints at what the river might have looked like (minus the electrical wires and tower) before Europeans arrived.

◀ Museum ornithologist Kimball Garrett surveys the Narrows for bird life. Over 170 species of birds have been recorded in this section of the river.

won't find them on paths or in the lawns, but instead hiding under woody plants or sunning themselves amongst the boulders and cobbles. They never stray too far into the open, staying close to cover in case danger comes knocking. This mosaic of urban hardscape and newer, native plantings provides a good outdoor classroom for anyone interested in making urban Los Angeles more wildlife friendly.

Steelhead Park sits close to the southern end of the bike trail. Steelhead are a special kind of rainbow trout that live in the ocean most of their lives. Like salmon, they swim upriver to lay eggs. Unlike salmon, a steelhead doesn't die at this point, but returns to the ocean to continue its life. It can swim upstream every season for many years.

Today, the only steelhead in the park are sculpted on fences. But this native fish used to breed in the LA River and many other rivers along California's coast. Recently, scientists have seen them investigating the river's mouth in Long Beach. They were last confirmed in the LA River in the 1940s, but with luck, planning, and some changes to the riverbed, they could one day return.

Steelhead trout can lay thousands of eggs in their lifetime. Some large females can contain up to 10,000 eggs! Maybe these native fish will return to the LA River someday.

TRIP 11

Ernest E. Debs Regional Park

This hilly park offers spectacular views of downtown and the Arroyo Seco. Visit the Audubon Center, see native walnut trees, and experience the coolness of Peanut Lake.

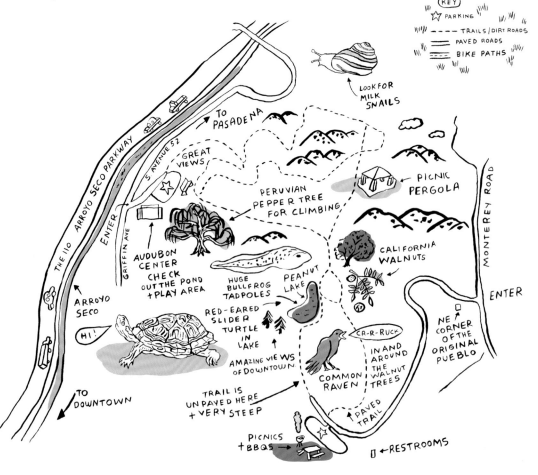

WHERE: Monterey Road Los Angeles, CA 90032
PARKING: Free parking at end of Monterey Road and at the Audubon Center, or a seventeen-minute walk from the Gold Line's Southwest Museum station.
DIFFICULTY, DISTANCE, ACCESS: Easy if only going to the Audubon Center, which has lots of kid-friendly amenities and one paved (but steep!) trail. Eight miles of trails course through the park, some steep, rough, and long.
FACILITIES: Lots of picnic tables and barbecues plus bathrooms. Also nature gardens and programs at the Audubon Center.
BEST TIME: Good year round, particularly in spring or to escape the heat of summer in the shaded areas around the water.

▲ The view of downtown from Debs Park.

Debs Park abuts the Arroyo Seco

just a few miles up from its confluence with the LA River near the intersection of the 5 and the 110 freeways. It also sits at a confluence of another sort, a place where two fault systems meet—the east-west–running Santa Monica fault system and the Whittier fault system which runs northwest-southeast. Water and earthquakes have worked together to form the topography here—uplifting at the faults created hills, and rivers carved out valleys.

Debs Park and the Mount Washington neighborhood immediately across the Arroyo Seco sit at the southwestern end of the San Rafael Hills, which extend north to Descanso Gardens. The park's 282 acres offer valuable open space for city dwellers and wildlife alike. They house charismatic fauna like secretive bobcats and soaring red-tailed hawks, spectacular flora like native California walnuts, and trails, benches, and shady spots to enjoy.

A Center for Birds

The Debs Park Audubon Center is the Audubon Society's very first urban nature center, built for the people of Northeast Los Angeles to help preserve local bird life. Today the center carries on its conservation mission with solar panels on the roof and a native plant garden that conserves water.

The gardens here were designed with wildlife and people in mind. A small pond provides places for dragonflies to lay eggs and thirsty animals to drink. Native sage and buckwheat plants, the same species that live naturally in the park, help extend habitat for the creatures that call Debs Park home.

For humans, there are benches to sit on and, under a towering Peruvian pepper tree, space for kids to play in the mulch and get their hands dirty. Audubon educators lead programs for children, families, and adults. Check their website for programming (debspark.audubon.org).

One hundred and thirty species of birds have been found in Debs Park. They build nests in the vegetation, visit bushes, flowers, and trees for seeds or nectar, and swim in Peanut Lake. The most common birds found on the lake are mallard ducks, but you'll also see black phoebes dipping through the air catching bugs and, in breeding season, collecting mud from the banks to build their nests. Other birds easily seen year-round include mourning doves looking for seeds on the ground, California scrub-jays flashing their blue feathers, and California towhees, which are brown with pumpkin-colored under-butts.

▼ A male mallard flashes his purple wing bars as he takes flight from Peanut Lake.

▲ At the top of Debs Park, Peanut Lake provides an unexpected aquatic habitat.

Eating Local

As in most parks, the mix of vegetation here is a patchwork of California natives and introduced species. At the top of the park, you may be greeted by ravens croaking from Southern California black walnut trees. After the zombie apocalypse, this is the tree you need to find. People in this region have eaten the Southern California black walnut for thousands of years. It'll require some effort, and your hands and clothes might get stained, but if you manage to pry open a walnut shell, you can eat the nut inside, just like the Gabrieleño/Tongva and Chumash have done for generations.

Entire hillsides in Debs Park can be covered in wild mustard, one of the area's earliest introduced plants. After spring rains, mustard plants explode into a bloom of bright yellow flowers. Some say European settlers purposefully planted coastal hillsides with the flowering mustard as a navigation tool for ship's captains. Others tell the story of Gaspar de Portolà's expedition planting them along the trail to mark the route of his expedition north from Mexico in 1769. Still others think the seeds were brought accidentally with imported livestock.

◀ Ravens frequently perch in the trees at the top of Debs Park, flying to the ground to grab a walnut or some carelessly discarded human food.

Whatever the mode of introduction, wild mustard now blankets much of California. Native people displaced by the incoming Spanish harvested the leaves and also collected the seeds, grinding them up to make a flavorful paste akin to whole grain mustards available in grocery stores today. Its raw leaves can be harvested for salads or cooking like other mustard greens.

Introduced snails are especially common in this park, including milk snails, which are descended from snails escaped from escargot farms. Even in dry summer months, the snails can be seen attached to plant stems, where they've sealed off their shell to wait out hot weather. After a rain, they unseal themselves to find food and a mate. Just like the wild mustard, these snails can be eaten. Wild mustard and California walnut pesto on snails, anyone?

Wild foraging has become a hip hobby, but please consider the rules and regulations in areas where you plan to collect, the likelihood of pesticide use, and the impact you may be having on native wildlife.

The Park's Elusive Bobcat(s)

In 2014, staff at the Audubon Center caught images of a bobcat on camera traps around the park. Bobcats can use this park because it's connected to wilder spaces—to Griffith Park via the LA River, and to the San Gabriel Mountains via the Arroyo Seco. River channels make handy nighttime highways.

You can retrace the steps the bobcat might have taken down from the San Gabriel Mountains. Start at the Red Box trailhead (4,640 feet in elevation) and follow the Gabrieleño Trail all the way down to Hahamongna Watershed Park. The Arroyo Seco eventually meets up with Debs Park. It's about twenty miles, a long trek whether you have human or bobcat legs!

Arlington Garden

A water-wise Mediterranean getaway featuring bright orange hooded orioles and other vivid birds.

If your favorite side of the crayon box had the oranges, reds, and yellows, this site will be a delicious treat. Flowers blossom year-round and orange trees remind us of Pasadena's agricultural heritage. Too sunny? Find an awning over a patio table. Feeling chilly? Move into the sun. Even on a quiet and foggy morning, the many chairs and stone-lined nooks invite visitors to dawdle, doodle, and daydream.

▲ Many plantings emphasize water-efficiency and ideal plants for a Mediterranean climate.

◄ The labyrinth is ever-popular for photo ops.

Thank You, Millionaires and Termites

This garden occupies a corner of a now-forgotten estate owned by the Durand family, whose fifty-room mansion was once the grandest house in Pasadena. Its three stories featured mahogany doors and gold-plated doorknobs. Tastes change, fortunes dwindle, and termites chew, chew, chew. The house had to be torn down, and thanks to unimaginative urban planning, the empty lot became a Caltrans yard.

Love, mulch, trowels, and persistence eventually transformed this site into a remarkable example of *xeriscaping*—landscaping with drought-tolerant, low-water plants. You can experience twenty-five "rooms" organized by theme, including the vernal pool, the arroyo, the succulent garden, the labyrinth, and the oak grove. The labyrinth was built by local schoolchildren and the seemingly ancient tree shading it is a thick-trunked, personality-rich Peruvian pepper. The flowers and shrubs that provide understory color include heuchera (coral bells), hummingbird sage, ceanothus, and California and European poppies.

Arlington Garden teaches us that public parks don't all need to be expanses of thirsty grass. On average, this garden uses 80 percent less water than a conventional park—and offers a great model for alternative park design.

WHERE: 275 Arlington Drive, Pasadena, CA 91105
PARKING: Street parking.
DIFFICULTY, DISTANCE, ACCESS: Small, intimate site, accessible to all—better for pausing and lingering than hiking.
FACILITIES: Many tables and small paths, no restrooms.
BEST TIME: Year-round but blooms are especially vivid in spring.

Oh, the Species You'll Meet

Many of the birds found at Arlington, including acorn woodpeckers and yellow-chevroned parakeets, can be found on multiple excursions in this book. One bird, though, is more likely here than anyplace else: the red-whiskered

◄ Arlington Garden features beautiful mixes of color, texture, and scent.

◄ An eastern fox squirrel surveys his empire from atop the boundary fence.

◄◄ Festive, red-whiskered bulbuls have lived in Pasadena since the 1960s.

bulbul, named after the red teardrop on its cheek. This medium-sized, black-and-white bird is native to Asia. Its head swoops upward into an over-gelled mohawk, and under the tail a flash of pure scarlet resembles very red underwear. Bulbuls usually flock together (or at least stick in pairs), exploring small, close-to-the-ground bushes or perching on phone lines or in the tippy-tops of trees. Their upswept hairdo is shared by only a few local birds, so even just in profile, they're easy to check off the list.

Other species found here include Anna's and Allen's hummingbirds (spring and summer), eastern fox squirrels (all year), western fence lizards, southern alligator lizards, and many different sparrows and warblers.

Close Your Eyes and Wander

As the saying goes, the nose knows. It can be a treat to let your nose take you through the gardens. Lavender and rosemary, three kinds of sage, blossoming orange trees, wisteria and climbing roses, and a dozen other traces and layers of smell that only a master perfumer could sort out—the senses receive a full workout here. As Ralph Waldo Emerson once said, "the earth laughs in flowers." At this site, the laughter is full and rich and lasts all day.

Oro Vista Park and Tujunga Wash

Los Angeles's top dragonfly site is reached by taking a stroll through a wild cactus garden. Search for scorpions with a black light or watch summer nighthawks zoom after moths.

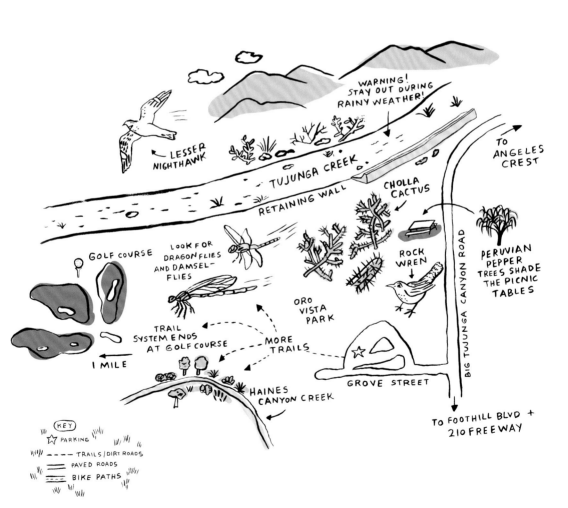

WARNING! STAY OUT DURING RAINY WEATHER!

TO ANGELES CREST

LESSER NIGHTHAWK

TUJUNGA CREEK

CHOLLA CACTUS

RETAINING WALL

ROCK WREN

PERUVIAN PEPPER TREES SHADE THE PICNIC TABLES

GOLF COURSE

LOOK FOR DRAGONFLIES AND DAMSELFLIES

ORO VISTA PARK

TRAIL SYSTEM ENDS AT GOLF COURSE

MORE TRAILS

BIG TUJUNGA CANYON ROAD

1 MILE

HAINES CANYON CREEK

GROVE STREET

TO FOOTHILL BLVD + 210 FREEWAY

KEY
☆ PARKING
- - - - TRAILS / DIRT ROADS
——— PAVED ROADS
═══ BIKE PATHS

Los Angeles is a mix of contradictions, and this trip is no exception. From some of the cactus-lined trails you can imagine you're in Baja California or an exotic desert. Yet after a short hike in summer, you come to a year-round stream where cottonwoods and dragonflies shimmer green in the sun, and, with a bit of imagination, you can picture the once-common grizzly bears last seen in Los Angeles at this exact spot in 1916.

Tujunga Wash is classic "flash flood landscape." Years of flood events have deposited a thick layer of gravel and water-polished boulders. As the canyon opens up and the ground levels out, the water slows and spreads out, dropping the interesting mix of rocks we can investigate today. Tujunga Wash is a giant library, but one of stones, not books. A close study reveals a galaxy of colors, textures, and geological processes.

The ground here is porous—it's super sandy—so there's little water available near the surface and no rich soil. This creates an alluvial wash, a mini-desert where the plants are more typical of a place like Joshua Tree National Park.

WHERE: 11101 Oro Vista Avenue, Sunland-Tujunga, CA 91040

PARKING: Free parking in Oro Vista Park or along residential streets.

DIFFICULTY, DISTANCE, ACCESS: Easy. Can be done as a half-hour trip, or up to a few hours. Not ideal for strollers and wheelchairs.

FACILITIES: Picnic area but no bathroom.

BEST TIME: There's year-round access, and any time of year is good to visit. Nighthawks are best April through September; dragonflies best May through October. If it's been raining or you see thunderclouds over the mountains, *stay out of the creek bed!*

SPECIAL NOTE: Dogs must be leashed. Warn kids to keep clear of spiny cholla cactus. At night, bring a UV flashlight to spot nocturnal scorpions.

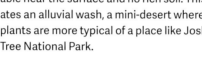

A Special Park for a Special Place

Oro Vista Park has a native plant garden, picnic tables shaded by pepper trees and eucalyptus, and plenty of parking. Dogs are welcome but must be leashed.

This is a special kind of park—you won't find green lawns or playgrounds, but instead an intact and too-rare community of chaparral yuccas, California quail, coast horned lizards, and golden cholla. The park is fenced but just follow the path to find openings where you can connect to trails that wander out into the wash and lead over to the stream. Your downstream turn-around point is the Angeles National Golf Club—you can't miss it.

In the stony maze of the wash, yucca plants, prickly pear, and cholla cactus thrive, as well as birds we don't often think of when we say Los Angeles, including rock wrens, lesser nighthawks, and phainopeplas.

NIGHTHAWKS AND ROCK WRENS

Another specialty of this site is a bird of dusk and dawn, the lesser nighthawk. Nighthawks are long-winged and acrobatic, swooping and banking as they chase down moths and other nocturnal insects. This is an easy bird to

▲ Tujunga Wash is a prime example of our ephemeral waterways—dry in summer and fall, filled with water from rain and snowmelt in winter and spring.

◀ The spines of this cholla cactus are beautiful in sunlight, but not in your toes. Watch your step.

learn because they have white bars near the ends of their slender wings, and their turning flight dips and rises over the horizon in the twilight sky. This flight style makes the night-hawk resemble a cross between an anxious falcon and a slightly drunk bat.

By day, look for rock wrens among the cactus and boulders. This dinky, ground-hugging bird with a slender beak about as long as its own head is a skilled spider-catcher and lives here because of the rocks, not the stream. Rock wrens get most of their water from their food, rarely needing to take a drink. They have an amazing range of songs—perhaps over one hundred—which the males give while doing deep knee bends.

ADVENTURES AFTER DARK: SCORPION EDITION

The chance to find scorpions in their native habitat makes this a nighttime adventure option. All you need is an ultraviolet flashlight (models can be purchased online for under twenty dollars). Scientists aren't exactly sure why, but scorpions glow under black lights, which makes them easy to find.

Researchers who study scorpions will sweep a beam of UV light across a sandy path as they walk. Pay attention to the space under bushes and rocks. You might have a few false positives with bits of trash, but keep at it. When you're finally lucky enough to see the brilliant glow of this nocturnal predator, it's worth it!

"Jumping cholla" is the folk name for one of the cactus species found here. The plant defends itself against browsing animals with a dense covering of barbed, fish hook spines. Some hikers claim you want to give the plant a wide berth, lest it "jump" on you, but they can't actually reach out in any way. The better tip is the usual one—look but don't touch.

STREAMSIDE JEWELS

After stepping through the fence, you can hike in several directions. Many people like to check out the stream first. Look to your right for the long, white concrete wall installed to control flooding. It tells you where the streambed is. As you get closer, you'll see arroyo willows and Fremont cottonwoods. All along the stream, dragonflies hover and dart.

Twenty-eight species of dragonflies and damselflies have been documented in Tujunga Wash, high diversity for such an urban-adjacent spot. Skimmers, darners, and amberwings prefer the calmer, vegetated sides of the stream, while ringtails and sanddragons prefer the running water in the middle of the rocky creekbed.

If the wash is dry in a drought year, head over to Haines Creek (check the map or just walk towards the line of tall trees between the neighborhood and the golf course), which is partially fed by urban runoff. Most of the dragons and damsels aren't picky—they'll go where the water is.

▲ This blue dasher dragonfly takes a rest from flying and basks in the sunlight. Dragonflies regulate their body temperature by moving from shade to sun.

▼ Neon skimmer dragonflies have eyes that cover almost their entire head. Not much can fly by without their noticing.

It's easy to tell dragonflies and damselflies apart: Adult dragonflies are stout and hold their wings out to the side when at rest. Damselflies are skinnier and usually hold their wings together above their body.

Hahamongna Watershed Park

Picnic under hundred-year-old trees, try your luck on the world's first disc golf course, or visit three different forests—oak, willow, and streamside—in a single hike.

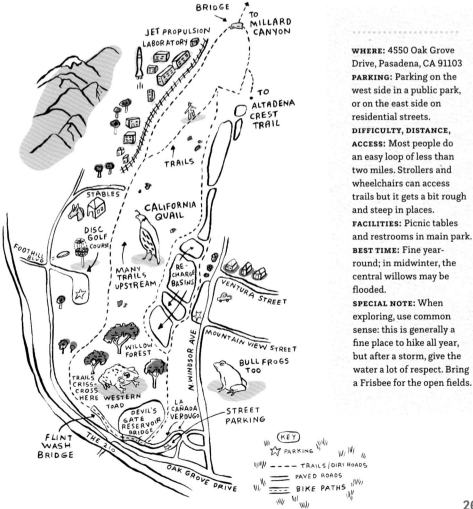

WHERE: 4550 Oak Grove Drive, Pasadena, CA 91103

PARKING: Parking on the west side in a public park, or on the east side on residential streets.

DIFFICULTY, DISTANCE, ACCESS: Most people do an easy loop of less than two miles. Strollers and wheelchairs can access trails but it gets a bit rough and steep in places.

FACILITIES: Picnic tables and restrooms in main park.

BEST TIME: Fine year-round; in midwinter, the central willows may be flooded.

SPECIAL NOTE: When exploring, use common sense: this is generally a fine place to hike all year, but after a storm, give the water a lot of respect. Bring a Frisbee for the open fields.

Hahamongna Watershed Park is a three hundred-acre preserve that provides a transition between foothill communities in Los Angeles and the vast open space of the Angeles National Forest. Lined with coast live oaks on each side, the central catchment basin protects an important willow forest. This open area is both storm control and recharge basin, meaning that water is collected in order to prevent flooding and also to replenish underground aquifers.

There's no wrong way to visit this site, which is open sunrise to sunset and offers different kinds of recreation. Trail runners come to crank out the miles, disc golfers (bags bulging with ten kinds of Frisbee) arc shots post to post, and birders check "lerp-filled" trees for visiting migrants. Of course, you don't really need a focus. Some people just come to walk the dog.

In rainy winters, a lake forms upstream from Devil's Gate Dam. Though it's usually gone by the end of spring, the dense thickets of willows, crisscrossed by dozens of game trails, remind us the water is just below the surface, flowing year round through the gravel and sand. If you listen closely, you can almost hear it. This site was once called Oak Grove Park, a name still found on some maps and signs.

> In nature, a lerp is the sugary protective covering produced by larvae of psyllid bugs. These bugs are commonly known as lerp insects, and when they infest a tree, birds like warblers swarm in to feast. Birders love to find lerpy eucs (eucalyptus trees)—that's where the birds are.

Three Forests

With spreading canopies and an enduring majesty, the thick-trunked coast live oaks here remind us of an older California. The biggest are hundreds of years old, so stop a moment to admire their longevity. They've lived through many cycles of flood and drought, fire and earthquake. Grizzly bears sharpened their claws on some, and their rich acorn crops have fed generations of scrub-jays, woodpeckers, and Native Americans.

Forest number two is at the bottom of the basin, where most of the densely packed, leafy trees are willows, thirty feet tall and ready for the next flood. You'll also find dense thickets of mulefat, interspersed with young cottonwoods. The boom or bust cycle of floods that fill this basin up with sand and scour the banks with rushing water turns out to be very good for maintaining a healthy mix of native plants. The willow forest here is one of Los Angeles's finest.

At the top end of the open space, starting at the short bridge next to the Jet Propulsion Laboratory, the Millard Canyon trail takes you upstream through forest number three, a riparian haven filled with sycamores and alders. The higher you go, the more terrain closes in, with mountains rising thousands of feet into the Angeles Crest high country.

At night, bears, bobcats, night birds called poorwills (a moth-eating owl-lookalike), and even the occasional mountain lion all use this canyon as their expressway connecting the lowlands to the highlands. In the morning, look for their tracks or droppings and see who has been passing through.

Who Hangs Here?

Over two hundred species of birds have been seen in the area. If you haven't added acorn woodpecker to your list yet, this is a good place to look, especially around the parking lot on the west side. Remember: you'll probably hear them before you see them.

The western toad is also found here. You won't see them very often though. Much of their lives are spent underground in mammal burrows. They do come above ground during the early spring breeding season or summer while looking for food, but they're often nocturnal. Besides habitat loss, their decline can be blamed on hungry non-native American bullfrogs, which you might also spot in some of these ponds.

The soft mud on the edges of ponds, lakes, and reservoirs is an excellent spot to search for animal tracks: raccoon feet, deer hooves, or large, round bobcat paws all leave impressions in the damp ground, revealing who comes out

▲ Disc golf started at this park and now is played all over the world (including the South Pole).

◀ Traversing the east side of the park, the trail crosses under oaks as it heads upstream toward the JPL campus.

▶ This western tiger swallowtail rests on an oak branch. You'll find its caterpillars feeding on the park's plentiful willow leaves.

after dark. Mornings bring bird song, including willow flycatchers in spring. By midday, a damp, salty stretch of earth will have attracted a cluster of eager butterflies looking for minerals, a behavior called puddling.

ROCKET FOLK AND SPACE DEER

This basin has some space age history. The collegiate-looking buildings along the upper border of the park make up NASA's Jet Propulsion Laboratory (JPL), the facility that sends rovers to Mars and cameras whizzing by Pluto. Although the campus is fenced off, it's okay to follow the trails on the public side of the fence.

JPL is here not for the good view or the lunchtime sessions of disc golf, but because this canyon used to be more isolated. Nearby science and engineering institute Caltech started out in the 1890s in what was then semi-rural Pasadena. As housing density grew around the main campus, so did the size of some of the experiments. When Caltech's Pasadena neighbors got tired of rocket engine experiments, all of which were loud and some of which blew up, the Upper Arroyo Seco, over the years a trash dump and a gravel mine, seemed like a good place to relocate. These days you won't find any exploding rocket engines, but JPL is now the center of some two dozen amazing space missions—some call it "the center of the universe"—and its lush campus provides good grazing for local mule deer herds.

▲ Raccoon pawprints look a lot like tiny human handprints.

Why Put a Dam Here?

Some dams are intended to make things happen, to generate electricity or store drinking water. Devil's Gate Dam was built to keep things *from* happening. It was built in 1920 to guard against flooding. It catches the massive debris flows that churn regularly out of the San Gabriels and helps keep mud off roadways and out of living rooms in Highland Park.

If there's no winter lake, you can hike up to the interior side of the dam and compare the 1920 version with the 1990 update just east. It sweeps up in a curl of truly impressive concrete. The large orange barriers tied down with chains help control trash.

◄ In the 1920s Devil's Gate Dam was a popular destination for those with access to cars.

TRIP 15

Eaton Canyon Natural Area

Hike to the base of a forty-foot waterfall, and in spring discover an amazing variety of wildflowers. Even more exciting, explore where Los Angeles's dirt came from!

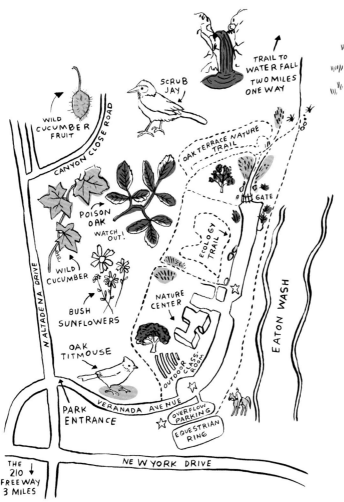

KEY
☆ PARKING
- - - - TRAILS / DIRT ROADS
====== PAVED ROADS
≡≡≡≡ BIKE PATHS

TRAIL TO WATER FALL TWO MILES ONE WAY

SCRUB JAY

WILD CUCUMBER FRUIT

CANYON CLOSE ROAD

OAK TERRACE NATURE TRAIL

GATE

POISON OAK WATCH OUT!

ECOLOGY TRAIL

WILD CUCUMBER

N ALTADENA DRIVE

BUSH SUNFLOWERS

NATURE CENTER

EATON WASH

OAK TITMOUSE

OUTDOOR CLASS ROOM

PARK ENTRANCE

VERANADA AVENUE

OVERFLOW PARKING

EQUESTRIAN RING

NEW YORK DRIVE

THE 210 FREEWAY 3 MILES

WHERE: 1750 North Altadena Drive, Pasadena, 91107

PARKING: During open hours, park in the paved lot and an overflow dirt lot; before hours, park on the street.

DIFFICULTY, DISTANCE, ACCESS: 3.7 miles to waterfall and back, not appropriate for strollers and wheelchairs; longer and shorter hikes possible.

FACILITIES: Restrooms and picnic tables at the nature center.

BEST TIME: Waterfall usually flows year-round; weekends can be very crowded.

Eaton Canyon extends down the Angeles Crest from high country into Altadena and is home to interesting plants, chittering flocks of birds, and a popular, stream-hopping hike that ends at a year-round (usually) waterfall. Called *El Precipicio* by the Spanish because of its steep gorges, this canyon was later named after Pasadena Judge Benjamin Smith Eaton. It has been home to many things in the past two hundred years, including an olive orchard, a gold mine, and a rocket-testing base during World War II. Now its popular nature center is a good place to learn about local wildlife and top off your water bottles before your hike.

Geology on Your Doorstep

From the parking lot, the open wash—also called an arroyo—looks like a rock garden. It was once a river that connected with the ocean at Long Beach, but now its water flows underground and is collected downstream, helping supply Pasadena and Altadena. As you hike upstream, water usually starts to flow above ground about halfway to the waterfall.

▲ This oak titmouse just scored a caterpillar lunch. As their name implies, these birds are common residents in oak woods.

The jumbled stones in dozens of shapes and colors remind us we are surrounded by young, active, very tall mountains, which are constantly in motion. For thousands of years, floods from Eaton Canyon sent walls of mud, water, and stones crashing down to spread out in the lowlands. If we could lift back foothill towns and freeways like a blanket, we'd see a series of interconnected *alluvial fans*—debris flows from mountain canyons fanned out across the top half of Los Angeles like a line of superhero capes.

In Glendale and Pasadena, the concrete sidewalks lie over layers of debris washed down from the San Gabriel Mountains. The concrete is maybe six inches thick. Outwash from canyons like Eaton can be nearly a thousand feet thick.

On the highest part of the eastern skyline, a cluster of antennas marks Mount Wilson, almost a vertical mile high and once home to the largest telescope in the world. You can still visit the observatory today and gaze upward at the cosmos.

Licorice-Scented Canyon

To reach the waterfall, follow any of the paths going up-canyon from the nature center. Stay on either the most well-traveled trail or the one that sticks truest to the stream. You might have to get your feet wet hopping back and forth across the stream at the upper end.

▶ Traversing stepping stones, looking for tiny creek dwelling insects, or just listening to the water tumble by in Eaton Creek is a fun, all-ages adventure.

Many of the native plants reviewed throughout this book are present, as well as newcomers from elsewhere. Fennel, once native to Europe and now a common weed along trails and roadsides, is a tall, airy bush with feathery leaves and small yellow flowers. If you crush the leaves and stems, you'll smell the distinct and delicious aroma of licorice.

Another plant worth a moment of olfactory pleasure is California sage-brush. Watch for a bush with feathery foliage and a pale, green-gray color—classic "sage green." Sagebrushes are different than sages, but both can be used in cooking and made into teas.

Some days, Eaton's bouquet bursts from every corner on the trail. A lovely spring flower to watch for is showy (also called royal) penstemon, a stalk-like flower with a row of fabulous violet blossoms, usually edged in a deep, saturated blue. The abundant yellow flowers that look like daisies go by the name brittlebush or California bush sunflower. In early spring they turn long sections of trail a vivid yellow.

Plants like these demonstrate that nature is not static. The last big fire here in the 1990s took away a lot of trees and chaparral plants (and burned down the previous nature center). Yet in doing so, it opened up space for fennel, sage, and other open-air vegetation.

KISSES AND WITCHES' HAIR

The dense green wads or tangles high up in the sycamores is mistletoe, the same kind you're supposed to kiss under at Christmas. Far from romantic, mistletoe is a parasite that taps into its host's nutrients, like a tick stuck on your dog. Birds eat mistletoe berries, but they can't digest the seeds. Instead, they poop them out onto the branches of other trees, where a new plant will grow.

Another parasite looks like somebody played a Silly String prank, sprawling over bushes like unraveled orange twine. This plant is known as dodder, but various folk names include devil guts and witches' hair. It grows by drilling into a host plant and sucking out water and nutrients. Unlike symbiotic partnerships, parasitic interactions are one sided. One critter wins, the other loses out.

▲ After sprouting from seeds in the ground, the dodder plant has five to ten days to find a host plant with its tendrils or it will die.

▼ The California scrub-jay is one of two native jay species in the region.

▲ Visiting Eaton Canyon after rain is a mushroom-lover's delight. Here we have turkey tail and an orange jelly fungus growing side by side on a fallen log.

► Eaton
Canyon Falls.

Waterfall U-Turn

Once you reach the waterfall, take pictures, maybe stop for a snack and a drink of water, then reverse your steps. This is the end of the trail. Don't climb the cliffs—the rocks are crumbly and will break off. *Believe the signs!* People get hurt here trying to climb. Enjoy the downhill hike back to the parking lot.

Charlton Flats

Escape summer heat by driving an hour up Angeles Crest Highway into the blue skies and green meadows of a mountain forest. Hike to a viewpoint or picnic under majestic pines.

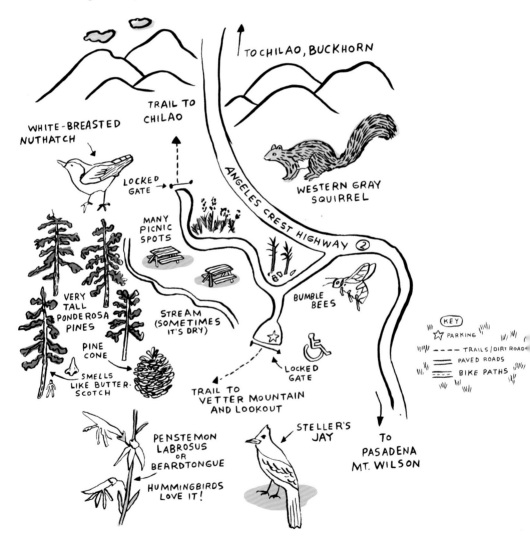

TO CHILAO, BUCKHORN

TRAIL TO CHILAO

WHITE-BREASTED NUTHATCH

LOCKED GATE

ANGELES CREST HIGHWAY 2

WESTERN GRAY SQUIRREL

MANY PICNIC SPOTS

VERY TALL PONDEROSA PINES

BUMBLE BEES

PINE CONE

STREAM (SOMETIMES IT'S DRY)

SMELLS LIKE BUTTERSCOTCH

LOCKED GATE

TRAIL TO VETTER MOUNTAIN AND LOOKOUT

PENSTEMON LABROSUS OR BEARDTONGUE

STELLER'S JAY

TO PASADENA MT. WILSON

HUMMINGBIRDS LOVE IT!

KEY
☆ PARKING
- - - - TRAILS / DIRT ROAD
═══ PAVED ROADS
▭▭▭ BIKE PATHS

WHERE: Forest Service Road 3N16, Falling Springs, CA 91789 (14 miles east of junction of Angeles Crest and Angeles Forest Highways)

PARKING: Handicap-accessible parking, multiple trailheads. Adventure Pass required.

DIFFICULTY, DISTANCE, ACCESS: Hike one mile or one week, as you wish. Trails not appropriate for strollers or wheelchairs.

FACILITIES: Vault toilets and many picnic sites.

BEST TIME: Spring, summer, fall (sometimes closed in winter).

SPECIAL NOTE: Be sure to purchase your Adventure Pass before arriving.

▲ The tall ponderosa, Jeffrey, and Coulter pines at Charlton Flats make it an excellent picnic ground. Be sure to get an up-close smell of the ponderosa's bark—can you detect its signature butterscotch scent?

Welcome to Los Angeles's Big Sky Country—big skies,

big trees, and big mountains. Angeles Crest—the collective name for the mountains between Los Angeles and the Mojave Desert—offers campgrounds and picnic sites year-round, snow play in the winter, and a cool and green getaway in the summer.

Although much of the high country was burned in the 2009 arson-sparked Station Fire, Charlton Flats has recovered well. Stately trees and scampering chipmunks make the case that you don't need to drive all the way to Yosemite for a quiet afternoon among the pines.

Tall or Small

As you pull off Angeles Crest Highway and into the site, you have two choices for parking. If you want to do a good four-mile roundtrip hike, park in the lot closest to the entrance then head up the fire road to Vetter Lookout. To explore more casually, do short hikes, birdwatch, or to have a picnic, turn right and follow the access road to the locked gate, stopping wherever is most attractive.

The Vetter Peak hike mostly follows a paved road, and to stay on the main route, keep left at the forks. You'll rise through forest to open brushy sections, until, at the summit, you can see in all directions. To the southwest, the mountain with the white domes and tall radio masts is Mount Wilson, home to a famous observatory and the transmission towers for many radio and TV stations. Go slowly because you're nearly six thousand feet above sea level. Don't be surprised if you huff and puff a bit.

FOLLOW THE STREAM

If you're not hiking Vetter Peak, turn your car right at the entrance and parallel the streambed, which is lined by willow and alder trees. This whole site was opened to the public in the 1930s. Facilities like toilets, parking pullouts, and picnic tables were installed by the Civilian Conservation Corps, a program created as part of President Roosevelt's New Deal.

Among the pines that tower over the stream, you'll find western bluebirds, Steller's jays, California scrub-jays, chickadees, brown creepers, and white-breasted nuthatches. Watch for the mountain-dwelling white-headed woodpecker, recognizable for its black body, all-white head, white wing patches, and in males, a little flick of red at the back of the head. Acorn woodpeckers are here too. In fact, nine different kinds of woodpeckers have been seen in and around the picnic grounds. In summer, listen for someone calling "Quick! Three beers!" That's the olive-sided flycatcher calling from treetops and really sounding like a thirsty bar patron.

▲ A Steller's jay rocks his jaunty mohawk. Watch your unattended food while camping or picnicking—Steller's are feisty and will grab what they can get!

► A bumblebee indulges in some nectar thievery.

Don't Be Plant Blind

Botanists often lament that people ignore plants in favor of animals—they call this plant blindness. Let's take a moment to honor the plants that feed the deer that mountain lions eat, the leaves that help caterpillars become butterflies, the flowers that make nectar for hummingbirds, and the forest that produces the oxygen we all breathe.

Most parking areas in Angeles Crest require an Adventure Pass, which you can purchase for the day or for the whole year. The Forest Service uses these fees to pay for facility maintenance and upgrades. Mount Baldy (Trip 17) also requires this permit. You can get them at the Chilao and Grassy Hollow visitor centers on weekends, or from sporting goods stores and some gas stations. Plan ahead, because you can rarely get them at the picnic grounds themselves.

The historic Vetter Lookout was built in 1935 and burned down in the 2009 Station Fire. Windows on all sides used to allow staff to watch for smoke in every direction. During lightning strikes, Ramona Merwin, a long-time lookout, would sit in a wooden chair whose legs had glass ball insulators for feet. Lightning once set her roof on fire. In her time on the mountain she saw all the wildlife possible, including mountain lions and black bears. The National Forest Service, which manages this land, may build a new station someday, but, in a rather bitter irony, they have less money these days for projects like rebuilding lookout towers because their budget is depleted by the cost of fighting so many wildfires.

Plants have inventive ways to get pollinated. One method is to create nectar and bury it deep in a flower. To get at the sugar, an insect or bird has to stick its head all the way into the flower and get covered with pollen. As the pollinator travels from plant to plant, the pollen from one fertilizes the flowers of another.

Unfortunately for some plants, certain insects don't always play by the rules. If a flower is too small, carpenter bees and honey bees have learned to perch at the base of the flower and chew a hole to get at the nectar. This is called nectar robbing—the bees get what they want but the flower doesn't get pollinated.

For years after the Station Fire, poodle-dog bush, also called turricula, was abundant around Charlton Flats and other parts of Angeles Crest high country. It's native to Southern California and Northern Baja, grows up to six feet tall, and has attractive purple flowers. It can also give you a terrible rash on par with poison oak (or worse). With time, it's becoming less common—though it will probably rebound after the next big fire. As a general rule, stick to the trail and don't handle unfamiliar plants, and all will be fine.

Other plants around Charlton Flats are much more pleasant. First, there's the sugar pine, John Muir's "king of the conifers," which boasts the longest cones of any pine in the world (rarely less than a foot long). You'll need both hands just to hold one. Coulter pines are here too. Watch for their hefty, barrel-shaped cones—large, hook-tipped, and big as a pineapple. You definitely want to avoid parking your car under these! The main pine in the picnic area is ponderosa—tall and straight, with bunches of long green needles that stay on the tree year-round. Look for colorful snow plants under the conifers in spring. They don't get their energy through photosynthesis; instead, they parasitize fungi that form around conifer roots.

All the trees make this site great for watching western gray squirrels and Merriam's chipmunks as they dart across fallen logs and spiral up tree trunks. Plus, there's always the hope of seeing a black bear or some mule deer.

Further up the Road

Just up the road is Chilao, a campground and picnic complex which has an open-on-weekends visitor center. If there's a dripping spigot or some bird seed, that's where all the birds will be. Higher up at Buckhorn Campground, even summer nights can be refreshingly chilly. It has a different set of trees and birds but a very narrow access road: don't try to drive a large RV into Buckhorn.

For most people, a visit to Charlton Flats is an excellent mountain day trip. You can cool off, enjoy the piney air, and take goofy selfies with immense pinecones. Bring hand wipes, since some cones will have a sticky resin on them. If you have a bird book, bring that too. You may be lucky enough to find some mountain forest exclusives.

▲ Keep an eye out for western gray squirrels, which you're unlikely to see lower down in the LA Basin.

▼ Snow plant's scientific name, *Sarcodes sanguinea*, translates to "bloody flesh-like thing."

TRIP 17

Mount Baldy

Take a ski lift to a subalpine habitat with epic views to the north and south. In summer and fall see bighorn sheep and chipmunks, in winter, hibernating ladybugs and a snowy wonderland.

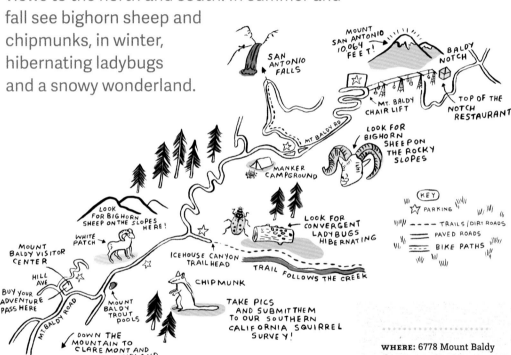

Mount Baldy, or as it is officially known, Mount San Antonio, is the highest peak in the San Gabriel Mountains, standing at a majestic 10,064 feet. Originally named for Saint Anthony of Padua, local settlers began to call it Baldy because of the bare bowl that dominates views from the city to the south. The nickname is so prevalent many locals don't even recognize the name Mount San Antonio.

Mount Baldy makes a great day trip. In the summer or fall, you can hike alongside a mountain stream, or take a ski lift to explore a snow-free subalpine habitat. In the winter you can visit the snow to play, ski, or look for overwintering ladybugs. In spring, check out a waterfall or join in the local bighorn sheep count.

WHERE: 6778 Mount Baldy Road, Mt. Baldy, CA 91759
PARKING: Many parking lots. All require an Adventure Pass (purchase at visitor center).
DIFFICULTY, DISTANCE, ACCESS: Icehouse Canyon Trail ranges from easy to difficult, depending on how far you hike. San Antonio Falls hike is easy. Ski lift to Top of the Notch is easiest! Trails are not stroller or wheelchair accessible.
FACILITIES: Bathrooms and drinking fountains at the visitor center.
BEST TIME: To avoid snow, visit in late spring through fall.

Every year in March, many organizations partner up to survey the local bighorn sheep population. Check the Department of Fish and Wildlife's website (wildlife.ca.gov) for information on how to get involved.

As you gain elevation on the journey up to Baldy Village, the scenery changes and the temperature drops—a welcome treat in the hot summer months. The rule of thumb for a sunny day is to subtract 5.4 degrees Fahrenheit for every 1,000 feet of elevation gain, though clouds, snow, or rain change the calculation. Keep an eye out for wildlife (and cyclists—this is a popular biking destination) on the drive, particularly if you're traveling in early morning or at dusk. Animals often slink across the road, and you may see snakes, deer, coyotes, bobcats, or (if you're incredibly lucky) a mountain lion, bear, or bighorn sheep. Storms are often intense here, so be sure to check the weather report. Even in the middle of summer, thunderstorms can be fierce.

▼ A bighorn sheep family makes easy work of a roadside barrier.

From Big Horns to Tiny Feet

According to rangers and village residents, you can often spot the bighorn sheep herd teetering on mountainsides above the trout pools or drinking at the creek below (see map). They can also sometimes be seen or heard from the ski lift parking lot. As males smash their horns together (each sporting a pair of horns that can weigh up to thirty pounds) trying to impress females, the sound echoes across the valley. When the sheep aren't being so obvious, look for other telltale signs. Stand still and scan the surrounding canyon walls for movement or sound (the sheep sometimes dislodge loose rocks). Binoculars can be helpful—don't leave them at home for this trip.

One guaranteed way to see a bighorn sheep on this trip is to look inside

▲ Check the weather before visiting Mount Baldy, storms can come on fast.

◄ Although signs warn motorists to limit their speed, only the luckiest visitors will get a glimpse of the resident black bears.

the Mount Baldy Visitor Center, though the sheep here are of the taxidermy variety. For up-to-the-minute sheep-spotting tips, stop in and talk to the ranger on duty. Take a moment to explore the displays. They depict the changes in plants and animals as you come up the mountain. A short trail around the center explores the area's cultural history, from the Gabrieleño/Tongva people that moved seasonally up into the mountains during warm months, to miners that dug and panned for gold in the late 1800s.

Don't miss the small pond out front, often inhabited by water striders—insects able to walk on water. They are very light and spread their weight out over their legs, allowing them to skate over the water without breaking its surface tension. In bright sunlight, look for the six shadowed dimples caused by each tiny foot.

The visitor center is also the place to purchase an Adventure Pass, which must be displayed while exploring the area, or a wilderness permit if you plan on hiking into the Cucamonga Wilderness.

Visiting in August? Try to plan your trip around the Perseid meteor shower. Light pollution from the city is minimal here, so shooting stars are much more visible.

Ski Lift Subalpine Adventure

The ski lift runs year round and offers visitors a peaceful, one-mile, seventeen-minute scenic ride. As you glide up the mountain, enjoy stunning views of the scree (loose rock) and pine-covered slopes below. Peeking into the treetops offers a glimpse of birds going about their business from a vantage we rarely get.

Summiting Mount Baldy is a rite of passage for many local hikers. It's one of a six-pack of challenging regional peak hikes that includes Mount Wilson, Cucamonga Peak, San Bernardino Peak, Mount San Jacinto, and San Gorgonio, which, at 11,503 feet, is the highest in Southern California.

The view gets better at the top. Follow a short trail to the ridgeline for spectacular vistas of both sides of the mountain. Got a Frisbee? There's a disc golf course at the top. Ziplines too, if the ski lift wasn't adventure enough for you. The trail to the summit is a grueling 6.5 miles round trip from here.

Be wary of the altitude. The top of the lift is at 7,800 feet, near the point when many people begin to feel the effects of altitude sickness. As elevation increases, air pressure decreases, making the air thinner. Thin air means fewer molecules in every breath you take, making it harder for you to get oxygen. People experiencing altitude sickness report headaches, nausea, dizziness, and loss of appetite. If you're new to high-altitude adventures, take it easy and stay hydrated. Opt for the short hike to the ridgeline, then stop for a bite to eat at Top of the Notch Restaurant and Bar. If you feel a headache coming on, take the ski lift back down where the air has more oxygen!

▲ A Merriam's chipmunk surveys the view from a fallen log.

🌲 Winter snow storms make Mount Baldy a popular destination for snow play.

Easy Hikes

Scared of heights, or sensitive to altitude? There's a much shorter and easier hike further down the mountain. The trail is only 0.6 miles from the parking area and leads to the seventy-five-foot San Antonio Falls. Be warned that in the middle of summer, the falls may be dry or offer only the most meager of trickles. If spring-fed mountain water is a must-see for your group, take the Icehouse Canyon trail, which follows a burbling mountain creek as it cascades from one rocky pool to the next. Even in the driest months, the stream

► A year-round creek follows the Icehouse Canyon trail. In the hottest of summers, it will be a mere trickle connecting deeper pools, and in the winter months parts of it freeze.

flows and has a nice chill to it if you put your hands or feet in.

Icehouse Canyon trail travels 3.5 miles up to Icehouse Saddle, with about 2,500 feet elevation gain. To avoid snow, plan this hike between June and October. At about the two-mile marker, you'll reach the Cucamonga Wilderness area, beyond which a wilderness permit is required. Many groups decide to hike only the first half mile or mile of the trail, which is great for children or beginners.

Icehouse Canyon is named after an ice harvesting plant constructed in the 1860s to supply ice to wealthy homes in the lowlands below.

Frank G. Bonelli Regional Park

The best place in Los Angeles to see bald eagles, this large park also offers boating, trail riding, an inland beach, and hiking.

EQUESTRIAN STAGING AREA

EQUESTRIAN STAGING AREA

BALD EAGLE

RAGING WATERS

BRACKETT FIELD AIRPORT

TRAILS

PUDDINGSTONE LAKE

RV PARK

RACCOON PRINTS

FAIRPLEX DRIVE

MANY TRAILS HERE

BEACH

VIA VERDE DR

VIA VERDE DR

MANY TRAILS

PARK ENTRANCE

THE 57

AMAZING CHILDREN'S PLAYGROUND

THE 10 FREEWAY

THE 10

THE 71

KEY
☆ PARKING
- - - - TRAILS / DIRT ROADS
═══ PAVED ROADS
═══ BIKE PATHS

WHERE: 120 Via Verde, San Dimas, CA 91773
PARKING: Multiple parking lots and trailheads.
DIFFICULTY, DISTANCE, ACCESS: Most people walk a few miles or less on wheelchair and stroller accessible trails; longer options possible.
FACILITIES: Trails, restrooms, picnic areas, play areas, public beach (summer only).
BEST TIME: Summer for swimming, winter for bald eagles, and midweek in winter to avoid fees and crowds.

▲ Roadrunners are part of the cuckoo family. They're fast enough to run down delicious lizards and small snakes, birds, or mammals for food.

⚑ Puddingstone Reservoir at Bonelli Regional Park is a naturalist's playground.

Sometimes called Puddingstone

Reservoir (after the big lake in the middle of it), Frank G. Bonelli Regional Park is named for a long-serving county supervisor and seems to cover every recreation possibility. Birders know this is a reliable place to look for bald eagles, white pelicans, five kinds of heron and egret, year-round ducks and coots, gulls and terns, and even a chaparral species, the greater roadrunner, that's tricky to find anyplace else in the region. There's mountain biking (the park was selected as the mountain biking event site for the 2028 Olympics!) and horseback riding, kayak and bike rentals, a campground, and even a golf course. Fishing is popular but check the county's Parks and Recreation website for health advisories about what not to eat (parks.lacounty.gov). Guided bird walks help beginners learn; check the same website for schedules.

◄ A red-tailed hawk gathers sticks for its nest.

Raptors Rising

Two fish-loving birds of prey can be seen at Bonelli, especially in winter. One is the osprey, the long-winged, white-and-black fish snatcher that's easy to identify thanks to its black bandit mask. The second is the bald eagle, larger than an osprey, with a dark body and (in adults) a white head and bright yellow hooked bill. Perhaps you'll be lucky and one will nab a fish right in front of you. While bald eagles and ospreys can be seen in summer, they are more common from November to April.

Great horned owls live in the park year-round, as do red-tailed hawks, usually seen circling on currents of warm air, their broad wings and cinnamon-red tail helping show us what they are. Once the air warms up, turkey vultures appear, patrolling the open country for carrion.

The bald eagle is a major conservation success story. In the 1700s, the estimated population of bald eagles in the lower forty-eight states was over 100,000 nesting pairs. Because of hunting, habitat loss, lead poisoning from scavenging on gut piles (exactly what they sound like) left behind by hunters, and eggshell thinning due to DDT, there were only 417 pairs in 1963. Bans on DDT and protection under the federal Endangered Species Act reversed this trend. The species was removed from ESA protection in 2007 when there were nearly 10,000 breeding pairs.

These raptors (birds of prey) are a good indication of the size of the park and the mix of habitats. Lots of predators means there's enough prey for them to eat. Cooper's hawks also are common, with year-round resident mourning doves, starlings, robins, and bluebirds all on their menu.

Stabbing, Jabbing, Pinching, and Probing

Five kinds of herons and egrets live here: snowy and great egrets, the great blue heron, the green heron, and the black-crowned night heron, which is often hunched over with its neck pulled down into its shoulders, like a grumpy person waiting in the rain.

Most of these birds are patient hunters, standing still or walking very slowly watching for prey, then grabbing it with a sudden jolt of the neck and bill. Snowy egrets are more active, often foot-paddling to stir up prey and sometimes running and lunging after escaping food.

▲ Using binoculars, scan for great blue herons and other birds perched in shoreline vegetation.

Bugs and the History of the Color Red

Bonelli has a lot of prickly pear cactus, and you may notice many cactus pads are covered with fluffy white fuzz. It sometimes looks like barnacles on a whale's tale. This fuzz covers a small insect called the cochineal scale. When it is dried, crushed, and mixed with fixatives, it produces an astoundingly bright, permanent red dye—a secret the Aztecs knew and the Spanish conquistadors promptly stole.

Cochineal from Mexico became a very valuable export. In Europe, almost as soon as it was discovered, it was used to dye many things deep red, from cardinals' robes to British Redcoat uniforms. The Spanish empire was built on three things: gold, silver, and cochineal. Artisan weavers and dyers still use it today, even though synthetic replacements are used in most commercial products.

Cochineal is found all over Los Angeles, not just at Bonelli Park, but once you learn to spot the infestations here, you can watch for them on other hikes (like along the LA River on Trip 10). If you do find some, take the tip of your pocket knife and crush a small piece of the white crust against the side of the cactus to see the intense magenta color. Just don't wipe your knife on your clothes or you'll have a stain that might not come out in the wash.

◄ Cochineal
sometimes looks
like barnacles on a
whale's tale.

All Roads Lead to Rome

Cochineal is still used today in food coloring. When you see "carmine" on a food label, you're actually eating crushed up insects!

This site has so many options that where to start is a matter of personal preference. You can circle the whole lake if you want, though most people do an out-and-back route. The lake was formed by a dam built in 1928 to control the mudslides that periodically roar out of the nearby San Gabriel Mountains. Today, the shoreline's willows, pines, open grassy spots, and marshy areas are home to many kinds of birds. For your first visit, come in from the west entrance by the 57 Freeway and go straight to the far side of the lake, parking near the East Shore. From there you can walk north and east around the lake to the RV park, a path with good birdwatching. When done, come back the way you came.

Whittier Narrows Recreation Area

Willow forests and well-marked, accessible nature trails provide a window into Los Angeles's past, as does an old-school nature center—the first home of the LA Audubon Society.

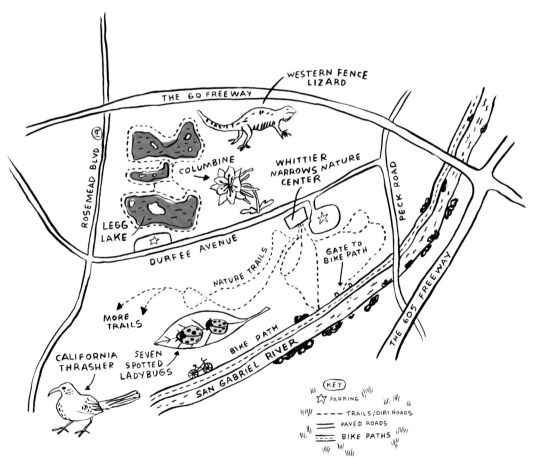

WESTERN FENCE LIZARD

THE 60 FREEWAY

ROSEMEAD BLVD (19)

COLUMBINE

WHITTIER NARROWS NATURE CENTER

PECK ROAD

LEGG LAKE

DURFEE AVENUE

NATURE TRAILS

GATE TO BIKE PATH

THE 605 FREEWAY

MORE TRAILS

CALIFORNIA THRASHER

SEVEN SPOTTED LADYBUGS

BIKE PATH

SAN GABRIEL RIVER

KEY
☆ PARKING
----- TRAILS / DIRT ROADS
═══ PAVED ROADS
═══ BIKE PATHS

WHERE: 1000 Durfee Road, South El Monte, CA 91733

PARKING: Parking lots at the nature center (no fee) or in nearby parks (fee).

DIFFICULTY, DISTANCE, ACCESS: Less than a mile (with much longer bike options).

FACILITIES: Restrooms and picnic tables at nature center.

BEST TIME: Late winter to late spring will have greenest plants, brightest birds.

SPECIAL NOTES: Check the schedule (parks.lacounty.gov) if you're interested in bird walks, family nature walks, or night hikes.

The San Gabriel Valley today has so many roads and houses it's hard to imagine anything natural survives. Yet survive it does, and Whittier Narrows helps prove it. Here, you can focus on getting your 10,000 steps or relax and explore each pond or cluster of flowers as you come upon them. The Whittier Narrows Nature Center has animal ambassadors to educate children. Birders check for migrants and rare arrivals, like the yellow-billed cuckoo that turned up one summer. And there's easy access to the San Gabriel River, where you can join a bike path that runs thiry-eight miles from the Santa Fe Dam to the Pacific Ocean at Seal Beach (coming out near Trip 22, the sea turtle site).

▲ Look closer at the blooming invasive mustard, and you may find it dotted with thousands of ladybugs.

Easy to Visit, Tricky to Describe

Whittier Narrows can refer to many things. On the geological level, it marks a "choke point" or "water gap" where the San Gabriel River forces its way between the Puente Hills to the east and Montebello Hills to the west, exiting the southern boundary of the San Gabriel Valley for the broad plain of the LA Basin. Historically, during winter storms, an unstoppable blast of brown water and screaming boulders rushed into the LA Basin. Where the 60 and 605 freeways now cross was once a flood zone too wild to build in. One hundred years ago even below-the-5 towns like Downey and Norwalk could be completely underwater during floods.

Dams and channelization changed all that. Protected from winter floods, farms, towns, and small cities grew. Yet this tangle of freeways and roads, parks, lakes, trails, power line rights-of-way, and sewage treatment plant outflows all combine to create a mosaic of wetland and upland habitat.

For naturalists, Whittier Narrows refers to a sequence of parks north and south of Durfee Avenue, between Rosemead Boulevard and the San Gabriel River. Habitats here include Legg Lake, where you might see a loon in winter

▲ Look for mating ladybugs on warm days.

⚓ The slow-moving water upstream of this weir dam is frequented by osprey, herons, egrets, and turtles.

◀ Phainopepla love mistletoe berries, and mistletoes love them right back—after eating lots of berries, the birds poop out the seeds, helping mistletoe to spread.

or hear the *witchy-witchy* call of a common yellowthroat, and the maze of nature trails and paths on the other side of Durfee, heading west from the nature center along the levee.

To visit, just park at the nature center and start walking. How green or brown it looks depends on how much rain there has been, but no matter which path you take, you'll find something delightful. It might be something common, like a red-eared slider turtle in the riverbed or a western fence lizard doing push-ups. It might be ladybugs in the mustard plants or a heron perched in the top of a tree. Or perhaps you'll see the phainopepla ("fay-no-PEP-la"), a desert and foothill bird whose name means "shining robe" in reference to the males' glossy black feathers. They sport a jaunty mohawk and intense red eyes. When they fly, white wing patches flash like small sunbursts.

The More It Changes, the More It Stays the Same

None of the excursions covered in this book will stay exactly the same year after year. Trails erode and get rebuilt; fires clear one vegetation regime and encourage another; funding priorities shift, closing one site while another opens. What is the future of the Whittier Narrows? A large discovery center has been in development for a while, one whose footprint would overlap with the present nature trails, but its future is unclear.

Whatever does or doesn't get built, out in the brush, along the Rio Hondo and San Gabriel Rivers, around Legg Lake and the small oasis near the current nature center, the California towhees and white-crowned sparrows will still hop and scratch, looking for seeds and carrying on as they always do. Swallows will soar and loop, gobbling up insects. A "discovery center" is a good idea, but the ultimate place to discover nature is nature itself.

Powder Canyon

A delightful island of habitat with a rich network of trails, large native oak trees, and (in winter) killer city views—popular with walkers, mountain bikers, and equestrians.

WHERE: 2345 Fullerton Road, La Habra Heights, CA 90631

PARKING: Gravel parking lot at trailhead.

DIFFICULTY, DISTANCE, ACCESS: One to five miles (or more), depending on your loop route. Not great for strollers or wheelchairs, but you can make it work if you are dirt-road ready.

FACILITIES: Port-a-potties at trailhead; picnic tables, restrooms in Schabarum Park.

BEST TIME: Good year-round; closed for forty-eight hours after rain to let trails recover.

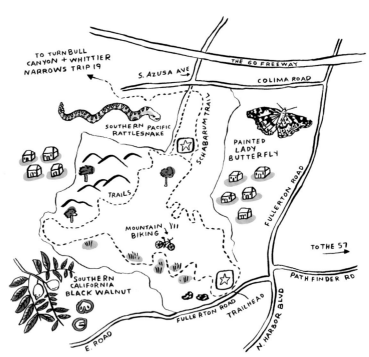

This island of habitat parallels the 60 Freeway between the 605 and Diamond Bar. The steep ridges and shady valleys offer a chance to experience oaks, rare Southern California black walnuts, chaparral plants, and open, grassy hillsides.

► Even if you don't see a snake, you might find evidence of them, like this shed skin.

🔍 Cheek pouches bulging, this California ground squirrel wonders if it can fit in just one more acorn.

Watch for mule deer here, red-tailed hawks, or maybe even the paw prints of a bobcat or mountain lion. The grassy slopes of Puente Hills are dotted with California ground squirrel burrows. This helps make it excellent snake habitat. Lucky hikers might see several rattlesnakes in a single morning, especially in the spring. Other times there seem to be none at all.

Interesting Trails, Interesting Trees

Start at the Powder Canyon Trailhead off of Fullerton Road. Check the kiosk for trail maps. If there aren't any maps left, just take a picture of the big map on the signboard with your smartphone. Trails here are well-marked, and you'll want to mix-and-match your loops to get just the right distance for you and your party.

No matter which way you want to go, everybody starts on the same entrance path. Almost immediately after leaving the trailhead you find yourself inside the shady canopy of oak and walnut trees. Both have dark brown trunks, but the walnuts are deciduous, dropping their leaves in winter, while these oaks keep leaves year-round. The oak leaves are dark green and smaller than a quarter, with sharp points and often curled up like saucers rather than flat. In contrast, a walnut tree's leaves are greener, slimmer, longer, more like the shape of a fern or willow. In spring, the nuts appear, looking like small green apples, but they turn brown and even black later in the season. Nowadays, native walnut trees can be hard to find in Southern California, but Puente Hills is a great place to spot them.

No matter how tempting the shade looks, stay on the trails. This not only helps maintain habitat integrity but also protects you from poison oak. After the oak and walnut grove, skip the Gray Squirrel Trail, which just connects back to the road, and instead take the Black Walnut Trail, which will come up on the right and creates a longer loop.

You also can stay on the Powder Canyon Trail to reach the stables at Schabarum Park. If you do, pause by the stables to look at the trees. In a perfect line there's a cottonwood tree, a pepper tree, a Mexican fan palm, and a coast live oak. It's like a botany lesson for the blended treescapes of Los Angeles, all in one tidy row.

Morning hikers wanting a workout can crank their way up the Purple Sage Trail. All routes are popular, and if you're not sure what connects to what, just ask some-body—on the weekends, there are always lots of people around.

It's Not My Fault: California Geology

As with so many LA parks, the Puente Hills are a steep island of undeveloped land rising out of the urban sea. Whenever you see hills sticking up like this, suspect an earthquake fault nearby, pushing and pulling the landscape like a baker kneading dough. The Puente Hills Fault made itself known with the Whittier Narrows Earthquake in 1987 (magnitude 5.9). Geologists call it a blind thrust fault because its presence was initially hidden beneath the surface; we now know it runs from Brea, northwest to downtown Los Angeles, and is yet another reason to have good earthquake insurance.

While hiking any of the trails here, study the hillsides. You're not only watching for a snake or resting deer but also a glimpse of ledges and

▲ In the warmer months, native oak and walnut trees provide welcome shade along the trail.

If you look at a map, the Puente Hills appear to be a northward extension of the Santa Ana Mountains. In fact, they belong to completely different sets of mountain ranges. The Puente Hills are one of the lower, smaller members of the Transverse Ranges, which run generally in an east-west orientation, and include the Santa Monica, San Gabriel, and San Bernardino Mountains. The Santa Anas are part of the Peninsular Ranges, which run generally in a north-south direction, include the San Jacinto Mountains, and run to the tip of the Baja Peninsula about 900 miles to the south.

▲ Many of the trails at Powder Canyon are multi-use and frequented by joggers, hikers, mountain bikers, and horseback riders.

exposed reefs (long ridges of normally underground stone). As the tilted bed-rock becomes visible through the soil and brush, it's like having x-ray vision, letting you see the bones of the planet in action.

Trail Etiquette

More than on any of our other excursions, expect to share the trails here with a mix of users. At all hours of the day there could be mountain bikers, joggers, and horseback riders on any of the trails, so we all have to practice common trail etiquette. Mountain bikers should know to give a shout or a tinkle of a bell to alert you when they're coming up from behind. Leave them room to get by and don't cross into the center of the trail unexpectedly.

Horses should always receive right of way from hikers and mountain bikers. Stand on the downhill side of the trail and wait for the horse to pass. Be friendly, use common sense, share the road—the same advice applies to hiking in popular areas as it does to living a generally good life.

El Dorado Nature Center

Two miles of winding trails, a stream, a nature center on an island, and two lakes filled with turtles bring some wilderness to the middle of Long Beach.

WHERE: 7550 East Spring Street, Long Beach, CA 90815

PARKING: Parking fees vary by day of the week.

DIFFICULTY, DISTANCE, ACCESS: Easy hikes from ¼–2 miles. ¼-mile trail is ADA and stroller accessible, trails close to lakes are also flat.

FACILITIES: Bathrooms and drinking fountains at nature center.

BEST TIME: This site is great to visit year round, with lots of shade on hot summer days.

SPECIAL NOTES: Closed Mondays. Admission to nature center requires cash.

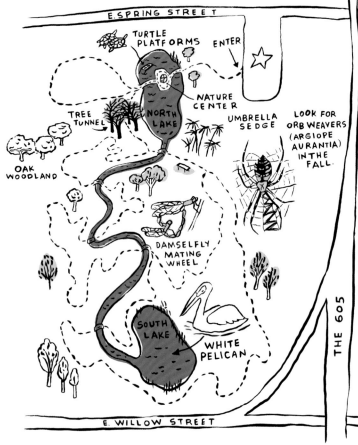

KEY
☆ PARKING
- - - - TRAILS / DIRT ROADS
═══ PAVED ROADS
━━━ BIKE PATHS

▲ One of El Dorado Park's two lakes.

Surrounded by suburbia, the San Gabriel River, and the 605 Freeway, El Dorado Nature Center is a 105-acre oasis in the heart of Long Beach. As soon as you step through the tall wooden gates, it feels as though you've left the city. This is a place where trees and waterfowl are more common than cars and buildings, where you walk on the Earth instead of concrete, and where the hum of electrical wires is drowned out by rustling leaves.

A Mini-Museum on an Island

The nature center is on an island in the middle of a lake and reached by crossing a wooden bridge. Inside, exhibits focus on the people, plants, and animals that call the area home. Outside, there's a porch with benches, hummingbird feeders, and great views of the north lake. For a closer look at wildlife on the water, gaze through the viewing scope. Heed the signs' warning: "Attention squirrels, human food can harm you." Don't let them trick you into feeding them. Use the restrooms, fill up your water bottles at the drinking fountains, and pick up a trail brochure before starting your hike.

El Dorado Park used to be part of the San Gabriel River floodplain and was covered with willows, cottonwood trees, and other riparian plants. Not long after Spanish explorers arrived, a number of Mexican land grants were issued for Rancho Los Alamitos, Los Cerritos, and Los Coyotes. Agriculture and livestock were big parts of early settlers' lives. Rancho Los Cerritos held 15,000 head of cattle, 7,000 sheep, and 3,000 horses. As human and livestock populations grew, native vegetation diminished. The nature center sits in an area once covered by bean fields.

In the 1960s, the local community came together to create a park. The center was constructed in 1969 as part of the larger El Dorado park system, which includes an archery range, golf course, tennis center, basketball courts, picnic areas, and fishing lakes. Soil excavated from the 605 Freeway construction was used to create hills and mounds for two miles of nature trails that wind past understory (ground level) vegetation and beneath an oak- and willow-tree canopy, hinting at the floodplain forest that used to line parts of the nearby San Gabriel River.

▲ Non-native eastern fox squirrels call this park home.

▼ A young goose is called a gosling.

Who Lives Here?

With a creek and two lakes, there are lots of banks and water edges to explore. Fishing isn't allowed, but look closely at still waters for bluegill and largemouth bass. There are also many colorful koi carp that might have been pets at some point. Canada geese breed in these lakes too. Look for their fluffy goslings in spring.

Although you can't catch the fish, plenty of birds do. You might see a great egret standing sentinel in the shallows, waiting for a fish to come within reach of its spearing beak. Or if you're lucky you'll spot a pelican swallowing a fish whole.

PELICAN BRIEF

Pelicans are showstoppers. Both brown and American white pelicans have been recorded here, usually in the fall and winter. These large, impressive birds are easy to identify because of their long necks and big bills with the fleshy undercarriage of their expandable throat pouch. To hunt, pelicans fly over water looking for fish. When they spot one, they dive in, twisting their necks against their body to protect their spines, then opening their bills wide to catch the fish. After resurfacing, before they can swallow the fish, they must drain their pouch of all the extra water. At this moment the pelican can lose its hard-won meal—sometimes the fish jumps out, and sometimes gulls or other birds swoop in and steal the fish right from the pelican's throat!

▲ American white pelicans are most often seen here in winter.

SEDGES HAVE EDGES

To hide from predatory birds like pelicans and egrets, fish and other prey often take to the shallows where various shore plants provide cover. The spiky-looking plant with umbrella-like leaves lining the water's edge might look like grass, but it's actually an umbrella sedge. Get close and touch the stems to feel their edges. Unlike grasses, which have round stems, if you were to cut a sedge stem in half you'd find a triangular cross section. The most well-known sedge in the world is papyrus, the plant ancient Egyptians used to make paper.

Also growing in the shallows or in the wet-soil along the water's edge is yerba mansa. It blooms each spring with showy white flowers that form a cone surrounded by white bracts (bracts look like petals, but they're actually mod-ified leaves). Dried yerba mansa has been used as a treatment for inflammation—from swollen gums and sore throats, to athlete's foot and diaper rash.

TURTLE POWER

As soon as you walk over the first bridge, look for the floating docks. On most days turtles sun themselves on these platforms. The most common turtles seen here are

Map turtles get their name from the yellow marking on their *carapace* (the upper part of their shell) that look like topography lines on a map.

► Hundreds of mostly non-native turtles live in the lakes and clamber out on warm days to bask on the floating docks. Here a western pond turtle basks atop a red-eared slider, while a yellow-bellied slider looks off to the right.

> The zig-zag designs in orb weaver webs give them the common name writing spider—just like the spider in *Charlotte's Web*, which was based on another type of orb weaver, *Araneus cavaticus.*

red-eared sliders, but you'll also find soft-shelled turtles, map turtles, and other non-native species common in the LA area. These are escaped or released pets, or their offspring. You may even spot the occasional native western pond turtle.

VISIT IN THE FALL FOR ORB WEBS

If you visit in the fall, keep a look out for the spectacular webs made by orb weaver spiders. Many species of spiders call the nature center home year-round, but they aren't always easy to find—preferring to hide under leaf litter or tree bark, or in rolled-up leaves. In contrast, orb weavers build their beautiful webs at eye level or higher. The park is a perfect habitat for them, and you can find lots of them in the fall. Small insects breed in the lakes, then hatch to fly through the air, collide with spider webs, and become spider food. The most common species of orb weaver in the park is *Neoscona crucifera,* also known as the spotted orb weaver or barn spider. It's about the size and color of a peanut, with a cross pattern on its back. Marvel at it from a distance, and imagine how much time it took to build that intricate web.

Choose Your Own Small, Medium, or Large Adventure

There are three trail options for visitors of all sizes and abilities. A short, quarter-mile trail is ADA accessible and offers handrails for anyone needing support. A longer, one-mile trail winds through shaded woody areas and crisscrosses over the stream multiple times with bridges at each crossing. The longest trail is two miles and leads all the way to the south lake on the other side of the park.

TRIP 22

Lower San Gabriel River

An endangered (and usually tropical) sea turtle lives in Long Beach. Try to spot one—and count the leaping fish and herons while you wait.

WHERE: San Gabriel River between Seal Beach and Long Beach.

PARKING: Free street parking on First Street near the Pacific Coast Highway; walk one block back to river.

DIFFICULTY, DISTANCE, ACCESS: Easy on foot. If on bike, you can ride up to thirty-eight miles each way to Azusa and back. Level, paved path is good for strollers and wheelchairs but watch out for bikes.

FACILITIES: Viewing platforms by the Haynes Generating Station allow you to get safely off the bike path. No bathrooms or picnic areas.

BEST TIME: Good year round but avoid the highest tides and just after heavy rains, when debris makes spotting harder, and water covers the lowest dips in the bike path.

SPECIAL NOTE: The turtles always make us feel like doing something nice for this area, so you might bring a bag to pick up some litter and throw it away later. Bring binoculars for bird watching on the walk to and from the best turtle-viewing locations.

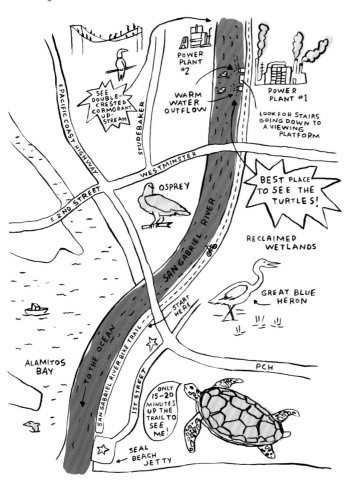

Ready for that sea turtle experience you thought you had to go to Hawaii to have? One of only two known groups of green sea turtles in California swims in the lower San Gabriel River (the other is in San Diego Bay). They've been spotted in the river since at least the 1970s. They

▲ Sea turtle spotting is a great group activity. Who can spot the first one?

don't nest here—that probably takes place on islands and beaches in Mexico—but they do spend a lot of time enjoying the warm water from the power plants and nearby shallow salt marshes.

The turtles look more brown than green. Though protected most places now, green turtles used to be dinner for many cultures, including Americans in the nineteenth century—a butchered turtle's fat is green and gave the species its name.

Park near the beach and follow the San Gabriel River bike path upstream to the power plants. The turtles are big fans of the Jacuzzi-like conditions of this part of the river, and the platforms by the power plants are the best place to look for them.

Sea Turtle Spotting 101

While sea turtles can be seen anywhere in Alamitos Bay, the most reliable place to spot them is in the San Gabriel River, upstream of the Second Street crossing. Unfortunately there

▲ ◀ You'll spot the turtles' heads first, but with practice, you can make out their flippers and saucer-shaped shells while they're still below the surface.

is often a lot of trash in the river, and you may get tricked a few times before you see your first sea turtle head break the surface. Be patient though, and you will very likely be rewarded.

Green sea turtles can grow to three feet across and weigh over five hundred pounds. Some will be smaller, and all can be tricky to find at first. Watch for their round heads poking out of the water when they come up for air. The head may look as small as a tennis ball or as big as a grapefruit. If you take a picture, don't forget to add it to the RASCals project on iNaturalist or email it to rascals@nhm.org.

WHY ARE THE GREEN TURTLES HERE?

Turtles haven't always lived here. Ocean temperatures were too cold for them in Southern California during the last glacial period when humans first settled the area, but the ocean has warmed. Because no group of green sea turtles along the Pacific Coast is found any farther north, we can assume this water is about as cold as they can tolerate. We also know sea turtle remains, common in archaeological digs further south, are very rare in local excavations of Native American settlements. Whether the turtles arrived one hundred or five hundred years ago is up for debate, but in ecological terms, they're new to the scene.

Young green sea turtles are omnivorous (they eat plants and animals), but as they get older, they become herbivorous—salad only, please! You can see them grazing along the river bottom and plucking algae and plants from the rocks by the power plants.

Turtles were probably using the wetlands before this area became developed, but the power plants along the river, built in the mid-1960s to provide electricity for Los Angeles, encourage them to stay in this narrow stretch. The generators are cooled with water pumped in from the ocean, which, once it has absorbed the heat, is then pumped out into the river. Turtles are cold-blooded—the scientific term is *ectothermic*—meaning they get body warmth from their environment. The warm water here is comfortable for them, and it encourages the growth of plants they like to eat.

An elegant tern flashes past, slim and agile.

Double-crested cormorants stand stoically on power lines crisscrossing the river. When they see a tasty fish, they're off like a rocket.

Do fish breathe water? Yes and no. They need the dissolved oxygen that's *in* the water to live. Mullets, common fish in the lower San Gabriel River, feed on the river bottom where there's not much oxygen in the water. They may be jumping out of the river to stock up their oxygen supply before returning to their basement habitat.

WHAT HAPPENS WHEN THE HOT WATER TURNS OFF?

The turtles congregate at the power plants because of the warm water pumps. But the power plants are being upgraded now, and in coming years, they will probably be converted to air-cooled (instead of water-cooled) systems. Will the sea turtles still gather at the river?

Probably. When power plants in San Diego Bay were upgraded, the turtles stayed. They just spread out more. The shallow, slow-moving water of our Alamitos Bay and Seal Beach National Wildlife Refuge is still warmer than other water along the coast. If the power plants change up, turtles are likely to stay in the general area, but they will be a bit harder to find.

It's Not All about the Turtles

The river here is a blend of water coming from two directions. Fresh water flows down the San Gabriel River, combining snowmelt, rain runoff, treated discharge from sewage plants, and flow from natural springs. When it meets the ocean, the mix of fresh and salt water is called brackish. Many species like this mix, and it offers lots to look for while you scan the river for turtle heads.

Striped mullet is a silver fish the size and shape of a small salmon. Normally it mucks around the river bottom, eating bits of dead plants and small animals called zooplankton, but you'll periodically see them leaping and splashing out of the water. Scientists aren't *entirely* sure, but they think the fish do this to grab extra oxygen from the air.

With luck, you may spot sea lions in the river too, and up to twenty kinds of water birds, from the stately great blue heron to fast-flying terns and black, snake-necked cormorants.

What Was Here before the Concrete and the Power Plants?

This land is always changing. Historically, water in the lower San Gabriel River slowed down and spread out as it approached the coast, expanding into the Los Cerritos Wetlands. High flows from winter rains spread out along the flat parts of Seal Beach and Long Beach, creating pools, marshes, and salt flats. As the water evaporated in summer, the soil would be caked with salt, allowing only certain plants to survive.

Then came the hallmarks of a growing Los Angeles—first grazing animals, then farms, and finally urban development. To provide security from the frequent floods, the channel was deepened and lined with concrete to contain the river.

Today, we value open space differently, and we recognize the importance of tidal marshes for animals—fish incubate and migrating birds eat here. Community-based efforts have secured land on both sides of the river and there are active efforts to restore portions of the Los Cerritos Wetlands. Just like a hundred years ago, the land is in flux. Each year you come back, it may look a little different.

Lower LA River at Willow Street

Saltwater meets fresh at this soft-bottomed section of the LA River. Come for birds and more birds—especially during fall migration.

WHERE: De Forest Avenue, between W. 27th Street and 26th Way.
PARKING: Street parking.
DIFFICULTY, DISTANCE, ACCESS: Walk just fifty yards or do a fifty-mile round trip bike ride. Bike path and river view are handicap accessible.
FACILITIES: No facilities.
BEST TIME: Mornings from mid-August to late-September are best for shorebirds.

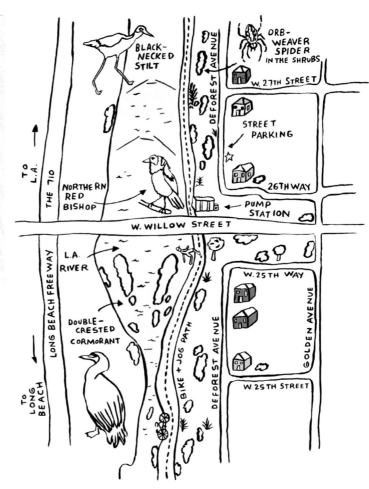

The last stretch of the LA River in Long Beach offers a different experience from Frogtown and Sepulveda Basin (Trips 3 and 10), because it's more heavily influenced by tides and has a different mix of bird species. After bending around downtown LA, the river is confined to concrete all the way to Willow Street. Here salt and fresh water create a brackish mix over a soft-bottom. This habitat is sometimes called estuarine, from the word estuary, which is a tidal lagoon.

During the fall migration, ten thousand or more shorebirds stop over. Introduced birds like red bishops and scaly-breasted munias (also called nutmeg mannikins) mix with natives for a typical SoCal blend of east meets west.

Hike Uphill to Find the Water

Your first visit to the river may seem strange—as you turn in from Willow Street to park, you're under a row of Peruvian pepper trees on a block of nice homes—it doesn't seem like a nature reserve at all. Where's the water? This neighborhood is protected from flooding (everybody hopes) by the tall levee between the houses and the 710 Freeway. You'll find the river by hiking up the levee's diagonal ramp to the channel on the other side.

A Rest Stop for Birds

Willow Street marks the divide: concrete above, vegetation and mudflats below. But a quirk of design makes the concrete a more hospitable rest stop for migrating birds than you might think. This stretch of channel boasts a narrow chute down the center. It ranges from 12–20 feet across, about the size of a car lane, and was designed to send water rapidly out to sea while the wider main channel stood available to gather heavy floodwaters when necessary. As Los Angeles grew, more water flowed through the chute than expected. Today, a small bit of water overflows and spreads out across the flat riverbed. Just a few inches deep, the water warms in the sun and creates a great place for algae mats to grow. The algae attracts snails and insects, which in turn provide a tasty buffet for migrating birds.

GOTTA SPOT THEM ALL

Serious birdwatchers travel upstream to Del Amo Boulevard or beyond, hoping to find out-of-range shorebirds that will add gold stars to their life lists. The hardest of hardcore birders survey thousands of small sandpipers, sometimes called peeps, feather by feather, looking for subtle differences.

Most people will be more interested in the river south of the access ramp, where you can bike or walk all the way to the Port of Long Beach. Water levels change and storms deposit sandbars different places each season, but there will almost always be a great mix of ducks, herons, and waders starting right at the access ramp.

Mid-winter and late summer are the most reliable times to observe thirty species in thirty minutes, but any month offers at least half a dozen species. As you go downstream, brown pelicans indicate where the river meets the ocean. The concrete sides give way to sharp, jumbled stone called riprap, which protects against erosion. From here out, the water gets increasingly salty.

In the willows and weedy grass, you may spot northern red bishops, a stout-billed mega sparrow with a closet full of crazy patterns. Females and non-breeding males are yellowish and black-streaked, like any of the dozen sparrows in your bird book. But breeding males turn on the open-for-business sign full force, with a blazing red-and-black full-body pattern visible from a distance.

American avocets also change color with the seasons. Their heads are gray in winter but in spring and summer turn a warm cinnamon orange. Avocets feed in shallow water by sweeping their bill side to side. In deeper water, cormorants chase down fish. You'll see them perched near the water with their wings spread towards sun (or into a light wind) to help them dry faster.

How do so many species of shorebird share the same area without fighting over food? Each species has a different bill—straight or curved, long or short—depending on their target food. Some beaks are good for hunting deeper things (like a buried clam), while others are better suited for finding insect larvae, shallow-water fish, or baby crabs. No single species is good at finding all possible prey, but each is an expert on a portion. Ecologists call this "resource partitioning." Taken as a whole, the bills in a shorebird community represent a set of Swiss army knife tools.

▲ Look for brown pelicans once you reach the riprap downstream towards the ocean.

▼ American avocets (this one has summer plumage) are often seen along the lower LA River.

◄ A cormorant drying its wings.

▶ At the lower LA River, bikers can get 35+ miles for their tires, and birders can get 215+ species of birds for their life lists.

Perfect Pocket Parks

Historically this section of the LA River would have been comprised of meandering channels, willow and cottonwood forests, deep pools and shady glens, wet marshes and dryer, seasonally flooded sections. Arroyo and white willows grew in luxurious thickets and forests, hence the modern town Willowbrook, and Willow Avenue.

Willows are still found in the river south of the bridge despite the densely populated neighborhoods. Between the 405 Freeway and the ocean at Long Beach, multiple pocket parks create space for sycamores and coastal sage, and therefore for warblers and flycatchers. Pocket parks offer great benefits for relatively low cost—once created, even the smallest pieces of open space generate an uptick in physical activity among local (human) residents, not to mention the benefit for wildlife.

Mixed Use—Birders and Bikes

Most visitors have one goal in mind. Birders come to bird; bikers come to bike. But there's great pleasure in combining goals. Riders cranking out a serious workout can still notice and appreciate avocets, stilts, and ospreys. Surprises await us on each trip, from a rock wren in the riprap to half a dozen butterflies species.

If you see somebody standing beside a telescope, jumping up and down like a giddy lunatic, have a stroll over and ask what's been spotted. You may have turned up just in time to celebrate the first North American record of a wandering Siberian shorebird. If it's going to happen anywhere in Los Angeles, it'll probably be here.

Earvin "Magic" Johnson Park

Ducks, geese, squirrels, and migrant birds gather around two small lakes. A fitness trail helps with New Year's exercise resolutions.

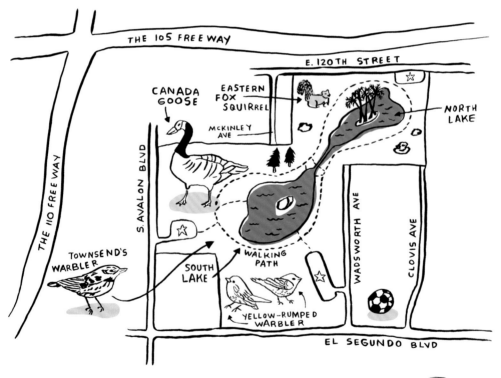

Basketball legend Earvin "Magic" Johnson works his magic as a businessman, philanthropist, AIDS-awareness spokesman, and co-owner of the Dodgers, Sparks, and Los Angeles Football Club. His magic extends to the park that bears his name, an oasis of calm, water, and nature in the heart of South Los Angeles.

KEY

☆ PARKING

---- TRAILS / DIRT ROADS

PAVED ROADS

BIKE PATHS

WHERE: 905 East El Segundo Boulevard, Willowbrook, CA 90059
PARKING: Paved parking lots plus street parking.
DIFFICULTY, DISTANCE, ACCESS: Most people do less than a one-mile loop. Trails are wheelchair and stroller accessible.
FACILITIES: Restrooms and picnic tables.
BEST TIME: Fine year-round; waterfowl best in winter.

▲ A small palm-covered island in the middle of the fishing lake is a valuable retreat for many of the park's birds.

As soon as you step out of your car, especially if it's early on a weekday, begin listening. The park will be alive with the chirps of warblers, the honks of geese, and the chittering calls of dozens of small birds too active and vroomy to stick a name on. The yellow-bellied, gray-headed flycatcher that's calling *kweer, kweer* on a winter morning is the lively and social Cassin's kingbird; look for it grabbing moths from trees around the lake. The long-tailed, all-black birds that whistle and gargle are grackles, a new arrival in California. They look like crows who dressed for prom while a bit tipsy and put on one tail too many. This Mexican and Central American bird follows quickly on the heels of urban and agricultural development, and its range continues to expand north and westward.

Dr. Nature

Most people walk the paths around the two lakes, knowing that a little exercise gets the body and mind energized. It can be hard work, living in the city. Spending time in nature can help lower blood pressure and anxiety. If you want a pleasant, low-stress way to start your exercise routine, this park is a lovely place to begin. It's impossible to get lost here, there's no entrance fee or membership card, it has many parking lots and restrooms, and if you bring binoculars, you just might spot a rare bird.

Plans are afoot for an ambitious expansion that would add amenities like a community event center, sculpture garden, and picnic shelters over the next several years. The idea is to grow this oasis to 120 acres.

One Duck, Two Ducks, Red Ducks, Blue Ducks

The park lakes are full of ducks. Some have arrived on their own, and others are abandoned domestic ducks. Mallards have been domesticated by people for thousands of years, and many of the big white ducks in the park had mallard ancestors. The ones with bumpy red faces are called Muscovy ducks and are originally from Mexico. Mid-winter brings other, wilder species to the park, including the American wigeon. It has a pale blue bill, blond forehead, speckled chin, and bright, iridescent green stripe blazing backwards from the middle of its face and down the side of its neck. Nothing else in the park looks like it.

▲ A domesticated Muscovy duck, with its distinctive red face.

It's worth studying the seagulls, since this can be a good inland site to compare large, gray-backed western gulls to the paler, slim-billed California and ring-billed gulls. You'll find American coots at the water's edge. Look for their specialized lobed feet, more useful on muddy ground than fully webbed feet. They're easy to see near the south lake, at least until somebody starts feeding the ducks popcorn—then everything becomes a flurry of feathers and squawks in a feeding-frenzy madness.

> Feeding wildlife is never a good idea, but if you're going to feed ducks, choose corn, lettuce, peas, oats, rice, or birdseed. They're happy to scarf down your bread, crackers, and popcorn, but it's not very good for them.

A Lakeside Who's Who

Though we discourage feeding wildlife here or anywhere else, not everybody gets the memo. Previous encounters with handouts from people have made the eastern fox squirrels here bold and curious. Up close, you can admire the subtle ways their reddish undercoat glows beneath gray outer hairs. Once you can identify this color palette, you'll recognize the species in other areas where it may overlap with western gray squirrels or California ground squirrels.

Black phoebes are also common in this park. Look for them perched on branches and fence posts. Though there may be several across the park, you'll probably only see one at a time, perhaps wagging its tail up and down. Yellow-rumped warblers, ruby-crowned kinglets, and white-crowned sparrows are common, winter-only birds. Their names tell you how to identify them.

▲ American wigeons are winter visitors to the park.

◀ American coot, with its rather large feet.

▶ Large flocks of Canada geese hang here year-round.

The park quiets down in summer. Still, there are usually a few gulls present, some geese that decided to stay in town and not bother with flying back to Canada, and some grackles, house sparrows, and starlings. As you do your walk around the lakes, watch for small things too, like ladybugs and honey bees. Look down as often as you look up. As naturalist Henry David Thoreau once said, "Heaven is under our feet as well as over our heads."

TRIP 25

Point Vicente Park

An interpretive center, lighthouse, miles of trails along coastal bluffs, and an annual gray whale migration. The Palos Verdes Peninsula boasts a unique nature experience.

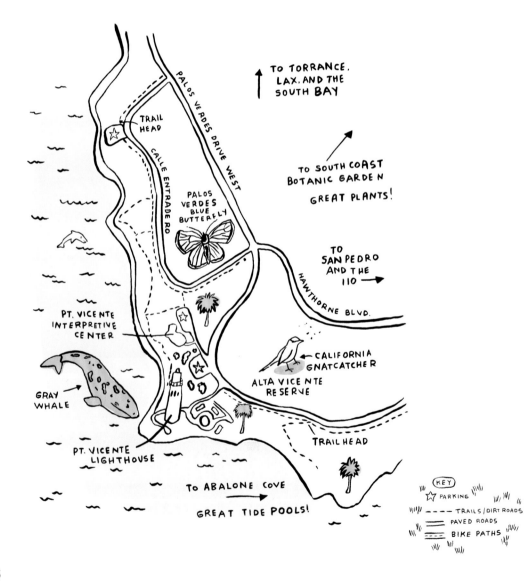

TO TORRANCE, LAX, AND THE SOUTH BAY

TRAIL HEAD

PALOS VERDES DRIVE WEST

CALLE ENTRADE RD

TO SOUTH COAST BOTANIC GARDEN
GREAT PLANTS!

PALOS VERDES BLUE BUTTERFLY

TO SAN PEDRO AND THE 110 →

HAWTHORNE BLVD.

PT. VICENTE INTERPRETIVE CENTER

CALIFORNIA GNATCATCHER

ALTA VICENTE RESERVE

GRAY WHALE

PT. VICENTE LIGHTHOUSE

TRAILHEAD

TO ABALONE COVE
GREAT TIDE POOLS!

KEY
☆ PARKING
---- TRAILS/DIRT ROADS
═══ PAVED ROADS
═══ BIKE PATHS

▲ The cliffs around the interpretive center provide great views.

As you drive or take the bus to Point Vicente, you'll be wowed by views of the Pacific Ocean. The road along the Palos Verdes Peninsula coast is one of Southern California's most scenic. On a clear day you can see Catalina Island twenty miles out to sea! Even though the peninsula is firmly attached to the mainland, it's sometimes called the ninth Channel Island because it first emerged from the ocean floor a few million years ago and has been an island, off and on, since then as sea levels fluctuated. The peninsula and the islands share plant and animal species that exist nowhere else on the mainland.

Start Your Trip at the Center

The Point Vicente Interpretive Center can be your jumping off point for exploring the entire Palos Verdes Peninsula, or it can be the main attraction. The center has free parking and, as soon as you pull into the lot, stunning ocean views. There are plenty of picnic benches in the grassy areas around the center, and inside there are restrooms, drinking fountains, a gift shop, exhibits, and the fossilized remains of a giant mako shark. December through May is whale migration season. Stop inside and borrow a pair of binoculars to see the whales chugging by.

WHERE: 30940 Hawthorne Boulevard, Rancho Palos Verdes, CA 90275

PARKING: Large parking lot with no fee.

DIFFICULTY, DISTANCE, ACCESS: Easy and short, but you can easily connect to longer trails. Two short trails near the interpretive center are stroller and wheelchair accessible.

FACILITIES: Picnic facilities outside. Bathrooms and drinking fountains inside.

BEST TIME: Gray whale migration is December through May.

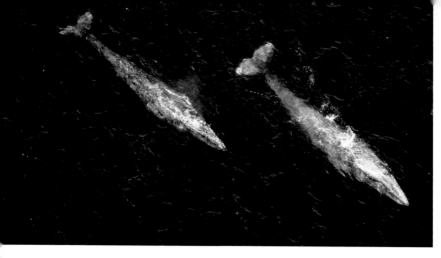

◄ Gray whales on their long migration.

An Incredible Journey

Today people capture images of whales with binoculars and cameras, but in the past this was a place for another sort of capture. Whale hunting used to be a worldwide activity, because the animals provided raw materials for daily life. *Spermaceti* (the semi-solid crystalline wax found in the head cavity of sperm whales) was used for candles, and baleen (the filter feeding device made of keratin in some whales' mouths) was used to make all manner of objects from backscratchers to corsets. Gray whales were hunted primarily for lamp oil, which helped illuminate the wealthier houses in Los Angeles.

Starting in the mid-1930s, international and then federal agencies banned the commercial harvest of gray whales. Thanks to conservation efforts, the eastern Pacific population has rebounded from 2,000 to between 20,000 and 22,000 individuals living on the West Coast and making their annual migration from feeding grounds in Alaska to breeding grounds in Baja California.

Point Vicente is ideal for watching gray whales on their long journeys. They begin their southward trip in December and pass by the center at the rate of about fifteen a day in January. As March rolls around, an average of twenty-four whales a day can be seen heading back from Mexico, including newly born calves. These young whales and their mothers usually stick close to shore, where shallower water makes it harder for predators to sneak up on them. The calves' presence means this is also prime time for spotting orcas (also called killer whales, even though they're actually dolphins). Orcas work together to hunt gray whale calves, a favorite food.

▲ Volunteers scan the ocean looking for migrating whales.

◀ The buildings surrounding the lighthouse support its operations. One houses a large foghorn that automatically turns on when visibility drops below three miles.

Life on the Coast

Imagine being a plant on a coastal bluff. You're happy because the ocean helps keep you cool in summer and warm in winter. But there are tradeoffs. The wind can be fierce, so you need strong roots to keep you in place. If you're a small plant, being low to the ground helps too. When it's hot, the wind can dry you out, so you develop waxy coverings for your leaves. Added bonus: the waxy covering also protects you from salty sea spray. Thanks to the unique challenges of survival, some plants found on the peninsula grow nowhere else on the mainland.

Take the island green dudleya, a type of cliff-adapted succulent. Unlike your garden-variety succulents that can live almost anywhere, this plant grows on Palos Verde sea cliffs, on two of the Channel Islands, and nowhere else in the entire world.

THE LIGHTHOUSE

Point Vicente is the most southwestern part of the Palos Verdes Peninsula, with dangerous rocky shoals (areas where the ocean floor rises close to the surface) in the surrounding waters. Shipwrecks were common. In 1926, after shipmasters petitioned the federal government, the Point Vicente Lighthouse was constructed, immediately becoming the brightest light on the Southern California coastline.

The steep cliffs here, so useful for lighthouses, also attract peregrine falcons, which nest on this section of coast. They vary their usual diet of pigeons and feast on seabirds as well. You can see them waiting on a ledge or flying past—maybe at one hundred miles per hour.

RARE BUTTERFLIES AND RARE HABITAT

In summer, explore the native plant garden and trails behind the center. Some of the pollinators visiting flowers around here are rare butterflies like the Palos Verdes and El Segundo blue. As caterpillars, both species feed on only one or two types of plants that grow in a very limited area. Both are on the endangered species list, and efforts by local conservation groups are helping protect their remaining habitat and cultivate their host plants.

Los Angeles is home to many fascinating species. Some have found clever ways to adapt, but others, like these bobcat kittens, may need a little help to thrive in this new kind of urban ecosystem. We can all do our part.

INDEX

IMAGE CREDITS

All illustrations by Martha Rich unless otherwise noted
Deer head icon on page 139 by Focus Lab
Watershed map on pages 206–207 by David Deis

Bledsoe Collection, Los Angeles Department of Water and Power, page 35 bottom
Jim Boone, page 109 bottom
Carol Bornstein, page 39 left
Peter J. Bryant, pages 126 bottom left, 149, 157
Jay Cossey, pages 106 left, 114, 115 top right, 128 left
Mario DeLopez, pages 29 right, 162, 238 left, 252 right, 254, 255, 258 left, 302
Deniz Durmus, pages 14, 19, 22 left, 25 bottom, 77, 98, 115 bottom, 163, 178 bottom, 199 left, 236–237 top, 238–239, 239 right,
Mark Esguerra, pages 16–17
Dennis Ghaitis, page 43
Jim Glenwright, page 317
Mark Hallett, page 21
Jim Hogue, pages 33, 107, 110, 113, 119 top, 124
Charles Hood, pages 16 left, 22–23, 27, 28, 30, 33 right, 37 left, 38, 39 right, 40–41, 41, 46, 54, 55, 59, 61 top, 62, 65 top, 67, 69, 71, 74, 82, 83, 84, 85, 86, 87, 89, 90, 91, 92, 93, 95, 96, 97, 99, 100, 101, 102, 103, 104, 112 bottom, 133, 134, 135, 141, 142, 145, 152, 156, 159, 164, 170, 173, 174, 175, 176, 177, 178 top, 179, 180 left, 182, 183, 184, 185, 186, 187, 189, 190 bottom, 191, 192, 193, 194 right, 195 right, 196, 197, 199 top right and bottom, 200, 201 bottom, 202 left, 203, 209, 211, 212, 214, 215, 216, 218, 220, 222, 223, 224, 226, 227, 228, 229, 234, 241, 243, 246 top, 248, 252 left, 252, 258–259, 259, 261, 262, 265, 266 left, 269, 272, 273, 274, 275, 277, 278, 279, 280 right, 283, 284 bottom, 285, 287, 288, 289, 290, 292, 293, 295, 296, 297, 299, 300, 301 top, 304, 305, 306, 310, 311, 313, 314, 315, 319
Robert Jensen, pages 123, 126 bottom right, 144
Dorothea Lange, page 53 top
Christopher Lequang, pages 256–257
Jose G. Martinez-Fonseca, page 63
Elliot McGucken, page 211

Kim Moore, pages 129, 132, 148, 242
Gary Nafis, pages 150, 153, 154, 155
The Natural History Museums of Los Angeles County, pages 23 right, 70, 71 bottom, 78, 237,
Miguel Ordenana, page 250
Seaver Center for Natural History Research, Natural History Museum of Los Angeles County, pages 25 top, 29, 32, 246 bottom,
Security Pacific National Bank Collection, page 31
Xan Sonn, page 76
Karen Strauss, page 51
Maureen Sullivan, page 301
Dick Wilkins, page 130 left and right
Harmut Wisch, pages 122, 119 bottom, 120
Michael Wood, pages 166, 167

Alamy
Adwo, page 65 bottom left
age fotostock, pages 117, 172
Max Allen, 270 top
Arco Images GmbH, page 318
B LaRue, page 64
Tom Bean, page 194 left
BIOSPHOTO, page 139
blickwinkel, pages 35, 105, 118, 112 top, 53 right
Ryan M. Bolton, page 156 bottom
Ger Bosma, page 109
Rick & Nora Bowers, pages 126 top, 115
Veronica Carter, page 169
Nigel Cattlin, page 53 bottom left
Citizen of the Planet, page 34–35
Steve Cukrov, page 188
Phil Degginger, page 58
Design Pics Inc, page 121
Trent Dietsche, page 280 left
Everett Collection Historical, pages 233 left and right
F1online digitale Bildagentur GmbH, page 68
Flame, page 125 bottom
Bob Gibbons, page 128
neil hardwick, page 167 bottom
Frank Hecker, page 107 top

imageBROKER, page 131
Al Kancello, page 247
Ivan Kuzmin, page 65 bottom right
Itsik Marom, page 73
Marvin Lo, page 116 bottom
Skip Moody, page 111
Rolf Nussbaumer Photography, page 94, 108
David L. Moore, page 196
NaturaLight, page 201 top
James Peake, page 106 right
Yvan Plamondon, page 88
sirichai raksue, page Michael Rose, page 190 top
Stephanie Starr, page 125
Stone Nature Photography, page 138
John Sullivan, page 160
SuperStock, page 13
Tito Wong, page 249
YAY Media AS, page 202
ZUMA Press, Inc., page 37 right

Flickr
Used under a Creative Commons Attribution 2.0 Generic license
gailhampshire, page 168

iStock
Davel5957, page 232
Freder, page 143
Frank Hildebrand, page 4, 45
Ink Studios, page 49
jgareri, page 61
JHVE Photo, page 57
lillybell, page 147
northohana, page 44
Spondylolithesis, page 116
Stefonlinton, page 282 left
twildlife, page 136
wergodswarrior, page 15

Shutterstock
Jijo Devasia, page 56
Kaianni, page 266
Les Delano, page 284
Warren Metcalf, page 17 right
Becky Sheridan, page 70

SCIENCE ADVISORS

Carol Bornstein, Botany
Brian Brown, Entomology
Jim Dines, Mammalogy
Aisling Farrell, Paleontology
Kimball Garrett, Ornithology
Lisa Gonzalez, Entomology

Amy Gusick, Anthropology
Emily Hartop, Entomology
Richard Hayden, Botany
Emily Lindsey, Paleontology
Miguel Ordeñana, Mammalogy
Jann Vendetti, Malacology

ACKNOWLEDGEMENTS

Sibylle Addotta, Katlen Abuata, Kim Baer, Nancy Batlin, Andrew Beckman, Lori Bettison-Varga, K. Victoria Brown, Daniel Caballero, John Cahoon, Carlos Carrillo, Emily Carlson, Jamie Cataldo, Luis Chiappe, Kate Clavijo, Chris Crockett, David Deis, Katy Delaney, Bailee Desrocher, Margot Dewar, Rick Feeney, Zach Feig, Heather Galles, Martha Garcia, Jessie George, James Gilson, Mark Hallett, Richard Hulser, Gretchen Humbert, Jacoba Lawson, Travis Loncore, Shawna Jones, Dawn McDivitt, Hanna Mesraty, Katie McKissick, Ilse Miller, Mara Naiditch, Jane Pisano, Maria Ponce, Martha Rich, Brent Riggs, Neil Sadler, Richard Salzman, Linda Sharp, Richard Smart, Juree Sondker, Karlee Swift, Gary Takeuchi, Christine Thacker, Jennifer Vaughn, Larry Walraven, Elizabeth Winchell, Emily Wittenberg, Karen Wise, Cynthia Wornham, Kelsey Ziff

About the Authors

Mario de Lopez

The Natural History Museum (NHM) was the first dedicated museum building in Los Angeles, opening its doors in 1913. It belongs now to the Natural History Museums of Los Angeles County, three indoor/outdoor destinations that include NHM, the La Brea Tar Pits, and the Hart Museum. Together they have amassed one of the world's most extensive collections of natural and cultural history, with more than 35 million objects. In addition to interpreting the planet's past, there is a new focus on the present—in particular, urban nature and the LA community's relationship with it. The museums serve more than one million visitors annually, concentrating on access and inclusion, and are national leaders in research, exhibitions, and education. Visit **nhm.org/wildla** for more information.

Deniz Durmus

Lila Higgins grew up on a farm in the United Kingdom, where she had lots of time for unstructured play in the wild. Her love for nature, especially insects, grew out of this time and led her to study entomology and environmental education. Her work at Mass Audubon Society's Drumlin Farms Sanctuary and at the Mary Vagle Nature Center focused on connecting people to nature, particularly in urban settings. Currently she oversees NHM's community science program and loves getting people involved in studying the plants, animals, and fungi that live in Los Angeles.

Deniz Durmus

Dr. Gregory B. Pauly is curator of herpetology and co-director of the Urban Nature Research Center at NHM. His research since joining the Museum in 2012 has focused on the impacts of urbanization on wildlife. He is an advocate for community science and believes partnerships between professional scientists and community members can revolutionize scientific research. His fieldwork has involved studying frogs in tropical rainforests, lizards in the Mojave Desert, and introduced geckos across Southern California neighborhoods. He has authored or coauthored numerous scientific publications, including several with community scientist coauthors.

Deniz Durmus

Dr. Jason G. Goldman is an award-winning science journalist, expedition leader, and public speaker. His writing has appeared in *Scientific American, National Geographic, Los Angeles Magazine, The Washington Post, BBC Earth, Audubon* and elsewhere. He's the director and co-founder of SciCommCamp, a camp-style retreat that brings scientists and science communicators together to inspire fresh, exciting ways to tell compelling science stories. As a founding member of the Nerd Brigade, he works to democratize access to and promote literacy in science, technology, engineering, and mathematics.

Deniz Durmus

Charles Hood grew up in Atwater beside the Los Angeles River. He has been a bird guide in Africa, a translator in New Guinea, and a National Science Foundation Artist-in-Residence in Antarctica. He is the author of many books and essays including *A Californian's Guide to the Birds among Us*. Three of his books have won national poetry awards; he also curates art exhibitions and is a Research Fellow with the Center for Art + Environment at the Nevada Museum of Art. A reformed birder, he stopped counting at 5,000 species, but he admits he's recently started a world mammal list.